People have been racing horses for thousands of years, all over the world. Yet horseracing is often presented as an English creation that was exported, unaltered, to the colonies. This *Companion* investigates the intersection of racing and literature, art, history and finance, casting the sport as the product of cross-class, cosmopolitan and international influences. Chapters on racing history and the origins of the thoroughbred demonstrate how the gift of a fast horse could forge alliances between nations, and the extent to which international power dynamics can be traced back to racetracks and breeding sheds. Leading scholars and journalists draw on original research and firsthand experience to create vivid portraits of the racetracks of Newmarket, Kentucky, the Curragh and Hunter Valley, exposing readers to new racing frontiers in China and Dubai as well. A unique resource for fans and scholars alike, this *Companion* reopens essential questions regarding the legacy and importance of horseracing today.

REBECCA CASSIDY is a professor of anthropology at Goldsmiths, University of London. She has written and edited a number of books on horseracing, animal domestication and gambling, including *Horse People* (2007) and *Sport of Kings: Kinship, Class and Thoroughbred Breeding in Newmarket* (2002).

THE CAMBRIDGE COMPANION TO
HORSERACING

EDITED BY
REBECCA CASSIDY
Goldsmiths, University of London

CAMBRIDGE UNIVERSITY PRESS
Cambridge, New York, Melbourne, Madrid, Cape Town,
Singapore, São Paulo, Delhi, Mexico City

Cambridge University Press
32 Avenue of the Americas, New York, NY 10013-2473, USA

www.cambridge.org
Information on this title: www.cambridge.org/9781107618367

First published 2013

Printed and bound in the United Kingdom by the MPG Books Group

A catalog record for this publication is available from the British Library.

Library of Congress Cataloging in Publication data
The Cambridge companion to horseracing / [edited by] Rebecca Cassidy,
Goldsmiths, University of London.
pages   cm
Includes bibliographical references and index.
ISBN 978-1-107-01385-8 (hardback) – ISBN 978-1-107-61836-7 (paperback)
1. Horse racing – Encyclopedias.   I. Cassidy, Rebecca, editor of compilation.
II. Title: Cambridge companion to horseracing.
SF321.5.C36   2013
798.4003–dc23   2012033216

ISBN 978-1-107-01385-8 Hardback
ISBN 978-1-107-61836-7 Paperback

CONTENTS

CONTENTS

ILLUSTRATIONS

CONTRIBUTORS

REBECCA CASSIDY is a professor of anthropology at Goldsmiths, University of London, and the author of two books about horseracing, *Sport of Kings* (2002) and *Horse People* (2007). In 1998, she led up the winner of the George Cleverley Memorial Handicap at Newmarket.

MARK DAVIES is a leading expert in the field of gambling, sports and finance. Having trained as a linguist, he worked in the City of London and as a sporting journalist and broadcaster. In June 2000, he became part of the team that launched Betfair, where he subsequently spent a decade. Since then, as well as advising numerous companies in the gambling space, from FTSE-250 to start-up, Mark has been running Camberton, a strategic consultancy specialising in reputation management.

DOUGLAS FORDHAM is an associate professor of art history at the University of Virginia. He is a co-editor of *Art and the British Empire* (2007) and the author of *British Art and the Seven Years' War: Allegiance and Autonomy* (2010).

MARK GODFREY has spent the last nine years in Beijing. Originally from the west of Ireland, he takes a keen interest in the development of China's equestrian scene and in horse welfare in particular. Mark has visited equestrian facilities all over China in the past decade. He works as a reporter at the *Financial Times*, on the newspaper's *China Confidential* publication.

JAMES HELMER is a lecturer in oral communication and Director of the Oral Communication Center at Hamilton College. He lives with his wife and two horses on a hilltop in central New York, where on certain nights he can almost make out the words of the announcer calling the races at the harness track below.

MICHAEL HINDS is Head of English and Coordinator of The Irish Centre for Poetry Studies at the Mater Dei Institute, Dublin City University. He edits the journal *POST: A Review of Poetry Studies* and has published widely on American and Irish poetry. He has followed racing since 1974, when a fast two-year-old called

Steel Heart at the Phoenix Park turned his head forever. He is currently working on a study of French racecourses.

SEAN MAGEE is the author of several books on horseracing, including *Ascot: The History* (2002), *Lester's Derbys* with Lester Piggott (2004) and *Arkle: The Life and Legacy of 'Himself'* (2005, revised edition 2009). In addition, he has collaborated on books with such racing luminaries as Sir Peter O'Sullevan, Richard Dunwoody, John Oaksey and Brough Scott.

JOHN MAYNARD is a Worimi man from the Port Stephens region of New South Wales. He currently holds an Australian Research Council Australian Research Fellowship (Indigenous). He is the author of five books, among them *Aboriginal Stars of the Turf*, *Fight for Liberty and Freedom* and *The Aboriginal Soccer Tribe*.

CHRIS MCCONVILLE lectures in sociology at the Footscray campus of Victoria University, Melbourne, Australia, which overlooks the Flemington racecourse. He recently edited a collection titled *A Global Racecourse* (2008) and co-authored *The Australian Pub* (2011). He has spent some time working in broadcasting, including presenting a history segment on Melbourne's racing radio station. At present, his research focuses on the provincial racing industries in Otago, New Zealand, and Western Victoria, Australia, as well as the vexed history of the rabbit in Australia.

RICHARD NASH is a professor of English at Indiana University, Bloomington, and the outgoing president of the Society for Literature, Science and the Arts. He is the author of several books and articles on eighteenth-century literature and culture. His racing silks are 'Gold with Black Chevrons with Diablo Sleeves'.

RACHEL PAGONES was the bloodstock editor of the *Racing Post* and a columnist for the *Financial Times* while living in England for a decade. She has written for numerous racing and bloodstock publications and is the author of *Dubai Millennium: A Vision Realised, a Dream Lost*, which was shortlisted for the Castleton Lyons/Thoroughbred Times Book Award of 2007. She has advised for many years on the purchase of young thoroughbreds, most recently putting her money where her mouth is by investing in three horses to race in California, where she lives and is working on a book of poetry.

WAYNE PEAKE works for the School of Humanities and Communication Arts, University of Western Sydney. He is the author of *Sydney's Pony Racecourses: An Alternative Racing History* and *The Gambler's Ghost and Other Racing Oddities*, a collection of humorous novellas and short stories. He has written on thoroughbred and standardbred racing in academic journals such as *Sporting Traditions* and popular racing magazines like *Turf Monthly*, *Harness Racing International* and *Bluebloods*. He has been a regular racegoer and punter since the age of eight, with declining success.

JONATHAN SILVERMAN is the author of *Nine Choices: Johnny Cash and American Culture* (2010). He is an assistant professor of English at the University of Massachusetts, Lowell, and received his PhD in American Studies from the University of Texas at Austin. He recently served as a Fulbright Roving Scholar in American Studies in Norway. He is the co-author (with Dean Rader) of the popular culture reader *The World Is a Text*, now in its fourth edition.

JANE SMILEY is the author of many books, including *Horse Heaven*, *A Year at the Races*, *A Thousand Acres* (which won the Pulitzer Prize in 1992), *Thirteen Ways of Looking at the Novel* and, most recently, *Private Life*. She lives in California and once bred racehorses, but came to her senses.

WRAY VAMPLEW is Emeritus Professor of sports history at the University of Stirling, Senior Research Fellow at the University of Central Lancashire and visiting professor at the Technological and Higher Education Institute in Hong Kong. Author or editor of 27 books, he has also published more than 150 articles and book chapters. His research has been awarded prizes by the North American Society for Sport History, the Australian Institute of Sport and the International Society for the History of Physical Education and Sport. He is the editor of the *Journal of Sport History* and managing editor of the *International Journal of the History of Sport*.

ACKNOWLEDGEMENTS

Thanks to Ray Ryan for commissioning *The Cambridge Companion to Horseracing*. I hope that we have done justice to a subject that I know is dear to his heart. Thanks also to Rebecca Taylor and Alison McMenemy at Cambridge University Press in the United Kingdom and to Louis Gulino in New York. Thanks also to Kate Fox and Jocelyn de Moubray.

The contributors to this book are not only tremendously knowledgeable but also unfailingly enthusiastic. Thanks in particular to Wray Vamplew who was first past the post with perfect copy, as well as to Jonathan Silverman and Mark Godfrey for fantastic late entries. Douglas Fordham found wonderful images and drove a hard bargain on rights, freeing up budget for the handsome cover.

We are grateful to Pat Lowe, the University of Melbourne, Yale Center for British Art, The British Museum, The National Gallery (London), The Tate Gallery (London), the National Gallery of Victoria (Melbourne) and Museum Victoria (Melbourne) for their generous permissions.

The chronology was a joint effort, although any mistakes are mine.

HORSERACING: A CHRONOLOGY

Eighth century BC	Homer describes a chariot race won by Diomedes (with some assistance from Athena).
16 BC	Ovid provides a literary account of a day at the races in book III of *Amores*.
1539	Henry Gee, mayor of Chester, replaces a violent football match with a horserace to be run for the prize of a silver bell donated by the Saddler's company on Shrove Tuesday on the Roodee at Chester.
c. 1560	*The Art of Riding*, an adaptation/translation of Frederico Grisone's Italian work of the same name, becomes the first work concerned with horsemanship to be published in England, reflecting the energetic exchanges of equine ideas and personnel that were taking place between England, Spain and Italy at the time.
1585	Horse races at Salisbury were attended by the Earls of Cumberland, Warwick, Pembroke and Essex. Prizes included a golden bell and a golden snaffle.
1593	Gervase Markham publishes *A Discourse of Horsemanship*, the first of several works on horses. Markham's *Cavalarice*, published in 1607, is thought to contain the first instructions for race riding.
1619	Salisbury Corporation takes charge of a fund 'for the encouragement of the races'.
1654	Cromwell bans horseracing for six months, citing 'the evil use made thereof by such ill-disposed Persons as watch for opportunities to raise New Troubles ... [and threaten] the Peace and Security of this Nation'.

1673 William Temple proposes to the Lord Lieutenant of Ireland that three days of horseracing should be held near Dublin.

c. 1674 Spanker is foaled and is later described as the best horse to run at Newmarket during the reign of Charles II. None of his achievements are recorded.

1680 Lord Monmouth, the oldest illegitimate son of Charles II, embarks on his 'progresses' around Britain, taking in several race meetings and competing himself, on horses provided by Thomas Wharton. He is arrested and banished in 1682 before leading an unsuccessful rebellion in 1685, after which he is beheaded on Tower Hill in London.

1683 Louis XVI hosts a race at Aix–St Germain, which is won by the Wharton gelding racing in the name of Lord Monmouth.

1683 The Rye House plot to assassinate Charles II and James, Duke of York, on their way back to London from racing at Newmarket is foiled when the races are cancelled after a fire in the town.

1690 The Byerley Turk carries English army officer Captain Robert Byerley (d. 1714) at the Battle of the Boyne. Legend has it that Byerley narrowly avoided capture while reconnoitring thanks to the great speed of his mount. The Byerley Turk dies, having been bred to relatively few mares, in 1703. His most important offspring was Basto.

1695 Catholics in England are prohibited from owning horses worth more than 5 pounds by the 'Act for the better securing the government, by disarming papists'.

1704 The Darley Arabian arrives at Aldby Park, Buttercrambe, Yorkshire, England, from Aleppo via Kinsale, Ireland. He is at stud between 1706 and 1715, and his most important progeny were Flying or Devonshire Childers and Bartlett's or Bleeding Childers.

1711 Queen Anne initiates racing at Ascot.

1715 Flying Childers is born and goes unbeaten in six races as a six- and seven-year-old, winning him the title of the first great racehorse.

1715	Lord Derwentwater assembles his forces at Dilston races in Northumbria. Tory gentry also converge on Bath races to take part in the Jacobite rebellion known as 'The Fifteen', but they are too late.
1727	John Cheny publishes the first annual *Historical Lists* of races; a pedigree index is added in 1743.
1730	The Godolphin Arabian produces his first crop for Edward Coke at Longford Hall in Derbyshire. The timing of his arrival in England is obscure. Romantic stories about him pulling a cart in Paris and fighting another stallion, Hobgoblin, for the right to cover Roxana are unsupported.
1733	Edward Coke dies and the Godolphin Arabian is passed to his friend, Roger Williams, who sells him to the second Earl of Godolphin. The horse is moved to a stud near Newmarket in Cambridgeshire. The focus of English horse breeding moves south.
1750	A reminder of a meeting of the Jockey Club appears in *The General Advertiser*, and Pond's *Sporting Kalender* refers to a race to be held between horses owned by members.
1752	Steeplechasing begins with a race between the parish churches of Buttevant and Doneraile in Cork.
1764	Eclipse is born. Unbeaten in eighteen starts, he becomes the best horse of the eighteenth century. Although he was never better than second (most often to Herod) in the leading sire list, he is a tail male ancestor of 95 per cent of modern thoroughbreds.
1766	George Stubbs publishes *The Anatomy of the Horse*.
1776	First running of the St Leger at Doncaster.
1777	The Madras Race Club is formed.
1779	The Oaks is staged at Epsom.
1780	The first running of the Derby is run over a mile at Epsom and won by Diomed, owned by Sir Charles Bunbury, the first great racing administrator.
1790	First publication of the *Irish Racing Calendar* by the Irish Turf Club.

1794	George Stubbs's Turf Gallery opens in Conduit Street, London.
1806	George Stubbs dies on 10 July, at the age of eighty-one.
1809	First running of the 2,000 Guineas at Newmarket.
1810	The first fully sanctioned race meeting occurs in Sydney.
1814	First running of the 1,000 Guineas at Newmarket.
1825	Brazil's first formal race meeting is held at Praia Vermelha in Botafogo, Rio de Janeiro.
1827	Great racing administrator and inventor of the weight-for-age scale in 1855, Admiral Rous arrives in Sydney from England to return in 1829 via a posting in India. While in Australia, he stands an English horse, the well-named Emigrant.
1829	The foundation stone for a racecourse at Aintree is laid by Lord Sefton. Historian John Pinfold has suggested that a race in 1836 should be recognised as the first Grand National. Other historians suggest that the first running of the race was in 1839, won by a horse called Lottery.
1830s	Races are held at Tirranna near Goulbourn, providing a template for picnic racing all over Australia. Tirranna is immortalised by George Lambert in 1929 in a painting that captures the bucolic pleasures of bush racing.
1833	Sheikh Maktoum bin Buti, of the Al Bu Falasah sector of the Bani Yas tribe, along with nearly 1,000 tribesmen, secedes from Abu Dhabi.
1844	The infamous Running Rein Derby. The winner is disqualified after it is discovered that he is an ineligible four-year-old named Maccabeus.
1845	Happy Valley Racecourse is built for the British in Hong Kong.
1848	Turf reformer Lord George Bentinck dies at age forty-six.
1848	Trollope publishes *The Kellys and the O'Kellys* in which the character of Dot Blake provides an early study of a canny professional trainer.

1849   Foreign Residents Club members pool resources to found Foreign Amateurs Racing Society to stage race meetings in Argentina.

1853   Western Australia becomes the first horse to win the English Triple Crown.

1856   The first running of the Viceroy's Cup is held at Hastings Racecourse in Calcutta.

1857   Longchamp racecourse opens, Paris's first metropolitan track.

1858   Exhibition of William Powell Frith's *The Derby Day* at the Royal Academy of Arts, London.

1861   The first Melbourne Cup is won by Archer who wins again the following year – the first of four horses to win consecutive cups.

1863   The first running of the Grand Prix de Paris, a champion race for three-year-olds held at Longchamp, is won by an English colt, The Ranger.

1863   John Hunter and William R. Travers build Saratoga racecourse following the success of a four-day meeting in the town organised by former bare knuckles boxing champion and congressman, John Morrissey. Saratoga claims to be the oldest organised sporting venue in the United States.

1864   The first Travers Stakes at Saratoga is won by Travers's horse, Kentucky.

1865   Gladiateur becomes the second winner of the English Triple Crown. The first foreign-bred winner of the Derby, he is dubbed 'the Avenger of Waterloo' by the French.

1867   Joseph Oller, a Catalonian bookmaker living in Paris, invents the pari-mutuel system of wagering. It is mechanised by Englishman George Julius, who had moved to New Zealand in 1889 when his father was nominated to the diocese of Christchurch.

1870   The Jockey Club assumes control over flat racing in Britain.

1880   Zola brings to life the excesses of the Parisian racecourse in *Nana*.

1881	Iroquois, owned by tobacco millionaire Pierre Lorillard IV, becomes the first American-owned and -bred winner of the Derby. He also wins the St Leger.
1882	The Argentinean Jockey Club is formed following a visit by four founding members to the French Derby at Chantilly. The first Argentinean Derby is run in 1884. The Hipódromo Argentino de Palermo, the first racecourse in Argentina, was established in 1876.
1884	Prolific English-born author Nat Gould embarks on an eleven-year sojourn to Australia, during which he chronicles the lives and times of the racing and betting industries.
1886	The most brilliant jockey of his generation, Fred Archer, known as The Tinman, commits suicide at age twenty-nine in a fit of depression caused by the death of his wife, Helen Rose. According to local legend, the ghost of Archer is said to ride a grey horse through Pegasus Stables in Newmarket.
1886	Ladbrokes is founded as commission agents for horses trained at Ladbroke Hall in Worcestershire. The name Ladbrokes was adopted in 1902 when operations were moved to London.
1886	Robert Black describes the Anglicisation of French racing, claiming that trainers in France are 'English to a man'.
1894	Novelist George Moore describes the mortal threat posed by horseracing for servants and stable boys in *Esther Waters*.
1894	Alexander Gray's single-strand barrier is used at a race meeting in Australia. It is used in the United Kingdom from 1897.
1903	The Jockey Club bans doping after trainer George Lambton dopes his own horses to draw attention to the problem, brought to Newmarket as part of what Lambton refers to as the 'American invasion'.
1905	Belmont Park opens in New York to a crowd of forty thousand.
1906	Sydney, with a population of less than half a million, stages more race meetings (236) annually on the flat than in all of the United Kingdom, with a population of around forty million.

1907	Toasted by the Protestant students of Trinity College and running with a rosary in his bridle, Orby becomes the first Irish-trained horse to win the Epsom Derby.
1908	The original stands in the Hipódromo Argentino de Palermo are replaced by a Beaux Arts tribute designed by Louis Faure-Dujarric.
1913	Suffragette Emily Davison dies after throwing herself in front of the king's horse in the Epsom Derby.
1913	The first totaliser system is installed at Ellerslie Racecourse, Auckland, New Zealand, and is manually operated. The second, at Gloucester Park Racetrack in Western Australia, is electrically driven.
1914	AB 'Banjo' Paterson hangs up his guitar long enough to write the first sociology of Australian racing, referring to the *cognoscenti* as 'knowledge boxes' and bemoaning the influence of 'the machine' (the pari-mutuel).
1915	Regret becomes the first filly to win the Kentucky Derby.
1918	Five hundred ninety people are killed in a fire after a temporary grandstand collapses at Happy Valley Racecourse, Hong Kong.
1919	Sir Barton is the first horse to win the American Triple Crown. After eleven unsuccessful seasons at stud, he served at the U.S. Army Remount service before being bought by a rancher from Wyoming.
1920	First running of the Prix de l'Arc de Triomphe at Longchamp is won by an English-bred and -owned colt, Comrade, ridden by the Australian Frank Bullock.
1924	First running of the Cheltenham Gold Cup is won by Red Splash.
1924	Skull caps become compulsory for jump jockeys in the United Kingdom after amateur rider Captain 'Tuppy' Bennett is killed at Wolverhampton racecourse after being kicked in a fall from Ardene in the Oteley Handicap Steeplechase.
1925	Gordon Richards wins the first UK jump jockeys' championship.

1926	UK trade papers agree on a starting price system to be determined by the betting market on course.
1926	Winston Churchill introduces a tax on betting, which is abandoned three years later. It was reintroduced in 1967.
1927	The Epsom Derby is broadcast on the radio for the first time.
1927	The first running of the Champion Hurdle at Cheltenham is won by Blaris.
1929	The UK Tote operates for the first time at Newmarket and Carlisle.
1930	Phar Lap wins the Melbourne Cup at 8–11.
1930	Irish Hospital Sweepstakes legalized by Public Charitable Hospitals Act.
1932	The first televised Epsom Derby.
1932	Australia mourns Phar Lap, aged only five, as he dies in the arms of his groom, Tommy Woodcock. Despite being born in New Zealand, Phar Lap had come to represent Depression-era Australia, battling back from finishing last in his first race to winning the Melbourne Cup and thirty-six of his other fifty starts.
1932	Golden Miller records the first of five consecutive triumphs in the Cheltenham Gold Cup.
1934	William Hill is founded as a telephone and postal betting service.
1934	Shirley Temple makes her debut in the film version of Runyon's *Little Miss Marker*. The shocking story of a little girl left as collateral with a bookie operating among the New York demimonde is leavened by the curls and dimples of the original child star.
1935	Foxbridge is imported to New Zealand from England. His progeny dominate New Zealand racing in the 1940s.
1935	*National Velvet* is published. Generations of girls grow up dreaming of winning a racehorse and riding it in the Grand National.

1939   Clay Puett's electric starting gate is used at Landsdowne Park, Vancouver. The design remains basically the same to this day. Starting gates were not introduced by the English Jockey Club until 1965.

1942   Wartime restrictions, including a ban on midweek racing and one raceless Saturday a month, are introduced in Sydney. Similar measures are enforced across Australia. The last-ever meeting is held on a Sydney 'pony' racecourse.

1943   A wartime restriction on fuel prevents Kentucky breeders from transporting their yearlings to Saratoga to be sold. Instead, a sale is held in a tent in the track paddock at Keeneland. Keeneland develops to become the most important sales company in the world.

1947   Sayajirao wins the St Leger for the Maharaja of Baroda, ridden by Australian Edgar Britt.

1948   *King of the Wind* adds another layer to the fantastical stories that surround the origin of the Godolphin Arabian. Author Marguerite Henry merges half-truths and fiction to dramatic effect.

1953   Vincent O'Brien trains the winners of the Cheltenham Gold Cup (Knock Hard), the Aintree Grand National (Early Mist) and The Irish Derby (Larkspur). He also wins the Grand National in 1954 (Royal Tan) and 1955 (Quare Times).

1955   The not-for-profit Greater New York Association (which became the New York Racing Association in 1958) is created.

1957   Bookies begin to bet 'each way' in Sydney.

1961   Betting shops are legalized in the United Kingdom. Cash betting off course is decriminalized overnight.

1961   Northern Dancer, the most successful sire of the twentieth century, is foaled in Canada. Having failed to meet his $25,000 reserve price as a yearling, he is retained by Windfields Farm for whom he wins fourteen out of his eighteen starts, including the Kentucky Derby and the Preakness. He stands at Windfields Farm in Maryland until his death in 1990.

1962	The first running of the Washington International takes place at Laurel Park.
1962	Vincent O'Brien wins the first of six Epsom Derbies with Larkspur, owned by Raymond Guest, U.S. ambassador to Ireland.
1963	The Betting, Gaming and Lotteries Act is passed, regulating betting in the United Kingdom, including defining the role of a 'bookmaker', until it is superseded by the 2005 Gambling Act.
1964	Arkle wins the first of three consecutive Cheltenham Gold Cups.
1964	Russian champion Anilin is allowed to run in the Washington International. He finishes third in 1964 and second in 1966.
1970	Nijinsky wins the English Triple Crown for trainer Vincent O'Brien.
1973	The first of Red Rum's three victories in the Grand National. In addition to winning in 1974 and 1977, he finishes second twice.
1976	The first yearling to be sold for more than $1 million goes through the Keeneland July Sale. Canadian Bound was sold by Nelson Bunker Hunt and bought for $1.5 million by a Canadian syndicate. He raced four times, without success.
1976	Wray Vamplew publishes *The Turf* and establishes a new direction for the study of horseracing.
1977	The trifecta comes to Australian racecourses.
1980	Irishmen Tommy Ryan and Joe Byrne are banned from riding in Britain for an unprecedented three months for misuse of the whip at the Cheltenham festival.
1981	Shergar wins the Epsom Derby by a record margin. In 1983, he is kidnapped from the Aga Khan's Ballymany stud by the Provisional Irish Republican Army (IRA). No ransom is paid, and his body is never found.
1981	First running of the Japan Cup. Participants were restricted to those trained in Japan, the United States, Australia, Canada, New Zealand and India, or by invitation. This restriction was dropped in 1982, but the race remains an invitational.

1984   Dawn Run becomes the only racehorse to have won both the Champion Hurdle and the Cheltenham Gold Cup. She also is the only horse to have won the English, French and Irish Champion hurdles.

1985   Seattle Dancer, a colt by Nijinsky, is sold at Keeneland for £13.1 million, the highest price ever paid for a yearling at public auction, and the high-water mark of the 1980s bloodstock bubble during which ten colts by Northern Dancer and his son Nijinsky realised $4 million or more each.

1990   U.S.-bred, Irish-owned Danehill becomes the first high-profile shuttle stallion, covering mares in both hemispheres. He goes on to be leading sire in Australia on nine occasions, in Britain and Ireland three times and in France on two occasions.

1993   The International Federation of Horseracing Authorities is established.

1993   Mark Wallinger acquires the racehorse which he names A Real Work of Art.

1994   Balanchine provides the first Group One winner for Godolphin.

1994   The National Lottery is launched in the United Kingdom. Bookies face extra competition, initially from prize draws and, after 1995, scratchcards.

1995   Happy Valley Racecourse is rebuilt.

1995   Northern Irish jockey A. P. McCoy begins his unbroken dominance of the British jump racing championship.

1996   Inaugural running of the Dubai World Cup, with prize money of $4 million, a figure intended to ensure the participation of the top U.S. horse and eventual winner, Cigar.

1996   Frankie Dettori wins all seven races on the card at Ascot. Bookmaker Gary Wiltshire sells his house and car in order to pay back the £800,000 he owes to winning punters.

1997   The Grand National is postponed after two coded bomb threats are received from the IRA.

1998   The first of Istabraq's three consecutive victories in the Champion Hurdle at the Cheltenham Festival.

2000	Betfair launches, offering its first market on the Oaks, won by Love Divine.
2001	Racing fiction gets its own equine narrators. *Horse Heaven* provides a nod to *Black Beauty* by reflecting on a horse's-eye view of racing in the United States and Europe.
2001	The UK government introduces a gross profits tax scheme designed to encourage the largest betting operators to return from their offshore locations. At the 2002 British Horseracing Board AGM, then-chairman of William Hill, John Brown, describes it as the 'single most important and influential development in betting and racing in 30 years'.
2002	In-running betting is offered by Betfair.
2003	Betfair agrees on a Memorandum of Understanding with the Jockey Club. The MoU allows the Jockey Club to request information that enables them to identify individuals behind activities that gave rise to a strong suspicion that the Rules of Racing have been broken.
2004	Australian Racing Board CEO Andrew Harding describes permitting betting exchanges as 'a suicide pill'.
2004	Emirates, the Dubai national airline, secures sponsorship of Arsenal football club's stadium and becomes a commonplace brand encountered throughout the sporting media.
2004	Ladbrokes' CEO Chris Bell tells the BBC's Money Program that 'at least a race a day, if not more, is now being corrupted by the availability of laying horses to lose on betting exchanges'.
2004	Kieren Fallon drops his hands, losing a nineteen-length lead on Ballinger Ridge at Lingfield Park. Sean Fox falls off Ice Saint at the first at Fontwell six days later. The two events prompt a flurry of media reports about corruption in racing, focusing particularly on the role of the recently established betting exchanges and their facility to bet against horses.
2005	The Gambling Act transforms laws dating back as far as 1845 and attempts to future-proof gambling regulation under the guidance of the newly created Gambling Commission.
2006	Sheikh Mohammed bin Rashid Al Maktoum becomes ruler of Dubai upon the death of his brother, Sheikh Maktoum bin Rashid Al Maktoum.

2007   Turf TV/Racing UK is created with the intention to foster competition in the market, on the basis that racecourses would be paid more for their rights if rival broadcasters had to bid against each other for contracts.

2008   Former Taoiseach, Bertie Ahern, tells the Mahon tribunal that substantial amounts of sterling deposited into his account are racecourse 'winnings'.

2008   The Green Monkey retires. Bought in 2006 for a record $16 million, he ran three times without winning. He joins Snaafi Dancer, bought for $10.2 million in 1983, as an example of a famous, and expensive, failure. Snaafi Dancer was unraced and suffered from fertility problems.

2009   Mark Wallinger is selected as the winner of the Ebbsfleet, Kent, public art competition, for his 50-foot-high sculpture of a white horse.

2010   A joint venture between the two British broadcasters, Racing UK and At The Races, called GBI, is formed to sell picture rights internationally.

2010   A law is passed in France whereby horseracing can only be bet on through the totalisator system or PMU.

2010   According to the BBC, 4,618 thoroughbreds are slaughtered in abattoirs in Ireland, casualties of overproduction and the economic crisis.

2010   Dick Francis, jockey and novelist, dies.

2010   Meydan opens. Sixty-seven million square feet of luxury and technology set new standards for racecourse construction, reinforcing the ongoing relevance of the connection between the fortunes of Dubai and international horseracing.

2011   Australian trainer Bart Cummings tells *The Racing Post* that racing in Ireland 'isn't worth two bob'.

2011   Betting firm BetFred buys the Horseracing Totalisator Board and with it the right to provide pari-mutuel betting in the United Kingdom.

2011   Queen Elizabeth II visits the Irish National Stud.

REBECCA CASSIDY

Introduction

Pathos and Poetry

The first episode of *Luck*, a television series created by David Milch (*NYPD Blue*, *Deadwood*), directed by Michael Mann (*Manhunter*, *Heat*) and filmed at Santa Anita Park in California, aired on Home Box Office in December 2011. It was immediately taken into a second season and broadcast in Britain in early 2012. In the conservative world of television writing, David Milch is regarded as a maverick genius, known for his uncompromising take on American life. *Luck* is no *Seabiscuit*. The first episode weaves together a number of stories: the release from prison of Chester 'Ace' Bernstein (Dustin Hoffman), a racehorse owner with links to organised crime; a pick-six attempt by four inveterate gamblers or 'railbirds'; and a hard boot trainer (Nick Nolte) with a dark horse. It also includes the humane destruction of a horse on the track, its head cradled in the arms of a tearful bug boy. *Luck* is a complex, unflinching portrayal of violence and corruption at the track. Dialogue- and character-driven, it invites reflection and understanding rather than judgement. Milch, a lifelong race fan and winner of two Breeders Cups, describes his series as 'a love letter', albeit an unsentimental one: 'To me, the track is what the river was to Mark Twain. Where you see the most life and interesting people, go there. That's what I've done.'[1] In March 2012, halfway through filming the second episode of the second season, production of *Luck* was permanently suspended by HBO, when a third horse had to be euthanized as a result of an accident on the set.[2]

As the brief lifespan of *Luck* indicates, representing racing is a fraught and complex endeavour. Death stalks the racecourse, along with joy and rapture – something that *Luck* confronted head on. When, in the first episode, the bug asks a ruined old jockey how to cope with the death of a horse, the jock, played with convincing bitterness by Hall of Famer Gary Stevens, replies, 'You'll get over it. That's why they make Jim Beam.' This was not a series that ignored or glorified the deaths of animals on the track, but one which encouraged us to confront the costs of our entanglements with animals in a thoughtful and progressive way. To cancel it because of the death of a horse, which died when she reared up, fell and banged her head while being led back to a barn, is to foreclose a potentially productive discussion about welfare. It allows people to return, chomping on cheap burgers, to a comfortable world in which the exploitation of animals can continue as long as it happens off screen.

The reactions of racing enthusiasts to the series, collected in the pages of the *Daily Racing Form*, were mixed.[3] Some complained that *Luck* was not an accurate representation of the track. Others lamented that this representation would not attract the new fans the sport craves. Although the jury is still out on *Luck*, part of the purpose of this book is to explore how the morally opaque, troubling image of racing that it presents coexists with alternative historical and contemporary representations which stress its elitist and conservative credentials.

Until recently, a division of labour existed between historians of racing and fiction writers exploring the same subject. As Jane Smiley shows in Chapter 3 of this volume, racing fiction includes murder, conspiracy, cross-class indiscretion and failure. Great authors including Anthony Trollope, George Moore and Ernest Hemingway have used racing as a backdrop to muse on inequality of opportunity, the small tragedies of ordinary lives blighted by bad decisions and the blindness of fate. Many horses and jockeys have died in tragic circumstances on the fictional tracks created by racing's greatest writers. Historians, until recently, stuck to lists of winners, descriptions of famous races, horses, owners and breeders. Artists fell into both categories. As Douglas Fordham describes in Chapter 2 of the present volume, many painted order and hierarchy, in the image of the establishment they served. Some, like William Powell Frith in *Derby Day*, turned their backs on the horses and depicted crowds that included thimble riggers, mistresses and infamous murderers. *Derby Day* is the Victorian equivalent of an episode of *Luck*, and when the National Gallery first exhibited it in 1858, it had to erect a barrier to protect it from the large crowds it drew. The Queen loved it too.

New writing about racing is beginning to look beyond descriptions of regal influence and equine heroism to more nuanced, inclusive representations. In North America, Edward Hotaling has described the contribution made by black jockeys to the sport and Steven Riess has exposed the relationship between racing administration and organised crime in New York between 1865 and 1913. In the United Kingdom, Mike Huggins has meticulously documented the often overlooked participation of the middle classes and women in the sport and Donna Landry has unravelled the connections between the Middle East and Europe that framed the creation of the thoroughbred. In Australia, John Maynard has written about Aboriginal jockeys and Wayne Peake has told the story of Sydney's pony racecourses, the one-time competitor to thoroughbred racing. These and other works urge us to rethink conventional descriptions of racing as an invention of the English aristocracy, which has been exported, unchanged, to the New World. Part of the purpose of this volume is to understand why ideas such as these have endured in place of cosmopolitan alternatives.[4]

A National Sport?

According to Thomas Egerton, the second Earl of Wilton, writing in 1868, horseracing was a reflection of the essential character of the Englishman in the same way as the theatre represented the French and the bullfight the Spanish. This vision included fair play, muscular athleticism, determination and beauty, indeed: 'Sportsmanship is the ideal of racing. It is its foundation.'[5] In practice, twenty-four years after the Running Rein Derby, when the winner was found to be an ineligible horse named Maccabeus, English racing was still far from pristine. However, the idea of racing as a quintessentially English sporting tradition, nurtured through administration by a private club for 250 years, was remarkably resilient. This idea retarded changes to the sport and underplayed the cosmopolitan and cross-class exchanges that characterised the development of the thoroughbred and racing in England and beyond.[6]

At the start of the twentieth century, a row broke out about the status of the thoroughbred racehorse. In some ways it was clearly an English horse, racing in England, bred on English studs, patronised by kings and queens. But in another, it was the offspring of imported stallions, described as Barbs, Turks and Arabian, and mares of indeterminate origin. In what sense could it be claimed as 'English' at all? One of the primary characters in this battle was the Arabian horse enthusiast Lady Wentworth, who, in 1945, published a vast volume, the purpose of which was to prove that the thoroughbred was descended entirely from Arab horses and was indeed an Arabian horse itself (of a kind inferior to those bred in the desert). She called this topic 'historical dynamite', and said that in raising it she risked 'receiving a bomb by post the day after publication'.[7] Richard Nash's chapter, which opens this volume, provides a new perspective on this incendiary argument. He shows how ideas of 'Englishness', continuity and descent battled with environmental determinism in the succession of kings as well as stallions. In Nash's chapter, racing is a form of politics: race meetings serve as rallies for Jacobite rebellions, and gifts of horses communicate diplomatic messages between international allies. According to Nash, 'the "sport of kings" is born from the same cultural ferment that marked the end of absolute monarchy'.

The thoroughbred was the product of international exchanges of horses, people and ideas which had taken place since at least 1576 when Elizabeth I commissioned the Neapolitan Prospero d'Osma to report on the state of the royal studs.[8] Once the breed was established, through the crossing of Arab and other horses, English racing and the thoroughbred became more insular, exporting a template and horses to the colonies and seeking to preserve a breed and practice that had always been hybrid, according to a new ideal of purity. The Jersey Act of 1913, which restricted entry to the *General Stud Book (GSB)* to horses who could trace their ancestry without flaw to those already registered, epitomised this insularity and was repealed in 1949. The Jersey Act proved that the Jockey Club was out of touch. Horses had travelled for stud purposes for several centuries. Horses bred overseas had also successfully competed in the European blue-ribbon events for more than thirty years: the American horse Iroquois won the Epsom Derby in 1881. Post–Second World War, French horses won nineteen classics between 1947 and 1959. The repeal of the Jersey Act was partly motivated by the ridiculousness of having French and then American Epsom Derby winners in 1947 and 1948, neither of which were eligible for entry in the *GSB*.[9]

Soon after the repeal of the Jersey Act, the movement of horses by air became routine, and racing entered a new era of internationalism, reflected in the international flat race pattern created by Lord Porchester and agreed by the French, Irish and English authorities in 1970.[10] Various races and series, with 'World Championship' pretensions including the Breeders Cup (first run in 1984) and the Dubai World Cup (first run in 1996), have since emerged. The internationalism of these competitions has been moderated by the continuing importance of local conditions ranging from epidemiology and breeding incentives to track conditions and race tactics. Chapters in this volume by Wayne Peake (Chapter 9) and Chris McConville (Chapter 14) show that the New World has produced influential horses, techniques and personnel, as well as vital technology including the starting stalls and pari-mutuel. Racing is not simply exported and replicated wholesale in new jurisdictions, colonial or otherwise.

The increased availability of air transport since the 1960s also profoundly affected the bloodstock industry. Northern Dancer (1961–1990) the most influential sire of the twentieth century, was a Canadian-bred Kentucky Derby winner who stood only in North America, but nevertheless produced North American, Japanese, European and Australian champions. Among his many grandson stallions, High Chaparral (b.1999) is typically well travelled. He was bred in Ireland, bought by Coolmore at Tattersalls in Newmarket, returned to Ireland to be trained by Aiden O'Brien, raced in England, Ireland and the United States and has stood as a stallion in New Zealand, Australia and Ireland. Ease of transport has not, however, created a single type of 'international' thoroughbred, valued equally in all jurisdictions. The preference for dirt sprinters in North America and stayers in Europe still produces different kinds of horses, with recognisable pedigrees and phenotypes. As McConville argues in his chapter, the majority of horses and races continue to be produced for regional markets that serve geographically proximate national racing cultures. The animated discussions regarding the relative merits of horses in England and the United States that took place when Diomed won the Epsom Derby in 1881 are just as lively today, although they take place online rather than in the pages of the racing press.[11]

Making Racing

The fusion of betting – an anarchic means of distributing wealth which has no minimum price – with the expensive business of producing and maintaining fragile thoroughbred horses generates many of the paradoxes that enliven racing. Nevertheless, in the eighteenth and nineteenth centuries, racing historians distinguished sharply between these activities. Egerton's vision of racing as epitomising the English character, for example, explicitly excludes betting, which he sees as an unfortunate side effect of the sport, reluctantly acknowledging that 'turf gambling has arisen from horseracing ... and to a very alarming extent; but it does not belong to racing as a sport'.[12] Fifteen years earlier, in the *Sporting Review* of 1853, Craven (John Carleton) had complained that 'Epsom's "pride, pomp and circumstance" are on the wane, no longer as of yore may it be said – "there all is gentle and aristocratic."' Systematic bookmaking or 'betting in the round' was emerging at the time, replacing matched bets between known individuals. Craven described this new system as having 'elbowed a way to place and power wholly unbeseeming'. He concluded by reinforcing the distinction made by Egerton: 'The turf is not intended for the trade of tout or tapster. ... As already aforesaid, betting has nothing to do with racing.'[13]

At times, this distinction has been politically expedient and even necessary for racing to survive. In post-Revolutionary New York, for example, 'Knickerbockers' – racing supporters drawn from the Long Island gentry – formed the Society for the Promotion of the Useful Arts and exhibited racehorses at agricultural fairs. They were rewarded in 1821 by a bill which permitted two racing seasons in Queens County.[14] In the United Kingdom, the distinction between racing and betting endured in divisions between regulatory bodies including the Jockey Club, the National Bookmakers

Protection Association (formed in 1932) and the Horserace Betting Levy Board (formed in 1961 to raise and distribute a levy from bookmakers on behalf of racing). In 1975, Phil Bull, the founder of Timeform and one of the great racing minds, told journalist Hugh McIlvanney that 'what is so sad and alarming regarding the future of racing is the refusal to admit the obvious, that the vital audience for the sport is no longer on the course but in the betting shops.... This is, above all, an entertainment industry and it is the audience that matters.'[15] The Jockey Club relinquished its control over English racing in 2006, but the administrative and regulatory structure of racing continued to reproduce the divisions between racing and betting that concerned Bull in the 1970s. In 2011, the government minister responsible for managing negotiations between racing and the betting industry likened his role to finding peace in the Middle East. The consequences of these structural divisions are discussed in more detail in Mark Davies's chapter in this volume (Chapter 13).

It has been conventional to present betting and breeding and testing horses against one another for the purposes of their improvement as mutually exclusive and even antagonistic. However, these different activities do not produce an exclusive set of binary oppositions between, for example, lower-class gamblers and upper-class owners. On the contrary, these categories are blurred and overlapping. Eclipse (1764–1789) – who appears in the pedigrees of more than 90 per cent of thoroughbreds racing today – was owned by a meat salesman and a madam at various points in his career. Eclipse's most famous owner was the son of an Irish smallholder whose first job was carrying the front half of a sedan chair. Dennis O'Kelly was mocked by the English establishment for his Irish accent, but, unlike ruined eighteenth-century aristocrats such as John Damer, eldest son of Lord Milton, who committed suicide after building up gambling debts of £60,000, O'Kelly left his heirs a fortune based on Eclipse's stud fees. More recently, Londoner Michael Tabor sold his betting shop chain for a reported £27 million in 2003 and has since won two Epsom Derbies (with Galileo and High Chaparral) and a Kentucky Derby (with Thunder Gulch). Irishman J.P. McManus, currently the most powerful owner in British jumps racing, became a bookmaker at a greyhound track at the age of twenty.

Wealth creators and the international super rich have had at least as much influence over the development of the thoroughbred as have royalty and the local establishment. The Rothschild family, their vast fortune based on Nathan Mayer von Rothschild's role in organising the financing of the Napoleonic Wars, were hugely successful owners-breeders in England and France throughout the nineteenth and twentieth centuries.[16] Nineteen-time leading owner and seventeen-time leading breeder Marcel Boussac dominated French racing in the twentieth century and made his fortune in textiles and newspapers. Colonel Hall-Walker (later Lord Wavertree), whose wealth came from the brewing industry in Liverpool, is known among the racing fraternity for using astrology to guide his breeding plans. He was also responsible for introducing the third Aga Khan to racing on a visit to his stud in Tully, initiating a successful and ongoing involvement in racing by the Imams of the Shia Ismaili Muslims. In 2011, the extent of the involvement of the royal families of Saudi Arabia and Dubai (and particularly Sheikh Mohammed, Prince Hamdan bin Rashid Al Maktoum and Khalid Abdullah) led Newmarket trainer Jon Scargill to describe British racing as 'three funerals away from a holocaust'.[17]

In the United States, influential owners and breeders have been drawn from a mix of established wealth, including Guggenheims, Mellons, Hunts and Hancocks, and self-made men. John Mabee, tireless promoter of California racing and breeding, moved from Iowa in the 1950s because of ill health and made his fortune from a chain of grocery stores. Breeder and racetrack owner Frank Stronach dominated Canadian racing, having emigrated from Austria in 1954 to make a fortune from manufacturing automotive parts in Montreal. In the past twenty years, Internet millionaire Satish Sanan has spent an estimated $150 million on bloodstock in North America, having discovered racing as a student in the betting shops of England. In 2011, the top five buyers at the Keeneland September Sale included two members of the Dubai ruling family, Florida health care executive Ben Leon, telemarketing billionaires Gary and Mary West and Irishman John Magnier's breeding and racing operation, Coolmore.[18] In Australia, the Melbourne Cup has been won four times (in 1974, 1975, 1996 and 2008) by Malaysian entrepreneur Dato Tan Chin Nam, whose first venture was selling chickens on the side of the road after leaving school at age sixteen. This cosmopolitan mix of new and more established wealth is *de rigueur* on racecourses and at bloodstock auctions all over the world.

Old Histories, New Histories

Despite good claims to having been a national sport at one time or another in England, Australia and the United States, to many people today racing is a complete mystery, couched in an arcane and mysterious language of 'odds', 'distaff lines', 'blinkers', 'fetlocks' and 'Furosemide'. For some enthusiasts it appears to encapsulate the whole challenging business of life, but racing is a relatively small village. The population is boosted annually by events such as the Grand National in England or the Melbourne Cup, 'the race that stops a nation', in Australia. The sport has not lost the elegant simplicity that attracted a crowd of seventy thousand people to see Seabiscuit win the Santa Anita in 1940: 106,322 came to a Tokyo racecourse in 2010 to watch Rose Kingdom win the Japan Cup in the stewards' room, and in the United Kingdom annual racecourse attendance figures reached record levels in 2011.[19] Interest in racing has recently been boosted by two wonder horses – Frankel in Europe and Black Caviar in Australia. Black Caviar's incredible unbeaten run has drawn vast crowds, and this mare is truly modern – she Tweets and has her own Facebook page. Despite these lifts, the size of the racing village is dwindling, and new investors and audiences must be found, perhaps in new markets, including China, considered in Mark Godfrey's chapter of this volume (Chapter 12), or through appealing to new kinds of fans. Racing faces stiff competition from sports which are more accessible to amateur participation and simpler to understand, as well as from increasingly diverse and accessible gambling products.

The United Kingdom recently modernised its gambling laws, enabling bookmakers to advertise, but also opening up the market to competition from other sports and online competition.[20] Neither racecourses nor High Street shops hold monopolies on off-course betting any longer: this generation can bet on the majority of sports at home, online, or through their telephones or televisions. Those who have remained in the shops to bet in cash are able to choose between machines, virtual racing and sports with much higher public profiles, better returns and simpler rules than racing. As Davies describes in his chapter, changes in technology and regulation have affected racing all over the world. In the United States, 'handle' (the total amount wagered) is down 37 per cent and attendance by 30 per cent over the past decade. Racing in the United States faces competition from casinos, which grew by 34 per cent between 2001 and 2010 and now outnumber racetracks by a ratio of 6 to 1.[21] Even in Hong Kong, where a phenomenal average of HK$150 million is bet on every race (fifty times the average at U.S. tracks in 2010), Winfried Engelbrecht-Bresges, the Jockey Club's CEO, estimates that the annual revenue lost to illegal online gambling is between one-third and 100 per cent of the Jockey Club's receipts. Worldwide, having once dominated the field, racing now competes with other betting media, legal and illegal, for air time, customers and investors.

Racing administrators are aware that in order to widen the appeal of horseracing to a new generation of potential investors, the product must both be 'clean' and also be perceived as such. This problem is particularly acute in the United States where federal bodies lack authority and the use of race-day medication is an established local practice. In 2012, the

Thoroughbred Owners and Breeders Association's American Graded Stakes
Committee announced that a ban on race-day medication for two-year-olds
in graded stakes races would not be enforced because of 'the nature of the
various entities involved in implementation of rules governing racing'.[22] In
the United Kingdom, where race-day medication has not been permitted
since 1904, new whip rules show that administrators have begun to engage
with arguments about horse welfare.[23] The popularity of the play and film
War Horse shows that people are fascinated by animals and their relationships with people, and that, under certain circumstances, sacrifices made by
animals can be viewed as heroic. The extreme demands placed on racehorses
are more likely to be understood and accepted by a wider audience if the
horse is seen as a willing participant. Race-day medication, surgical proce-
dures and whips alienate people, including the vast numbers who own pets
or ride horses, because they militate against the idea that racing is the natural expression of instinctive competition.

If racing is to reach out to new audiences, it also needs to be mindful of
the heuristic effects of the ways in which it presents itself. In the introduction to a book of short stories published in the United States in 1986, the
editor describes racing as

> an integral part of British history, a vivid and colourful pageant of people,
> courses and, above all, great horses, stretching back over three hundred years
> to the reign of that great sporting monarch, Charles II. He it was who first
> instituted races across the glorious heath at Newmarket which has rightly
> come to be known as the 'Horse Racing Capital of the World'. In Britain too,
> we created the thoroughbred racehorse.[24]

This description makes racing sound irrelevant and parochial: a white,
Anglophile, upper-class sport. It was written twenty-five years ago, but similar ideas are still recycled on racecourse Web sites and in sundry media.
The alternatives presented in this collection (and in *Luck*) are so much more
interesting. Isn't it time to ditch old histories in favour of more exciting,
accurate and inclusive alternatives?

This book examines thoroughbred racing as it developed in Britain and
was adopted and adapted elsewhere. Each chapter allows an expert in his
or her field to unpick the diverse interests and priorities of racing's participants, undermining common misapprehensions and opening up new
topics for academic and popular debate. The chapters may be read in any
order, and no attempt has been made to standardise opinions because,
as Mark Twain said, 'it is difference of opinion that make horse-races'.[25]
Nevertheless, certain common themes emerge, including: cosmopolitanism

and cross-class contributions to racing; internationalism, regionalism and localism; racing and politics; the commercialisation of racing and breeding; the funding of racing by betting; and the depiction of racing in popular culture. Several chapters illustrate how these shared themes are instantiated differently 'on the ground' at different times and in various racing jurisdictions.

Why bother to scrutinise racing in this way? Won't claims of Englishness, stories about great victories and the intrinsic beauty and power of individual thoroughbreds be sufficient to ensure a future for the sport? The response presented in this collection is that more critical, dynamic and inclusive writing about racing is not only more accurate but also more likely to interest new audiences. From this perspective, *Luck* is not an exposé of the underbelly of track life, as some have suggested, but an invitation to hang out with the crooks and rogues, horses, heroes and ordinary people who between them create the racing spectacle.

NOTES

1 L. Pugmire, 'Q&A: David Milch on horse racing and iconic TV series', *Los Angeles Times*, 25 December 2011. Available at: www.articles.latimes.com/2011/dec/25/sports/la-sp-pugmire-qa-20111226. Accessed 6 February 2012.

2 BBC News, 'HBO cancels Dustin Hoffman drama Luck after horse death', 15 March 2012. Available at: www.bbc.co.uk/news/entertainment-arts-17364029. Accessed 19 March 2012.

3 For mixed reactions to *Luck* in the pages of the *Daily Racing Form*, see, for example: www.drf.com/blogs/luck-episode-3-recap-ace-bernstein-takes-reins. For reactions on a UK-hosted racing forum, see: www.theracingforum.co.uk/horse-racing-forum/viewtopic.php?f=3&t=89554&start=0. Both accessed 27 February 2012.

4 E. Hotaling, *The Great Black Jockeys: The Lives and Times of the Men Who Dominated America's First National Sport* (New York: Prima, 1999); S. Reiss, *The Sport of Kings and the Kings of Crime: Horse Racing, Politics and Organised Crime in New York 1865–1913* (Syracuse, NY: Syracuse University Press, 2011); M. Huggins, *Flat Racing and British Society 1790–1914* (London: Frank Cass, 2000); M. Huggins, *Horseracing and the British, 1919–1939* (Manchester: Manchester University Press, 2003); D. Landry, *Noble Brutes: How Eastern Horses Transformed English Culture* (Baltimore: Johns Hopkins University Press, 2008); J. Maynard, *Aboriginal Stars of the Turf* (Canberra: Aboriginal Studies Press, 2007); W. Peake, *Sydney's Pony Racecourses: An Alternative Racing History* (Sydney, N.S.W.: Walla Walla Press, 2006).

5 T. Egerton, *On the Sports and Pursuits of the English, as Bearing upon Their National Character* (Unknown binding, 1868), p. 1.

6 For the invention of the thoroughbred, see D. Landry, *Noble Brutes*. For a description of the cross-class development of horseracing in England, see M. Huggins, *Flat Racing and British Society* and *Horseracing and the British*.

7 J. Blunt-Lytton (Lady Wentworth), *The Authentic Arabian Horse and His Descendents* (London: Allen and Unwin, 1945), p. 31.

8 For an authoritative description of the exchanges of ideas, horses and personnel between Europe and England at this time, see J. Thirsk, *Horses in Early Modern England: For Service, for Pleasure, for Power* (Reading: University of Reading Press, 1978).

9 For a discussion of the Jersey Act, see C. Leicester, *Bloodstock Breeding*, 2nd ed., revised by H. Wright (1957; London: J.A. Allen, 1983).

10 C. Hill, *Horse Power: The Politics of the Turf* (Manchester: Manchester University Press, 1988), p. 188.

11 For discussions of the relative merits of the North American thoroughbred, see: http://cs.bloodhorse.com/blogs/market-watch/archive/2010/09/23/is-the-americ an-thoroughbred-a-separate-breed.aspx. Accessed 29 February 2012.

12 Egerton, *Sports and Pursuits*, p. 1.

13 Carleton, J. (Craven) (ed.), *The Sporting Review* (London, 1854), pp. 6, 12.

14 Reiss, *The Sport of Kings and the Kings of Crime*, p. 9.

15 H. McIlvanney, *McIlvanney on Horseracing* (Edinburgh: Mainstream Publishing Company, 1995), p. 64. Math teacher and chess player turned professional gambler Phil Bull formed Portway Press in 1948 and began to publish annuals containing statistical information about every horse running. After Bull's death in 1989, Timeform has continued to give each horse in training a rating expressed as a single number. The company was sold to Betfair for a reported £15 million in December 2006. For more information about this important racing figure, see H. Wright, *Bull – The Biography* (Halifax: Timeform, 1995).

16 Nathaniel de Rothschild was one of the first Jews to be elected to the notoriously exclusive French Jockey Club. For more details, see D. Stone, 'The Racing Rothschilds: The Sportsmen, the Maverick and the Legend', *Rothschild Archive Review of the Year, April 2008–March 2009*. Available at: www.rothschildarchive.org/ib/articles/AR2009Stone.pdf. Accessed 5 March 2012.

17 Quoted by M. Engel, 'British Institutions: Horse Racing', *Financial Times*, 10 June 2011. The relationship between Sheik Mohammed, tourism in Dubai and international racing is discussed by Rachel Pagones in this volume (Chapter 11).

18 More information about Coolmore can be found in Michael Hinds's chapter in this volume (Chapter 8).

19 M. Curry, 'Rose Kingdom Stuns Buena Vista via DQ in Japan Cup', *Thoroughbred Times*, 28 November 2010. The Racecourse Association Limited, 'Racecourse attendances hit record high in 2011', 24 January 2012. Available at: britishrace-courses.org/news/racecourse-attendances-hit-record-high-in-2011/. Accessed 5 March 2012.

20 The text of the United Kingdom Gambling Act 2005 can be accessed here: www.legislation.gov.uk/ukpga/2005/19/contents. Accessed 5 March 2012.

21 For more statistics about racing in North America, see: www.jockeyclub.com/ROUNDTABLE.asp. Accessed 5 March 2012.

22 Blood-Horse Staff, 'AGSC will not enact raceday medication ban' *The Blood-Horse*, 26 February 2012. Available at: www.bloodhorse.com/horse-racing/articles/67648/agsc-will-not-enact-race-day-medication-ban. Accessed 28 February 2012.

23 British Horseracing Authority policy on whip use and specification is available at: www.britishhorseracing.com/inside_horseracing/about/whatwedo/disciplinary/whipuse.asp. Accessed 29 February 2012.

24 R. Peyton, *At the Track: A Treasury of Horse Racing Stories* (New York: Bonanza Books, 1986), p. 9.

25 M. Twain, *Pudd'nhead Wilson* (London: Charles L. Webster, 1894).

I

RICHARD NASH

Sporting with Kings

What is a thoroughbred? The very notion is bound up with curious formulations and identities that span the improbable and impossible. Commonly encountered responses include: a breed of horse; a horse whose sire and dam were both registered thoroughbreds, whose pedigrees are recorded for several generations in the *General Stud Book*; a breed of race-horse, originating in England, with pedigrees recorded in a *General Stud Book*, whose origins can be traced in continuous tail-male descent back to one of three foundation stallions, imported from the Orient: the Byerley Turk, the Darley Arabian, and the Godolphin Arabian. Closely associated is the idea that racing between thoroughbreds so defined originated in England during the reign of Charles II, who instituted a series of races for Royal Plates following his restoration to the throne, to be contested on the heath at Newmarket. To one degree or another, each of these is true, and none, to the extent that it is true, entirely discredits another. And yet they cannot all be made to work. For instance, given that Charles II died in February of 1685, it is utterly impossible for him to have ever seen a thoroughbred in any of those races he established, if by thoroughbred we mean a horse descended from the foundation sires, who only arrived in England after his death. In this sense, thoroughbred racing predates the thoroughbred.

A larger, but related, imprecision occurs when we juxtapose the 'breed of horse' designation with registry in the *General Stud Book*. We want ideas like 'breed of horse' to refer to something in nature, but the *General Stud Book* is a cultural artefact. The notion of 'breed' in animals, in the same way as the notion of 'race' as it is applied to people, is one of those conceptual slippages, in which cultural perceptions of difference are reified as naturally occurring. This is particularly true of the breed identity of the thoroughbred which emerges over the nearly two-hundred-year span that also sees the rise of modern notions of racial identity. In many ways, the cultural transformation that ushers in modern conceptions of racial identity, and at the same time introduces modern democratic notions of state organization, follows closely – and is inextricably entangled with – the historical process during which the horses who raced for Charles II became the racehorses whose 'purebred identities' were recorded in an official breed registry roughly a century and a half after the restoration of that happy monarch. The 'sport of kings'[1] is born from the same cultural ferment that marked the end of absolute monarchy. From the outset, there has been a subversive, carnivalesque current to horse racing, as important as the more often noted royalist pretensions.

While we have anecdotal references to racing in the seventeenth century, those events were not recorded systematically, and it is unclear if they were intended as tests for the results of systematic breeding practices, or if systematic breeding practices developed in pursuit of greater success in these events. Geohumoral breeding theories (the idea that different environments produced variations in people and animals) were dominant before the Restoration, supported by Galen's doctrine of the four humours. In the later seventeenth century, Galenic models diminished in influence, the role of individual agents became more valued, and the model of inheritance that emerged shared much with legal and political theories of inheritance and succession.[2] We can see something of a turning point at the very moment of Restoration itself, when Charles II rode in his coronation parade on a horse given to him by the Parliamentary General, Lord Fairfax, who, after defeating the Royalist forces in 1648, then parted company with the regicides over the execution of Charles I. Fairfax sat out the interregnum in rural retirement, breeding horses and writing a treatise on the breeding of horses and a volume of verses, most of which remain deservedly unpublished. One brief, rough verse that he wrote concerning the horse he gave to Charles II to ride at his coronation captures a moment of cultural reversal:

> 'Upon the Horse wch hhis Matie Rode Upon att his Coronation 1660'
> Hence then Dispaire my hopes why should itt bury
> Sence this brave steed Bredd first was in my Query
> Now thus advance's with highest honors Laden
> Whilst his that bredd him by most Men's trodden
> But tis noe matter Seeing tho' hast gott th'Advance
> Then please the Royal Rider with thy Prance
> Soe may thy Fame much rayse thy Prayses higher
> Then Chesnut that begott thee or Brid La-dore -the- ^his^ sire[3]

[Bridla-dore (Anglice): Golden Bridle]

There is but one horse in this poem, but the title insists on placing two burdens 'upon' him – both the monarch at his coronation and the verses themselves, announced as 'upon' the horse rather than the rider – only to collapse the distinction between horse and rider with a royal compliment at the conclusion. The first stanza wittily restores the horse to his royal owner, who is now restored to his throne, while at the same time acknowledging that henceforth, the advances of the horse he bred must come at the expense of the breeder, who has been humbled. Acknowledging a double restoration – Charles to the throne, the horse to Charles – the first stanza announces a separation: the horse bred by Fairfax is separated from the one who bred him. The second stanza, then, by the conceit of the two final lines, collapses a desire to praise the horse into a complementary compliment to the new rider. The correction in the manuscript from 'the' to 'his' in the final line not only clarifies the pedigree of the horse Fairfax bred from the remnants of the Royal Stud, but does so in a language that evokes an identity of lineage between horse and rider: portraits of the auburn-haired Charles I and blonde, bearded James I illustrate how aptly 'Chesnut that begott thee or Brid La-dore his sire' describes the lineage of Charles II himself, enabling 'thee' to signify both horse and king. The poem's final word, 'sire', plays on all three senses active in the poem, and in the context of horseracing in the decades that follow: monarch, father and breeding stallion. The stud, like the state, is to be identified by notions of paternity, inheritance and succession.

Spanker and Monmouth

If the sport of horseracing that we now identify with the thoroughbred came into being during the reign of Charles II, it did so in advance of those imported stallions who came to be known as 'foundation stallions'. And it also began in advance of the record keeping and registration that constituted the sport's history. No better illustration of the ambiguities of the sport's early history exists than the horse universally acknowledged to be 'the best horse who ran at Newmarket during the reign of Charles II', Spanker, a son of the Darcy Yellow Turk. Although racing results begin to appear in the press early in the eighteenth century, and are recorded systematically in some areas as early as 1709, and nationally via Historical Registers from 1727 onwards, the results of those races established during the Restoration are, at best, haphazard and are more likely to focus on the human than the equine agent. So, although some results of individual matches and plates exist from the reign of Charles – including matches won by the monarch himself – there is not a single result of any race involving a horse named Spanker. Spanker's career – at once celebrated and anonymous – testifies most strongly to the extent to which the sport's earliest achievements were unrecorded. He was foaled around 1674 and his racing career is likely to have belonged to the last third of the quarter-century Charles spent on the throne, during that portion of his reign that was marked by strident political controversy and an anxiety over succession that touched the racing world as well.

When Monmouth conducted his 'progresses' in 1680 and 1682, while Shaftesbury sought the passage of an Exclusion Bill, thousands thronged to follow him in an impressive display of protestant populism that served as a none-too-subtle suggestion of the possibility of rebellion should James ascend the throne. As these displays became more vigorous in 1682, Charles was forced to act. After it was reported that Monmouth's followers were drinking toasts to a protestant succession, Monmouth was arrested and brought before the king, who forgave him but banished him from court. The ostensible occasion for this progress was that Monmouth was proceeding from race meet to race meet, in each case riding to victory on horses provided for him by Thomas Wharton, whose most accomplished horse, the Wharton Gelding, was at the time the best racehorse in England. Decades later, in his *Tour*, Defoe recounts on several occasions the great crowds that rallied to follow Monmouth, including a race that he won for 'the Great Prize at Quainton Meadow', created by Thomas Wharton specifically to showcase Monmouth's skills: 'It was my hap formerly, to be at Aylesbury, when there was a mighty confluence of noblemen and gentlemen, at a famous horse race at Quainton-Meadow, not far off, where was then the late Duke of Monmouth, and a great many persons of the first rank, and a prodigious concourse of people.'[4]

Defoe, who we know was among Monmouth's forces in the rebellion of 1685, was also clearly amongst those drawn to the progresses as a dress rehearsal for that rebellion, as forty years later he vividly recalls not only the race at Quainton Meadow, but other triumphs: '[S]ometimes indeed the gentlemen ride themselves, as I have often seen the Duke of Monmouth, natural son to King Charles II ride his own horses at a match, and win it too, though he was a large man, and must weigh heavy.'[5] After Charles banished Monmouth for the excessive and potentially treasonous display of his progresses, in the following February, Louis XVI hosted the first international horse race at Aix-St. Germain, and it was won by the Wharton gelding, racing in the name of the Duke of Monmouth.[6] Following the race, Louis said he would pay a thousand pistoles to own such a horse, and Thomas Wharton immediately replied that the horse was not for sale, but that Louis could have him as a gift. When Louis declined the gift, it may have signalled to Monmouth and Wharton that his support was already committed elsewhere and Monmouth's only remaining path to the throne was through open rebellion.

The following spring, Charles and James travelled together to the spring meeting of Newmarket races, but this time the two-week meet was cut short when the town caught fire. While there were no casualties, and the royal party was never in jeopardy, the conflagration was intense and destroyed half the town, putting an end to the race meet and sending Charles and James back to London a week ahead of schedule. For the next two years, while Newmarket was rebuilt, racing was conducted elsewhere. More importantly, the fire and the hasty return to London disrupted the Rye House Plot that was only revealed later that summer. The previous year, before his banishment, Monmouth had met with several extreme protestant supporters at Rye House on the road between London and Newmarket, where plans had been hatched to ambush the king and his brother on their return from Newmarket the following spring. Monmouth begged the king's pardon, claiming that he had never known the full intent of the plot, nor approved designs against the king's life. This time, Charles sent him into an exile from which he never returned until in open rebellion against James in 1685. Other Rye House plotters were executed.

Foundations

The most vigorous years of Charles's support of the sport of horseracing coincide with the final half-dozen years of his reign, when amongst the most active participants in that sport is his illegitimate son, Monmouth. All of these activities predate the earliest of the so-called foundation stallions. The foundation stallions – Byerley Turk, Darley Arabian and Godolphin Arabian – were not, of course, identified as such during their own lifetimes, and only began to be thought of as foundational in the early nineteenth century, by which time their descendants had demonstrated significant ability in comparison to the progeny of the dozens of other imported stallions. Rather than being contemporaries, these three stallions lived successively, and indeed, there is almost a seamless transition from the end of one career to the beginning of the next. In many ways, the era described by their three successive careers may be thought of as the transitional period in which England articulated, as a settled and secure compromise, the parliamentary monarchy that followed the death of Charles and finally and definitively established itself with the final defeat of the Jacobite uprising of 1745.

The Byerley Turk was, in the eighteenth century, identified as Captain Byerley's charging horse at the Battle of the Boyne in 1690. Only in the early twentieth century did the widely credited, but recently challenged, notion arise that he had been captured as spoils of war during the siege of Vienna. No record exists of Byerley ever serving at the sieges of Buda or at Vienna. The account of the Turk being captured as a spoil of war began as a conjecture of the twentieth-century historian, C.F. Prior, and was too quickly adopted as true. That narrative, in fact, merely followed an eighteenth-century account of the importation of another horse (the Lister Turk). I have recently argued for the likelihood that the horse now known as 'the Byerley Turk' (though probably of imported ancestry) was bred in England.[7] His career as a stallion was relatively brief, lasting only about a dozen years, during which he was bred to relatively few mares in North Yorkshire before his death in about 1703, soon after the death of William, the monarch in whose service he had charged at the Boyne. In December of that year, Thomas Darley wrote from Aleppo to his brother, saying that he was sending home as a gift to his father (from whom he appears to have been estranged) an Arabian stallion who would be four years old the following spring. The Darley Arabian arrived (via Kinsale, Ireland) in May 1704, and his earliest progeny seem to date from 1706. He, too, was bred to relatively few mares in North Yorkshire, and his most famous progeny were two full brothers – Flying or Devonshire Childers and Bartlett's or Bleeding Childers – who seem to have been bred from the same dam in the final two years of his career as a stallion, 1714 and 1715, the final year of Stuart rule and the first year of the Hanoverian succession. Very few outliers have been assigned to the Darley Arabian after 1715, but in each case the evidence is weak and contradictory and no confidence can be had in his having sired any offspring after 1715.

The precise origins of the Godolphin Arabian are quite obscure and have been encrusted with the absurd legends and tales that grew up around him at the end of the eighteenth and into the nineteenth centuries. But his earliest known activity was in the stud of Edward Coke of Longford, Derby, and seems to have begun with a crop of 1730, although it is possible that he arrived in England as a young horse as early as 1726. Accounts have long echoed the statement in the *Sportsman's Pocket Companion* (c. 1766) that the Godolphin Arabian's death on Christmas Day, 1753 came 'in his 29th year'. However, A.J. Hibbard (personal communication) has recently called to my attention a death notice in the *Derby Mercury*, which places his birth as early as 1721.[8] As a foal of 1721, it becomes more plausible that he may have been one of the half-dozen horses who appear to have been brought to England as diplomatic gifts of the ambassador of the Emperor of Morocco in August 1725.[9] Edward Coke's brother was Lord Lovel, who acquired at this time Lord Lovel's Arabian, who appears to be the same horse later known as Sir Michael Newton's Grey Arabian, who, according to an advertisement of 1760, 'came over with the Godolphin Arabian'.[10] After Coke's early death in 1733, he became the property of Lord Godolphin; and it was at Lord Godolphin's stud, Gogmagog, in Cambridge, that he came to such prominence that his death in 1753 was reported in the newspapers.

At the times when these three arrived in England, each was considered only one of many representatives of 'southern blood' being brought into a northern climate to revitalize a stagnant breed; of the three, only the last achieved significant acclaim during his own lifetime. What had been, during the Restoration, primarily a regional sport, centred in North Yorkshire, where family loyalties were often strained between Catholic and Protestant, Royalist and Parliamentarian, was becoming (albeit gradually) a national pastime that would be identified with a southern centre at Newmarket by the 1770s. Coke's death in 1733 was the occasion for Lord Godolphin's stud at Gogmagog to become the most significant racing stud not located in the north. Moreover, dramatic changes were occurring on the national stages of both politics and sport. The year 1727 saw the death of George I and the succession of his son, George II. This had not been the happiest of father-son relationships, and the younger George had given clear signals that he might well return to a Tory ministry when he ascended the throne, cultivating both Court and Opposition camps during the extended anticipation of the death of his father. In the end, those hopes were dashed when the younger George consolidated the 'Whig supremacy' and extended the career of Prime Minister Robert Walpole. In racing news that year, John Cheny began publishing by subscription an annual 'Historical List' of races run during the previous year, initiating the systematic recording of the sport at a national level. From the very outset, Cheny planned to include pedigree information, but it was not until 1743 that he was able to go beyond simply keeping up with the races themselves, and add an index that included pedigree information for the most significant horses to that point. Although Weatherby did not credit Cheny, it is undeniable that when the *General Stud Book* finally made its appearance at the end of the eighteenth century, much of the early pedigree records were those that had been compiled by Cheny between 1727 and 1743.

The monarch has always had an interest in the breeding and racing of horses, presented as a matter of national security. As early as Henry's attempts to acquire horses from the Gonzagan stud at Mantua, the Royal interest in both breeding better horses and in sporting contests that would test that breeding were rationalized by a call to improve the breed of horses in England, so as to better mount a cavalry for national defence. But such a strategy has an obvious downside. If those who take the lead in developing better horses become disaffected with the monarch, the horses they produce become (quite literally) the breeding ground for potential rebellion.

In the shifting political terrain of late-seventeenth-century England, as tensions and hostilities simmered over uncertainties of succession between Protestant and Papist, Whig and Tory, the competition for breeding (and possessing) better horses became a matter of concern; and in what amounted to a seventeenth-century Homeland Security Act ('An Act for the better securing the government, by disarming papists'), Catholics were prohibited in 1695 from owning horses valued at more than five pounds. Until the act was modified during Anne's reign to allow Catholics to possess breeding stock of that value, a protestant could under law compel a Catholic to sell any horse or mare for which he was willing to pay five pounds and five shillings; and many did, exacerbating tensions between Catholic and Protestant families in Yorkshire horse-breeding districts.

If the breeding of quality horses posed (or was perceived to pose) a potential threat to the monarch, then the assemblages created by the race meets themselves must have seemed distinctly menacing. By their very nature, these events brought together many well-mounted individuals. Owners would generally bring several top horses to compete, and standard practice called for the horses to race in four-mile heats, with a large part of the crowd accompanying the racers through the final half-mile or mile run to the finishing post. Not infrequently, race meets would attract a partisan crowd, as was certainly the case during Monmouth's progresses. As those progresses grew and the numbers of followers, both mounted and on foot, increased, they effectively became rehearsals for rebellion. In the end, of course, it was Monmouth himself who suffered when the many who had come out for the rehearsals stayed home for the main event. But the potential for these race meets to prove subversive had long been recognized. One of Cromwell's first acts had banned horse races for sixth months because 'of the evil use made thereof by such ill-disposed Persons as watch for opportunities to raise New Troubles ... [and threaten] the Peace and Security of this Nation'.[11]

Even after the execution of Monmouth, race meets continued to be useful rallies for rebels. At the time of the 1715 Jacobite rebellion, a number of Tory gentry assembled at the Bath race meet, only to be told that it was already too late and they should return home. In the north, however, not long before, Lord Derwentwater assembled the Northumbrian Jacobites at the Dilston race meeting, from where they began the rising. The failure of that Jacobite rising did not, of course, put a final end to Jacobite ambitions; in 1743, James Butler, a kinsman of the Duke of Ormonde, who was then serving as Master of the Horse to Louis XV, visited England, ostensibly to buy bloodstock. In fact, he was taking the pulse of Jacobite sympathy among Tories in England. After a meeting with Jacobite sympathizers at the Lichfield races that September, Butler returned to France, and plans for

French support for 'The Forty-Five' began, following his report to Louis XV. Far from being simply occasions for manifesting state authority, race meets conformed more closely to the subversive and riotous potential theorized by Bakhtin in his notion of the carnivalesque.[12] Defoe's description of 'nobility and gentry' in Newmarket in 1722 behaving like 'so many horse-coursers in Smithfield' also captures this topsy-turvy disruption of order.[13]

Clubs and Calendars

The failure of The Forty-Five settled, for all but the most stubborn of Jacobites, the succession question that had lingered to varying degrees as part of English political life from the latter days of the reign of Charles II. No event was more emphatic in determining that outcome than Culloden, and the hero of Protestant Royalism was the Duke of Cumberland, younger son of George II, who became known to Jacobites as the 'Butcher of Culloden' for the aftermath of that battle. Cumberland's subsequent military career was notably less successful, and following his disgrace in 1757, he focused his ambitions primarily on horseracing. Even before then, however, from the early 1750s, we can see the Duke taking an active interest in horseracing. Historians have long identified the formation of the Jockey Club as occurring in either 1750 or 1751, and the earliest record of its existence appears to be a notice in Pond's *Sporting Kalendar* of 1751, where he notes a race to run the following spring at Newmarket 'by horses the property of the Noblemen and Gentlemen belonging to the Jockey Club at the Star and Garter in Pall Mall'. In fact, the Jockey Club was formed a generation earlier in the 1720s and may have initially motivated and supported Cheny's *An Historical List of Races*. That manifestation of the Jockey Club underwent some reform in response to various events of 1750–51, and by the meeting of November 21, 1751 had established a more formal institutional presence that would, over the next quarter-century, constitute itself as the national centre of racing that it remains today.[14] Cheny had died in 1750, and his son had enlisted the assistance of Reginald Heber in bringing out that year's volume, with an apology for the delay; from this time forward, the list was published by Heber under his own name. But during that first year, when the *Historical List* was delayed, a competitor appeared in the form of John Pond's *Sporting Kalendar*. While Pond only published his volume for eight years, for that period of time there appears to have been a divided market with considerable overlap in the subscriber lists. One glaring difference in those subscriber lists is that while he does not appear in Heber's list (as he had not in Cheny's), Pond's list always began with, in slightly larger font: 'His Royal Highness, the Duke.' The Duke of Cumberland was not only the first member of the royal family to belong to the Jockey Club, but he is likely to have been involved from the beginning (or shortly after the beginning) of the 1751 reform movement. Certainly, he was a member by 1753, since he won the following year's renewal of the Club's Subscription Plate (entry to which was limited to Club members) with Marske. Marske's principal claim to fame was as sire of the greatest racehorse of the eighteenth century, Eclipse, a direct descendant of the Darley Arabian, through Bleeding Childers. Eclipse is known as 'a conduit stallion', because it is through him that more than 90 per cent of the world's thoroughbreds today trace back to the Darley Arabian along the sire line. But the Duke was also responsible for breeding Herod, the conduit through whom the Byerley Turk's sire line persists into the present.

By breeding two of the three conduit stallions of the later eighteenth century, the Duke might be described as the most important breeder of the century (the third conduit, Matchem, a grandson of the Godolphin Arabian, was bred by John Holmes of Carlisle). In the shorter style of racing that emerged at the end of the eighteenth century, in which horses contested a single race of less than two miles, as opposed to the older style of competing in multiple heats of four miles, the most significant bloodlines have tended to trace to nicks produced by crossing the offspring of Eclipse and Herod. But the Duke did not witness the extent of that impact. Herod, foaled in 1758, was a significant, but not dominant, racehorse before the Duke's death in 1765; afterwards, he manifested serious respiratory bleeding problems and was retired to stud. It was in this role – particularly through the influence of his most successful son, Highflyer – that he left a lasting impression on the sport. The most important horse bred by the Duke was, of course, Eclipse, named for the solar eclipse during which he was foaled in 1764. The Duke died late in the following year and thus never saw his best horse run.

It seems incredible today that the dispersal sale following the death of the Duke of Cumberland included two of the three conduit stallions of the thoroughbred breed (Eclipse and Herod sold for a meagre total of 545 guineas). However, at the time, both of those two northern sire lines (Byerley Turk and Darley Arabian) had come to be overshadowed by the popularity of a more recent import, stabled in the south, the Godolphin Arabian. In those relative popularities, we can discern both a survival of an earlier breeding philosophy and the emergence of a new one. Geohumoral theory had originally advocated the importation of stallions, not so much because they were eastern as because they were southern; it was believed that hot, southern blood was necessary to revitalize the stock of northern climes. That philosophy, however, also required the perpetual replenishing of that southern influence, so the impact of the Darley Arabian and Byerley Turk that we now look back to as foundational would have been seen in the 1760s as too remote to be of great influence. Indeed, the Duke had acquired Marske, sire of Eclipse, by trading an imported Arabian for him, and throughout the remainder of the eighteenth century, imported Arabian stallions continued to be advertised year after year, yet none of them left a lasting influence on the breed. According to this theory, stallions would be more valuable for importation than mares (because a mare would produce only one offspring a year, while a stallion could be put to many mares in his first year or two when his blood would retain most of its native heat), and there would be a steady market for newly imported southern stallions. Although historians have sought many possible sources for the so-called Royal Mares of Charles II, those efforts have not been successful; in fact, importing mares would have run counter to what was the more orthodox breeding philosophy of the seventeenth century, given that one southern stallion could conceivably improve many mares, whereas each imported mare would quickly degenerate in her new northern climate.

The newer philosophy that was emerging and came to prominence with the success of sons of the Godolphin Arabian was the notion of 'prepotency'. The earlier notion of this term, of 'having superior power or influence', now began the migration to the specific biological sense that it would take on in the nineteenth century, as a contribution to emergent evolutionary ideas. Veterinarian Osmer wrote of the Godolphin Arabian, in 1756, 'There never was a horse (at least, that I have seen) so well entitled to get racers as the Godolphin Arabian.' Osmer was writing at the time very much against the emerging view that there was some attribute of blood that descended from sire to son, and the rest of his sentence about the Godolphin Arabian's excellence as a sire attributes that excellence to his physique rather than to some property transmitted by blood.[15] But the current he was resisting was stronger than his arguments, and the Godolphin Arabian was lionized throughout the final third of the eighteenth century for his 'prepotency,' which focused on a perceived ability not only to influence the next generation, but to carry that influence on into a third generation.

In the final third of the eighteenth century, James Weatherby took over the racing calendar begun by Cheny in 1727 and served as keeper of the match book at Newmarket; from that position, he set about collecting a *General Stud Book* that assembled the pedigree records of the most prominent equine families of the previous century. He managed to live to see, with the help of his nephew and namesake, the publication of an *Introduction to the General Stud Book* in 1791, with the first volume appearing a dozen years later and continuing (for the next 200 years) under the auspices of the Weatherby family. However much the *General Stud Book* (as its name suggests) may have begun with the idea of collecting an aggregate record of actual breeding practice, almost from the moment of its publication it became a document espousing logics of continuity, epitomized in ideas such as 'prepotency' and 'breeding back'.[16] The tumultuous, hybridized seventeenth-century origins were re-inscribed in a model of purity and coherence, in the stable as in the state.

NOTES

1 While 'the sport of kings' is today associated with horseracing in the eighteenth century, that phrase (rarely encountered) would be more likely ascribed to hunting (see Somerville's *The Chace* I, 14). Less well known outside the racing world than within is the nineteenth-century democratizing maxim that 'all men are equal on – and under – the Turf'.

2 For a discussion of geohumoralism with respect to early modern horse breeding, see I. F. MacInnes, 'Altering a Race of Jades: Horse Breeding and Geohumoralism in Shakespeare' in P. Edwards, K.A.E. Enenkel and E. Graham (eds.), *The Horse as Cultural Icon. The Real and Symbolic Horse in the Early Modern World* (Leiden-Boston: Brill, 2011), pp. 175–189.

3 M.S. Fairfax 40, Bodleian Library, Oxford.

4 D. Defoe, *A Tour through the Whole Island of Great Britain*, rev. edn. (London: Dent, 1974).

5 Defoe, *Tour*, p. 148.

6 J. Kent Clark, *Whig's Progress* (Cranbury, NJ: Associated University Presses, 2004), p. 165. Macauley retells this story, although by getting both the date and the horse wrong, he misses the association with Monmouth's political aspirations. For a fuller treatment of Wharton's racing interests and their importance to reconsiderations of the origins of the thoroughbred, see my "'Beware a Bastard Breed': Notes Towards a Revisionist History of the Thoroughbred Racehorse" in P. Edwards, K.A.E. Enenkel and E. Graham (eds.), *The Horse as Cultural Icon. The Real and Symbolic Horse in the Early Modern World* (Leiden-Boston: Brill, 2011), pp. 191–216.

7 See Nash, 'Beware a Bastard Breed'.

8 'We hear from Newmarket, that on Christmas-Day last died, in the 33d Year of his Age, the famous Horse known by the Name of the Godolphin Arabian.' *Derby Mercury*. Volume XXII. Number 41. From Friday, 28 December [1753] to Friday, 4 January 1754.

9 *Stamford Mercury*, Vol. XXXVI. No. 9, 26 August 1725.

10 *London Evening Post*, issue 5055, 27 March 1760. Sir Michael Newton was the uncle of Lord Lovel and Edward Coke.

11 *By His Highness: A Proclamation Prohibiting Horse-Races* (Henry Hills and John Field, 1654).

12 M. Bakhtin, 'Folk Humor and Carnival Laughter' and 'Carnival Ambivalence', from *Rabelais and His World*, in P. Morris (ed.), *The Bakhtin Reader* (London: Edward Arnold, 1994): pp. 194–226. See also Silverman, Chapter 10 in this volume.

13 Defoe, *Tour*, p. 75.

14 'This is to acquaint the Noblemen and Gentlemen of the Society call'd the Jockey Club that the first Weekly Meeting will be held on Thursday, as usual, at the Star and Garter in Pall Mall.' *General Advertiser*, Tuesday, 19 November 1751. I am working on an account of the formation of the Jockey Club that is too complex to include here.

15 W. Osmer, *A Dissertation on Horses: Wherein it is Demonstrated by Matters of Fact, as well as from the Principles of Philosophy, that Innate Qualities do not exist, and that the excellence of this Animal is altogether mechanical and not in the Blood* (London: T. Waller, 1756), p. 50.

16 R. Nash, 'The Book that Wrote an Animal' in L. Runge and P. Rogers (eds.), *Producing the Eighteenth-Century Book: Writers and Publishers in England, 1650–1800* (Newark: University of Delaware Press, 2009): pp. 117–134; R. Cassidy, *Horse People: Thoroughbred Culture in Lexington and Newmarket* (Baltimore: John Hopkins University Press, 2007), pp. 31–32.

2

DOUGLAS FORDHAM

The Thoroughbred in British Art

The history of art is replete with horses, from early representations in the caves of Chauvet, to the Bronze Age white horse carved into the hillside in Uffington, England, to the glistening miniatures of Mughal India. The survival of these images speaks to an ancient and enduring desire on the part of humankind to represent a species that has been a partner and a companion across diverse cultures and over many millennia.[1] And yet each culture's engagement with the horse, and their representation of it, reveals a unique conjunction of cultural forces. This essay examines a particularly dynamic moment in the representation of the horse, which coincided with the creation of the 'thoroughbred' horse in eighteenth-century Britain. The development is traced through Great Britain's imperial expansion in the nineteenth century to the globalization of its formal tropes and aesthetic premises in the twentieth. It is striking that an intensive process of animal breeding was seen to be coextensive with – or at least highly amenable to – fine art processes of painting, sculpting, and engraving. From the start, the thoroughbred horse was viewed as an achievement worthy of high cultural representation. And while thoroughbred portraiture entered a culvert in the nineteenth and twentieth centuries, it has reappeared in contemporary art as a major site of inquiry and contestation.

In Western painting traditions, equestrian portraiture typically paired an unnamed steed with an aristocratic or royal rider. Van Dyck's grand portraits of *Charles I at the Hunt* (1635) and *Charles I on Horseback* (c. 1637–38) constitute two particularly influential examples. But the notion of a horse portrait, in which the 'sitter' is a standing horse, belongs quite firmly to the eighteenth century and corresponds with the emergence of thoroughbred breeding, racing and bookkeeping. As Landry has argued:

> After his lordship's Arabian arrived on the scene, and only then, were horses considered worthy of painting, as subjects of portraits rather than objects in pictures about humans. There were Eastern – Persian, Mughul, and

Figure 2.1. John Wootton, *The Duke of Rutland's Bonny Black*, ca. 1715, Oil on canvas, 76.2 × 123.2 cm, Yale Center for British Art (YCBA).

Ottoman – precedents for this equine portraiture. But in the British Isles, it was the arrival of these exotic horses themselves that inspired a new genre of painting.[2]

Although earlier thoroughbred portraits can be found, John Wootton was the first widely celebrated horse portraitist in England, and to a striking extent his paintings lay out the basic parameters of the genre. His portrait of *The Duke of Rutland's Bonny Black*, painted around 1715, offers an excellent early example (Figure 2.1).

Capturing the horse in profile, Wootton painted distinctive visual markers such as the white rear fetlocks, clipped tail and light patches on a jet-black hide. The painting is set at Newmarket, with a vignette of Bonny Black at full gallop in the middle distance between the thoroughbred's legs. The painting captures a degree of class mingling often noted by contemporaries at Newmarket, particularly in the group of gentlemen surrounding a jockey on the right. The compositional template, in which a horse stands in profile against a naturalistically rendered setting, served eighteenth-century sporting artists exceedingly well. So well that it led to complaints like that by Rouquet: 'As soon as a race horse has acquired some fame, they have him immediately drawn to the life: this for the most part is a dry profile, but in other respects bearing a good resemblance; they generally clap the figure of some jockey or other upon his back, which is poorly done.'[3] Written in

1755, this passage demonstrates how quickly the genre took hold and also the artistic mediocrity with which it was already associated. Within a few years George Stubbs would move to London and greatly refine the genre, but not substantially alter its conventions.

One of the most commonly cited functions of the thoroughbred portrait was to record and celebrate a patron's material wealth. In 1775, the aspiring history painter James Barry railed against an excessive national taste for 'portraits of ourselves, of our horses, our dogs, and country seats', which implied a certain crass materialism and an egotistical self-regard.[4] It also constituted a critique of aristocratic taste, which conflicted with many of the aims and ideals of the 'public sphere'. The shift from aristocratic patronage in the early eighteenth century to a publicly oriented art market by the end of the century constitutes one of the grand narratives of Georgian art history, and it is a shift with significant implications for sporting art. Deuchar described eighteenth-century sporting art as 'an old ideal in a new world' and examined the need by Stubbs and his contemporaries to combat 'the sporting stigma' which had become acute by the end of the century.[5] When viewed as a distinctive category of elite consumption and as a marker of aristocratic wealth, horse portraiture seemed to have little to add to a polite and commercial nation.

This essay takes a different approach, emphasizing the popularity, global diffusion, and longevity of the genre. It is an approach driven by three basic arguments. First, historians have convincingly argued that the English aristocracy was more resilient and enterprising than the art historiography mentioned earlier might suggest.[6] Second, historians of sporting art have tended to focus on painting, artistic innovation and fine art patronage, while ignoring or dismissing the role of intaglio prints and other mass media in popularizing thoroughbred portraiture. Third, a number of contemporary artists from the English-speaking world resurrected horse portraiture in the late twentieth century as a means of interrogating a whole array of social and aesthetic questions. Mark Wallinger, Damien Hirst, Jeff Wall, Jimmy Pike and others have toyed with the conventions of horse portraiture, but often with an underlying seriousness about the ways in which the genre might inform 'Race Class Sex', to cite the title of Mark Wallinger's set of four thoroughbred portraits from 1992.

Returning to *The Duke of Rutland's Bonny Black*, it should be emphasized just how significant the title is to the work's purpose and meaning. The title and painting establish two parallel genealogical trees that inform and naturalize one another. Summarizing and extending an argument first put forward by Howard Bloch, Christopher Wood has stated:

Genealogy was a fiction designed to mask the incomprehensible realities of genetic dispersal and recombination and instead construct clean paths to the right ancestors. Genealogy was a theory of genetics propped up by naming magic. The persistence of the name through the male line, the various systems governing the transmission of aristocratic titles, the inalienability of property, the identification of family with a piece of land, and the possibility of advantageous renaming, perhaps through social elevation, at any point in the chain, were arbitrary conventions that needed all the magic they could get.[7]

Horse breeding was more tightly controlled than that of the aristocracy, but a similar 'naming magic' prevailed in both, establishing powerful analogies between landed aristocrats and their thoroughbreds. While eighteenth-century Britons largely accepted these medieval conventions as they applied to the landed aristocracy, the extension of these values to thoroughbred horses remained something of a novelty.

George Stubbs and Thoroughbred Portraiture

Stubbs' *Pumpkin with a Stable-Lad* (Figure 2.2) demonstrates a quantum leap in thoroughbred portraiture's evocative power and the intensity of its naturalistic observation. Stubbs stages a feeding ritual between an anonymous stable lad and a named horse that possesses a quiet poignancy given the youth of both. Horse and servant perform their allotted tasks with a placid, mutual understanding. Both individuals are portrayed in strict profile, and there is a wonderful equivalence between the white impasto highlights on the boy's collar and cuffs and those on the horse's face and eye.

In contrast to the horse handler in *Bonny Black*, Stubbs's stable lad is distinctive and almost certainly a portrait. As Blake has observed, 'England had never produced a more committed painter of the labouring class than Stubbs. His hunt servants, gamekeepers, stud-grooms, jockeys, stable-lads, tiger-boys, and farmworkers are neither patronized nor caricatured; they are studied presences, about whose features, clothing, and posture the artist has taken minute care.'[8] This description emphasizes a recurring motif in Stubbs's paintings, the labourer, as well as a characteristic of his own practice – Stubbs's paintings are quite literally *laboured*. Stubbs, alone in the eighteenth century, exhibited a complete mastery of oil painting and equine anatomy, and this had profound implications for the genre. No biography of the artist is complete without a description of the Herculean effort that Stubbs undertook in a barn in Horkstow where he toiled for eighteen months dissecting horses and producing drawings that would become the

Figure 2.2. George Stubbs, *Pumpkin with a Stable-lad*, 1774, oil on panel, 82.2 × 101.3 cm, YCBA.

cornerstone of his artistic practice and his monumental publication, the *Anatomy of the Horse*. There is very little record, unfortunately, of Stubbs's daily trials and triumphs with paint and brush.[9]

Actual labour, however, is nearly always sublimated in Stubbs's 'work', which is to say that labour is both acknowledged and elevated to a higher cultural plane. Stubbs's labourers are usually on display, standing or sitting in their finest livery, rather than sweating behind the scenes. The paradox of labour in Stubbs's paintings, both ubiquitous and latent, offers insight into the function of horse portraiture. More than documents of possession, like a will or an auction catalogue, these are records of the manpower and skill needed to breed and train horses. This was labour of a particularly non-utilitarian and symbolic kind, however, which distinguishes it from that celebrated by Ford Maddox Brown in the nineteenth century.[10] While horse handlers possessed indispensable skills in a horse-powered age, the breeding and training of thoroughbreds came closer to landscape gardening than to building or brewing. While the labour was real, the product was largely aesthetic.

Stubbs's thoroughbred portraits reside at the intersection of fine art, skilled labour, and the 'naming magic' of patronymics, both aristocratic and equine. But that is only part of the story, because the genre equally thrived on a vigorous print culture. An important episode in the 'democratization' of thoroughbred portraiture came with the opening of the Turf Gallery, which Stubbs undertook between 1790, and the project's demise in 1794. Akin to John Boydell's Shakespeare Gallery and Henry Fuseli's Milton Gallery, the Turf Gallery was planned as a London exhibition of fine art paintings. Whereas the Shakespeare and Milton galleries illustrated English classics in an expressive Romantic style, the Turf Gallery offered the public closely observed representations of 'every horse of note' in English racing since 1750. The final publication was to include 'upwards of one hundred and forty-five prints, engraved in the best manner from original portraits of the most famous racers, painted by G. Stubbs, R.A. at an immense expense, solely for this work', and this was where Stubbs hoped to turn a profit.

In a prospectus for the Turf Gallery, Stubbs offered a rare glimpse into his aims:

> although the numerous volumes of Cheney and Heber, downwards, may give critical knowledge to the diligent and deep explorer, they certainly do not impart sufficient information to a superficial observer; yet both may regret that there is not a regular series of paintings and engravings of these horses, with their histories, which have been, or are now, famous.[11]

Cheny and Heber published annual compendia of results, the forerunners to Weatherby's *Racing Calendar*, and eventually the *General Stud-Book*, first published in 1791. The Turf Gallery was an illustrated studbook of sorts, offering 'on-the-surface' clues into selective breeding, and perhaps even a leg up in the placing of bets. While a few of the prints show horses actually competing, the prints are mostly sideview portraits.

Stubbs's prospectus suggests that these portraits were intended as near-equivalents to human portraits. They were intended as autonomous 'subjects-of-a-life' in paint, to borrow a phrase from the philosopher Tom Regan, which is to say they are presented as individuals with their own agency and stories.[12] Stubbs's portrait of Dungannon provides a glimpse into this logic, here reproduced in the engraving made by the artist's son, George Townley Stubbs (Figure 2.3). Exhibited at the Turf Gallery in January 1794, the original painting appeared with the following catalogue entry:

> Dungannon, Esteemed amongst the most famous, if not the very best son of Eclipse, was both bred and trained by the late Col. O'Kelly, and is now a stallion; among the few of his get that have yet appeared, is Mr. Wilson's Lurcher.

Figure 2.3. George Townley Stubbs after George Stubbs, *Dungannon*, 1794, stipple and etching on paper, 40.6 × 50.5 cm., British Museum.

> The great attachment of this horse to a Sheep, which by some accident got into his paddock, is very singular.[13]

The sheep's side is marked with O'Kelly's initials, and the juxtaposition activates dissonant conceptions of possession, hierarchy and animal sentiment. The thoroughbred occupies a middle position in the 'Great Chain of Being' between human sentiment and industry and the sheep's passivity and objecthood. Dungannon is capable of 'great attachment', which renders this hero of the turf more than a product of scientific breeding, which aimed at superficial beauty and speed. Stubbs then capitalized on the emergence of provincial print shops by advertising for the series in Liverpool and Newcastle.[14]

The Turf Gallery was not the success that Stubbs had hoped, in part because of the crumbling financial support of the Prince of Wales.[15] But the conflicting aims of the gallery may have doomed it from the start. It certainly captured the professionalization of horseracing and the desire to document breeding and racing success. This modernizing urge came at the expense, however, of the agency with which Stubbs wished to endow his horses. There is significant confusion about whose agency the Turf Gallery was meant to celebrate – the horses that won major races, the steeds that

Figure 2.4. George Stubbs, *Whistlejacket*, c. 1762–65, oil on canvas,
National Gallery, London.

sired winning horses, the owners who bred and fostered the nation's racing
stock or the artist who represented them. Stubbs's contemporaries ultimately
proved unwilling to view thoroughbred portraits as worthy of the same kind
of public artistic investment as human portraits or history paintings. The
series did, however, contribute to a tradition of engraved thoroughbred portraiture that would continue to flourish. Indeed, reproductive print technology was uniquely suited to the replication of superficial differences between
thoroughbreds that simultaneously inscribed their unique racing feats.

It is fair to say that Stubbs is best known today for the august, aristocratic
portrait of *Whistlejacket* (Figure 2.4). Beginning in 1762, Stubbs painted a
series of horse portraits for the Second Marquess of Rockingham in which
subtly modelled horses were set against plain backgrounds of flat colour.
In one of the earliest of these, *Mares and Foals*, the rhythmic placement of
horses across the horizontal canvas intimates a classical frieze. The original

impetus behind these canvases may have been to leave the landscape background to a specialist.[16] As a keen collector of classical sculpture, Lord Rockingham possibly viewed the 'unfinished' canvas as classically appealing. Whether the formal innovation came from Stubbs or from Rockingham, the sculptural isolation of equestrian form reached its apogee in the rearing portrait of Whistlejacket.

The formal paradox at the heart of the painting is that it presents an equestrian portrait without a rider. It was a painting in which the mount had become the protagonist. The absence of a rider prompted debate as early as the eighteenth century when Horace Walpole suggested that the steed was intended to bear a portrait of King George III. Whether this accurately reflected the original commission, the painting was brought to an astonishing conclusion when it was framed and hung in Lord Rockingham's country house as we see it today. No longer a 'vehicle' for royal authority, the rearing horse nakedly asserted the aristocracy's hereditary rights, independent of the crown. In no other painting is the equivalence between aristocratic and thoroughbred breeding brought to such potent political purposes, for the painting thoroughly naturalized Lord Rockingham's landed authority.

More recently, *Whistlejacket* has been viewed as an icon of consensual English identity. This reached an apotheosis when the painting was 'saved for the nation' as part of the National Gallery of Art's public campaign to acquire the work in 1997.[17] This view of the painting distorts our understanding of thoroughbred portraiture in two key respects. First, it implies that this particular emblem of aristocratic power represented a single, unified nation, which it did not. It would be more accurate, albeit less memorable, to describe *Whistlejacket* as an emblem of Lord Rockingham's oppositional Whig identity in the 1760s.[18] Second, it obscures the actual breadth and popularity of thoroughbred portraiture in its conventional form, manifest through inexpensive paintings, painted copies and the intaglio print trade.[19] It is significant that Whistlejacket's formal and iconographic novelty remained precisely that, never gaining traction or spawning imitations in the eighteenth century. Only one extant print appears to reproduce the painting, but even that print locates Whistlejacket in a landscape rather than replicating its splendid isolation.[20] *Whistlejacket* is exceptional in nearly every way, and the painting was the product of a unique relationship between Lord Rockingham and George Stubbs.

Stubbs came of age as a painter in the 1760s, working tirelessly on behalf of the Rockingham Whigs, and it was in this tumultuous decade that contemporary art exhibitions began in London and the Royal Academy of Arts was founded. The unwillingness of the inaugural class of Royal Academicians to include George Stubbs among their number says a great deal about their desire to impose a French-style hierarchy of genres onto the fledgling academy.[21] Stubbs's experiments in 'animal history painting' and his rigorously scientific approach to the thoroughbred were effectively marginalized within this new institutional structure. His powerful example continued, however, to reverberate with individual artists over the next two centuries.

Thoroughbred Portraiture and Modernity

Sir Walter Gilbey observed: 'We might almost divide our British painters of horse pictures into two periods – those who lived before Stubbs, and those who followed him and profited by his monumental labours at the Horkstow farmhouse.'[22] This seems entirely valid, although the distinction has not been kind to those of the quarter-millennium-and-counting post-Stubbs era. The thoroughbred portraits of Sawrey Gilpin, James Ward, John Frederick Herring, Benjamin Marshall, John Ferneley and Alfred Munnings can be individually stunning and formally innovative, yet the overwhelming art-historical judgement has been that of redundancy and sterility. To this list of names could be added a great many horse portraitists from the English-speaking world, including the United States, Canada, Australia and India. While occasionally the beneficiaries of regional studies, horse portraitists tend to garner little critical discussion.[23]

The art-historical problem has not been one of quality per se, but rather a disastrous mismatch between the aims and ideals of thoroughbred portraiture and those of modernity. These values collided spectacularly in 1949 when Alfred Munnings, then president of the Royal Academy of Arts in London, turned the annual presidential address into a broadside against modern art.

> I find myself President of a body of men who are what I call shilly-shallying. They feel there is something in this so-called modern art.... If you paint a tree, for God's sake try to make it look like a tree and if you paint a sky try and make it look like a sky ... there has been a foolish interruption to all efforts in art, helped by foolish men writing in the press encouraging all this damned nonsense, putting all these younger men out of their stride. I am right.[24]

From the hauteur of his tone, to his appeal to common sense, to his absolute conviction in the final sentence, Munnings articulated a stark dichotomy between naturalistic observation and modernist stunt. While trees and sky constituted his examples, horses surely came to mind for his audience, for no artist was more thoroughly associated with equestrian painting.

It has been easy for art historians to dismiss Munnings's diatribe as just that, an embarrassing vestige of outdated artistic values. A bit of postmodern scepticism, however, lends Munnings's complaint a certain poignancy. It enables us to see the historical outlines of Munnings's predicament more clearly. George Stubbs elevated and popularized thoroughbred portraiture, although he proved unable to elevate the genre to genuine academic acceptance. Thoroughbred portraiture continued unabated in the Victorian period, but the spotlight tended to fall on either extreme of the nature-versus-nurture continuum, with thoroughbred portraiture occupying a somewhat bland middle.[25] The wild animal paintings of Edwin Landseer stand at the violent extreme of the spectrum and the social spectacles of William Powell Frith's *Derby Day* (1856–58) stand on the socialized extreme. *Derby Day* represents horseracing as a thoroughly human drama with hardly a horse to be seen, and this human spectacle was compounded by the exhibition audience of 1858, which pressed so eagerly around the painting that barriers were erected.

It was the anti-academic impulses of the French *plein-air* and impressionist painters that liberated thoroughbred portraiture from its lowly status in the hierarchy of genres. Munnings had a deep appreciation for Edouard Manet and he undertook a painting career guided by a series of avant-garde principles including the fleeting quality of natural light, the instability of local colour and the suitability of common life to artistic representation. In his autobiography Munnings contrasted Stubbs's *Whistlejacket*, then a little-known painting, with his own powers of observation: 'I was watching one of the finest displays of horse agility, power, and strength that anyone would ever see. There is a large picture at Wentworth Woodhouse, titled 'Whistlepacket' [sic], by George Stubbs. It is a life-size painting of a horse rearing, but Stubbs' horse is dead as mutton compared with the live, rearing Coronach that I was staring at that morning.'[26] It is a fair critique; at least to the extent that *Whistlejacket* expressed a platonic, sculptural ideal, while Munnings captured the fleeting quality of light on flesh. As Charles Simpson wrote, 'A painter like Munnings will take a horse out to get the colour of one shadow, or to study the infinite variations of light as it is reflected in the whorls of the hair, as the coat turns over with a sheen like silk on the modelling of the quarters.'[27] Stubbs, preoccupied with the documentation of a natural world exterior to himself, left hardly a scrap of writing about his own thoughts and feelings. Munnings believed that subjective impressions of light and colour were the very substance of art, and his three-volume autobiography copiously recorded fleeting thoughts and jotted notes. Just as horse portraiture became ripe for rejuvenation as a fine art subject, a new avant-garde challenged the aims and ideals of representational painting. Even though Munnings's work continued to fare well on

Figure 2.5. S.T. Gill, *The Inquiry*, c. 1860–84, watercolour on paper, 39.3 × 66.5 cm, National Gallery of Victoria, Melbourne.

the art market, it went into the same art-historical void as thoroughbred portraiture more generally.

Thoroughbreds and the British Empire

In the aftermath of these battles, new questions have begun to be asked about sporting art, and a great many still need to be posed.[28] What insights, for example, might horse portraiture offer into the relationship between art and the British Empire? Take, for example, S.T. Gill's watercolour, *The Inquiry*, which was painted in the third quarter of the nineteenth century in Southern Australia (Figure 2.5).

Two white settlers approach a group of four Aborigines with an unspecified inquiry. A clear power differential is manifest in the sword, rifles, the blue uniform of the constable and, just as importantly, in the powerful bodies of the horses. Unlike the American West, where Native American tribes integrated horses into their cultures over centuries, the sudden arrival of vast numbers of white squatters and their horses overwhelmed Aboriginal modes of life. As Gill wrote in his diary from an expedition that he took into southern Australia in 1846, the Aborigines 'stood with us some time but appeared afraid of the horses more than us'.[29] Gill drew upon that expedition for the rest of his career, and while his intention may have been to show a paternalistic regard for the Aborigines, the effect is to bring the thoroughbred's 'good breeding' to bear on Australian settlement. As if to emphasize the point, Gill paints a sleek greyhound staring at a dingo, contrasting another instance of careful breeding with the 'unimproved'.

It is interesting to speculate whether tensions within early Australian society, including a volatile mix of convicts, freemen, prospectors, opportunists and Aborigines, endowed thoroughbred horses and racing with a particularly potent charge. By the time Mark Twain attended the Melbourne Cup in 1895, he could barely conceal his astonishment:

> The Melbourne Cup is the Australasian National Day. It would be difficult to overstate its importance .... I can call to mind no specialized annual day, in any country, which can be named by that large name – Supreme.[30]

Along similar lines, Australia's supreme national hero may be a thoroughbred named Phar Lap who won the Melbourne Cup in 1930. Phar Lap then won the lucrative race of Agua Caliente, located in a Mexican oasis just south of the border from prohibition America. Although Phar Lap succumbed to poisoning under suspicious circumstances shortly thereafter, he had already proved himself on the world stage. And he did so in the early age of 'talking' motion pictures when a significant percentage of depression-hit Australians tuned in to watch him race. Australian institutions scrambled for a piece of the true cross, and an ingenious division of parts was made with Phar Lap's skeleton going to Wellington's Dominion Museum where it honoured the steed's birthplace, Phar Lap's heart going to the National Institute of Anatomy in Canberra and his taxidermied hide going to the National Museum in Melbourne. The latter retains pride of place in the Melbourne Museum where 'Phar Lap' remains one of its biggest draws.[31]

Stuart Reid's oil portrait of Phar Lap is the most impressive of the portraits taken from the life. The Tasmanian artist Joseph Fleury painted a remarkable image of *Phar Lap Before the Chariot of the Sun* in 1932, which was widely reproduced as a print where it joined a flood of commemorative and advertising imagery. Particularly astonishing is a recent portrait on canvas by an Aboriginal artist who was given the English name Jimmy Pike when he began work on a cattle station in Kimberley in the 1950s. Titled *My Horse Phar Lap*, the painting transposes the centuries' old convention of the thoroughbred portrait into a uniquely personal key with undertones of Aboriginal art (Figure 2.6). Intrigued to learn late in his life that his English name was based on the famed jockey who had ridden Phar Lap to victory, Jimmy Pike reappropriated his totem animal and thoroughly subverted thoroughbred painting in the process. He also joined the ranks of numerous contemporary artists from the English-speaking

Figure 2.6. Jimmy Pike, *My Horse Phar Lap*, c. 2000, acrylic on canvas, 30 × 26 cm. Donated by Jimmy Pike, Museum Victoria, Melbourne.

world who were appropriating and invigorating the genre of thoroughbred portraiture.

The Postmodern Thoroughbred

In a beautiful moment of sympathetic convergence, the thoroughbred portrait became a genre through which far-flung artists tested national identities and asserted new hybridities in the late twentieth century. The British artist Mark Wallinger has taken this exploration furthest, creating a whole series of works in which the thoroughbred constitutes both content and question mark. Wallinger's *Half-Brother (Exit to Nowhere/Machiavellian)* is a beautifully rendered oil painting in which two thoroughbreds who shared the same sire and who are named parenthetically in the title are split and juxtaposed on canvas (Figure 2.7).

In what might be termed the postmodern thoroughbred, the series queries the patrimonial 'naming logic' of the thoroughbred horse and the venerable genre of art that rendered selective breeding superficially evident. Wallinger identifies a potent synchronicity between the thoroughbred as an artistic

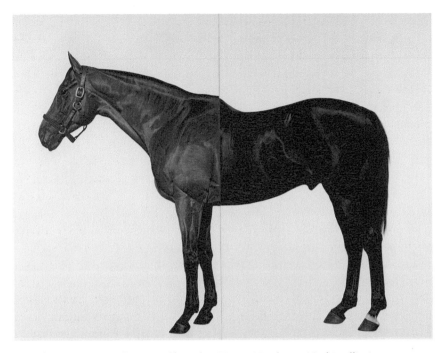

Figure 2.7. Mark Wallinger, *Half-Brother (Exit to Nowhere – Machiavellian)*, 1994–95, oil on canvas, 230 × 300 cm, Tate Britain.

subject and the equally embattled medium of oil painting, saying, 'I think that painting probably died in the early 1960s, but for some reason we remain in its thrall.' Echoing Christopher Wood's observations about the transference of aristocratic 'naming magic' to that of fine art, Wallinger continues, 'There's still a bit of magic left in painting and I wouldn't like to overstate my scepticism.'[32]

Wallinger's critique of thoroughbred ideology and Western fine art is appealing and potent precisely because it reveals a genuine fondness for both. This can be seen in a Duchampian gesture that Wallinger made in 1993 when he persuaded a consortium of artistic institutions and collectors to field a chestnut filly in the following year's flat racing season under the direction of the Newmarket trainer Sir Mark Prescott. Named (and titled) A Real Work of Art, the filly took Stubbs's investment in the subculture of the horse to a new level. Parallels between an overheated contemporary art market and racetrack gambling were difficult to miss. Direct engagement with Stubbs came in 2001, when Wallinger exhibited a photographic transparency of what appeared to be *Whistlejacket* under X-ray. Titled *Ghost*, the negative reveals a unicorn's horn atop Whistlejacket's head. The

Photoshopped photograph would have us believe that Stubbs overpainted the horn before delivering the work to Lord Rockingham.[33] *Ghost* cleverly imagines that the 'ideology of the thoroughbred', so powerfully embodied in *Whistlejacket's* idealized form, was actually an elitist fantasy imposed on the public from the beginning. But there is also a sense of self-discovery and even loss in these works, as thoroughbred portraiture becomes a lens through which British national identity is interrogated in the postcolonial era. Wallinger notes that the four thoroughbred portraits in *Race Class Sex* were owned by the ruler of Dubai, Sheikh Mohammed, and thereby signalled a return of the thoroughbred to its Arabian origins.[34] Once again, thoroughbred portraiture appears fundamentally bound to the history of the British Empire and its representational practices.

Pike and Wallinger demonstrate the surprising contemporaneity of thoroughbred portraiture, particularly in its capacity to interrogate national identity, social stratification and fine art. It remains to be seen, however, if the genre retains the power to promote and bind new communities. Mark Wallinger's recent commission for a public sculpture in Ebbsfleet, England offers a remarkable test case. Intended to provide a sculptural landmark for a planned community adjacent to a Eurostar station, Wallinger proposed a 50-metre-high 'White Horse' standing placidly on a hill with four hooves planted firmly on the ground, wearing a bridle. The popular response in North Kent has been positive, while the critical response has been mixed.[35] It is particularly striking that Wallinger has rendered the horse within the conventions of the thoroughbred portrait. It contains two key modifications, however, which help to shift the genre fully into the public realm. The first is its scale and the second is the absence of a name, and therefore of a lineage. Wallinger's *White Horse* offers itself as a shared, communal symbol rather than as a private possession or as the bearer of an aristocratic ideology. If *Whistlejacket* appeared to lack a royal rider, the *White Horse* claims, at least rhetorically, to be big enough for everyone to sit on.

It is tempting to posit a neat trajectory from the Bronze Age white horse at Uffington to Wallinger's white horse at Ebbsfleet. But the story traced here is an exclusively modern one, and it runs from the English Enlightenment to the European Union. Adjacent to Eurotunnel, Wallinger could have sculpted a giant mole to symbolize modern tunnelling efficacy, or a cheetah to symbolize the speed of Eurostar and of contemporary life. But the thoroughbred horse, like the tradition of oil painting and representational sculpture, remains deeply resonant in the West and constitutive of a whole range of positive associations. As a genre, thoroughbred portraiture has survived 300 years, and today it seems as beleaguered and as pugnaciously resilient as ever.

Acknowledgements

I would like to thank Lisa Beaven, Alisa Bunbury, Adrian Jones, David Marshall and everyone at the David Nichol Smith Seminar in Melbourne, Australia for their encouragement, collegiality and advice.

NOTES

1 T. Pickeral, *The Horse: 30,000 Years of the Horse in Art* (London and New York: Merrell Publishers, 2006), N. Chudun et al., *The Horse: From Cave Paintings to Modern Art* (New York and London: Abbeville Press, 2008).

2 D. Landry, *Noble Brutes: How Eastern Horses Transformed English Culture* (Baltimore: The Johns Hopkins University Press, 2009), p. 160. See also E. Niemyer, *The Reign of the Horse: The Horse in Print, 1500–1715* (Washington, DC: Folger Library Publications, 1991).

3 A. Rouquet, *The Present State of the Arts in England* (London, 1755), p. 58.

4 J. Barry, 'An Inquiry into the real and imaginary obstructions to the acquisition of the arts in England,' *The Works of James Barry, Esq.*, vol. 2 (London, 1809), p. 246. The *Inquiry* was first published in 1775.

5 S. Deuchar, *Sporting Art in Eighteenth-Century England: A Social and Political History* (New Haven and London: Yale University Press, 1988); the quotes are section heads from pages 59 and 135.

6 P. Cain and A. Hopkins, *British Imperialism, 1688–2000*, second edition (London: Pearson Education Limited, 2001).

7 C. Wood, *Forgery, Replica, Fiction: Temporalities of German Renaissance Art* (Chicago and London: University of Chicago, 2008), pp. 58–59. See also H. Bloch, *Etymologies and Genealogies: A Literary Anthropology of the French Middle Ages* (Chicago and London: The University of Chicago Press, 1983).

8 M. Warner and R. Blake, *Stubbs & the Horse* (New Haven and London: Yale University Press, 2004), p. 82.

9 The best account of Stubbs's technique can be found in J. Egerton, *George Stubbs, Painter. Catalogue Raisonné* (New Haven and London: Yale University Press, 2007), pp. 72–89.

10 See T. Barringer, *Men at Work: Art and Labour in Victorian Britain* (New Haven and London: Yale University Press, 2005).

11 B. Taylor, *Stubbs* (New York: Harper & Row Publishers, 1971), p. 59.

12 T. Regan, *The Case for Animal Rights* (Berkeley: University of California Press, 1983).

13 Warner and Blake, *Stubbs & the Horse*, p. 207.

14 T. Clayton, *The English Print 1688–1802* (New Haven and London: Yale University Press, 1997), pp. 223–24.

15 Warner and Blake, *Stubbs and the Horse*, pp. 143–56.

16 Warner and Blake, *Stubbs and the Horse*, p. 176.

17 As Myrone has noted, the public campaign recreated the painting 'as a luminous emblem of a shared national culture' rather than 'a record of property', his own interpretative emphasis. See M. Myrone, *George Stubbs* (London: Tate Publishing, 2002), p. 38.

18 D. Fordham, 'George Stubbs's *Zoon Politikon*', *Oxford Art Journal* 33 (2010), 1–23.

19 For the remarkable tensions in British visual culture between the 'fervent adulation of the horse and cynical exploitation of it', see D. Donald, *Picturing Animals in Britain 1750–1850* (New Haven and London: Yale University Press, 2007), pp. 199–232.

20 C. Lennox-Boyd, R. Dixon and T. Clayton, *George Stubbs: The Complete Engraved Works* (London: Sotheby's Publications, 1989), p. 175.

21 For more on the political machinations and visual strategies employed by London artists in the 1760s, see D. Fordham, *British Art and the Seven Years' War: Allegiance and Autonomy* (Philadelphia: University of Pennsylvania Press, 2010).

22 W. Gilbey, *Animal Painters of England, From the Year 1650, A brief history of their lives and works*, Vol. 2 (London: Vinton & Co., 1900), p. 196.

23 See, for example, Walter Shaw Sparrow's *George Stubbs and Ben Marshall* (London: Cassell and Company, Ltd.), tellingly included in a series titled 'The Sport of our Fathers'.

24 Quoted in S. Booth, *Sir Alfred Munnings, 1878–1959* (London: Sotheby Parke Bernet Publications, 1978), pp. 9–10.

25 See A. Potts, 'Natural Order and the Call of the Wild: The Politics of Animal Picturing', *Oxford Art Journal* 13 (1990), 14, 30.

26 A. Munnings, *The Second Burst* (London: Museum Press Limited, 1951), p. 120.

27 Cited in J. Goodman, *AJ: The Life of Alfred Munnings, 1878–1959* (Norwich: The Erskine Press, 2000), p. 128.

28 The history of sporting art has begun to intersect with the emergent fields of animal studies and ecocriticism; see E. Drew and J. Sitter, 'Ecocriticism and Eighteenth-Century English Studies', *Literature Compass* 8 (2011), 227–239.

29 Cited in C. Clemente, *Australian Watercolours 1802–1926, in the Collection of the National Gallery of Victoria* (Melbourne: The National Gallery of Victoria, 1991), p. 38.

30 M. Twain, C. Dudley Warner and A. Bigelow Paine, *The Writings of Mark Twain*, Vol. 20 (New York: Gabriel Wells, 1923), p. 145.

31 See M. Reason, *Phar Lap: A True Legend* (Melbourne: Museum Victoria, 2009).

32 'Turf Accounting: Mark Wallinger Discusses *A Real Work of Art* with Paul Bonaventura', *Art Monthly* (1994), 175.

33 See *ArtNow: Interviews with Modern Artists* (London and New York: Continuum, 2002), p. 82.

34 'Mark Wallinger in conversation with Kathrin Rhomberg', in *Sculpsit: Contemporary Artists on Sculpture and Beyond*, K. Mey (ed.) (Manchester University Press, 2001), p. 41. See also Rachel Pagones, Chapter 11 in this volume.

35 See G. Stamp, 'Why Size Is Not Enough', *Apollo* 169 (2009), 48–49.

3

JANE SMILEY

The Fiction of Horseracing

He sighs, wondering why he bothers with horses at all. Every race hurts
him deep inside. The horse left behind is always himself. Always the
struggle is *his*![1]

In 1719, the year Daniel Defoe published *Robinson Crusoe*, Bartlett's
Childers, son of the Darley Arabian, was a three-year-old. In 1724, the year
Defoe published *Roxana*, the Godolphin Arabian was born, and in 1739,
a year before the publication of *Pamela*, he produced Regulus, the brood-
mare sire of Eclipse. The year 1749 saw the publication of *Tom Jones* and
the birth of Spilleta, Eclipse's dam. About halfway through the publication
of *Tristram Shandy* (let's say right about the time Tristram decides to relate
the story of Uncle Toby's amours), Eclipse was born. In 1780, when Jane
Austen was five years old, the Epsom Derby was run for the first time, a single heat, at a mile and a half, marking, for some, the beginning of modern
racing. There is no reason to believe that these first novelists cared about the
thoroughbred horse, and there is likewise no reason to believe that those
who were passionate about horseracing knew that a fresh art form was
developing in their midst. The novelists were members of the burgeoning
literate middle class, whereas the owners of the horses were mostly upper
class (educated in the classics) and those who cared for and rode them were
mostly servants, hardly educated at all. However, horseracing, fiction, and
capitalism came to form a mutually nurturing threesome, and it is easy to
see why. Each of the three is a form of speculation. Each of the three is a
complex endeavour that does not easily give up its secrets (and maybe there
are no secrets; maybe every success or failure is pure chance). Each of the
three is a microcosm of existence – a brief and intense series of lost or gained
fortunes and thrilling or terrifying plot twists. And without capitalism to
systematize betting, without capitalism to systematize the distribution of
printed narratives, we would not have the literary world or the racing world
we have today.[2]

Two examples from 1848 prefigure the eventual split in horseracing fiction between popular and the literary. The first of these is *Clement Lorimer, or The Book with the Iron Clasps*, by Angus Reach, in which the protagonist, Clement, is the unknowing victim of a two-hundred-year-old vendetta between his Sicilian ancestors and his Flemish ancestors. His father marries the last known descendent of the enemy family; once she gives birth to Clement, he kills her and puts Clement out to nurse, then manages the child's privileged life from afar. At twenty-three, Clement pursues a profligate existence – he dates a ballerina and owns the Derby favourite. His father sets Clement's destruction in motion when he extorts the jockey into giving the horse a mysterious drug that causes him to lose the race, thereby ruining Clement, who has heavily backed his horse. The novel then turns away from racing and conforms fairly closely to the traditions of the Gothic novel – horror, curses, uncanny events, happy ending.[3]

Also published in 1848 was Anthony Trollope's second novel, *The Kellys and the O'Kellys*, a social comedy principally concerned with two marriage plots. In one, the plain sister of a greedy and ruthless brother has been left an interest in the family estate. Her drink-addled brother thinks of killing her to get her money, so she takes refuge with some friends in a nearby village. In the other, a well-meaning young lord finds himself in over his head because of his racing bills. But instead of focusing on betting, Trollope focuses on character – the young lord's trainer, Dot Blake, has made a successful career for himself both training and betting. He is highly observant, always a realist, never impulsive, and expertly self-educated, a brilliant example of a certain type of intelligence. When the young lord finally goes to him for advice concerning his marital dilemma, Dot is both judicious and canny.[4]

Both *Clement Lorimer* and *The Kellys and the O'Kellys* depict social shifts: at the brokerage office where Clement's jockey's son is a clerk, the two principals are Shiner and Maggs. In his office, Maggs is contemplating various speculations in land. In the adjoining office, Shiner is contemplating various speculations in horse betting. Two characters who help to foil Clement's father are Spiffler and O'Keene, a writer and a publisher launching a weekly magazine. When they investigate the story and reveal the plot, they hit the tabloid jackpot. While Trollope's milieu is more traditional, his portrayal of Dot Blake marks the emergence of the horse trainer in his modern form, a self-employed entrepreneur with a set of proprietary skills, the middleman between the aristocratic owner and the working-class jockeys and grooms.

The five components of every piece of fiction are plot, setting, theme, character and language (which is sometimes individualised enough to be called 'style'). The fiction of horseracing begins with a given – a somewhat removed and exotic setting that not all readers are familiar with but some readers are passionate (and knowledgeable) about. It is a world that abounds in unknowns and is awash in money; it is corrupt to a degree that exists in the eye of the beholder. At the centre of this world is the horse. Writers think differently of horses – to some, they are symbols of hope or innocence, and to others they are symbols of despair or sin. Once every writer accepts the setting, he or she then chooses, in accordance partly with his or her intentions and partly with his or her predilections, one of the other components. Popular fiction most often chooses plot, which promises suspense, whereas literary fiction most often chooses character or theme, which promises understanding of wider issues. There is also the separate category of children's literature, basically pedagogical, which includes some of the most the famous and beloved horseracing books.

Trollope returned to horseracing towards the end of his career, in *The Duke's Children*, the last of the six Palliser novels that form the core of his mature contemplation of English political and social life. This time, Trollope is more aware of the dangers of the racing world. The Duke of Omnium is, upon the death of his wife, Lady Glencora, forced to confront the many activities of his children that he has not been aware of heretofore. Amongst other things, he is horrified by the profligacy of his son, Lord Silverbridge, who hopes to make a splash on the turf. Silverbridge attempts to maintain the secrecy of his relationship with Major Tifto, a classic turf character with multiple unsavoury connections, but eventually he bets so much money (70,000 pounds, equivalent to 5.6 million pounds in 2011) on his horse (named Prime Minister) in the St Leger, that when the horse does not run (because Major Tifto has seen to it that he picks up a nail in his hoof on the morning of the race), he has to confess to his father in his desperation for the money to settle his bets. Trollope is interested in the complexities of Silverbridge's dilemma and of Tifto's character – he is not quite a villain, but more like a spurned lover, hurt and insulted by Silverbridge's waning affection. He is both ruined and repentant when, after the horse fails to run, Silverbridge must disband his stable. Silverbridge finally pensions him off to 'some obscure corner of South Wales'. As with *The Kellys and the O'Kellys*, the racing plot is set against a similarly unorthodox pair of marriage plots.[5]

Also in 1880, Emile Zola published *Nana*, the ninth volume of his Rougon-Macquart series. Nana, a star of the Varieties, can neither sing nor dance, but she has plenty of sex appeal, and becomes the toast of Paris. Like many of the Rougon-Macquart series, *Nana* is about excess, in this case an excess of pleasure that can neither be tolerated nor resisted by the characters of the novel (wealthy men and ambitious inhabitants of the demimonde).

The climactic scene of debauchery takes place in the Bois de Boulogne, where one of Nana's aspiring lovers, Vandeuvres, runs two horses in the Grand Prix de Paris. Nana shows up to watch the race, dressed in her lover's stable colours and displayed in an ornate carriage drawn by four white horses. A frenzy of gambling, gossiping and showing off ensues, in which it is discovered that no one has bet on the filly named for Nana. When the filly wins, 'the real Nana' feels the frenzy of adoration for the horse lift her into a state of exalted triumph that lasts through a wild evening celebration. For Vandeuvres, however, the win is a disaster, revealing his scam and causing him to be warned off and ruined. He sets fire to his stables, burning himself and his horses to death, which prefigures Nana's own horrific end. Another famous scene in which events on the racecourse prefigure a character's fate occurs in *Anna Karenina* (1877). Shortly after taking up with Anna, Vronsky rides his beloved mare in an amateur race. Tolstoy is clear that it is through Vronsky's poor judgement that the horse breaks her back and must be destroyed. When Anna, watching the race, reacts to the accident, her husband confronts her, and she admits the affair. Anna, of course, is later destroyed by her relationship to, and dependence on, the dashing but flawed Vronsky.[6]

Perhaps the most thoughtful depiction of racing and betting in nineteenth-century English fiction is in George Moore's novel *Esther Waters* (1894). Whereas previous writers had focused on the damage racing presents for members of the upper classes, Moore's protagonist is an illiterate young woman who works as a housemaid. Her first job is at a training farm, and it is through her innocent eyes that we see trainers, grooms, exercise boys and jockeys. Once again, one of the farm's horses is a favourite, and all of the employees back him enthusiastically. After the celebration, Esther falls for and is impregnated by a fellow servant. She returns to her family in shame and ends up in the workhouse. When, after several crises, she finally does find steady employment and a good situation for her son, her old lover returns, now a bookmaker and a bar owner, reasonably well off, but addicted to gambling and, it turns out, unwell. Soon his shop is closed down and he dies. Esther eventually returns to the training farm, but that, too, has gone bust. Moore's style is simultaneously lyrical, honest and detailed, giving *Esther Waters* a palpable sense of doom from the beginning. The gist seems to be that for the upper classes, the dangers of racing can be avoided, if with difficulty (Lord Silverbridge's lesson is an expensive one, but it is only a lesson). For the lower classes, however, racing offers several kinds of seduction that may serve as relief from the uncertain drudgery of English life, but the ultimate destruction is total and inevitable.[7]

A British-born author who set many of his racing novels in Australia, Nat Gould wrote more than eighty novels between 1891 and his death in 1919. He went to Australia in 1884, worked on several newspapers, and returned to England in 1895. *The Second String* is semi-autobiographical – in it, Jack Redland finds himself broke in his early twenties. He has self-confidence and savoir faire, but all he is good at is riding amateur races. A trainer friend suggests that he rides well enough to become a professional jockey, but he wants to marry into the landed gentry, so he decides instead to take the winnings from his last race and accompany an old school friend to Australia. In Fremantle, he is introduced to a wealthy investor and horse owner, who involves him in pearl fishing. Jack performs several feats of daring and regains a stolen black pearl for his beloved back in England. He invests the proceeds from pearl diving in both a gold mine and a horse, which he backs in the Sydney Cup. The horse is not highly considered, but Jack sees something in his plodding persistence, and he does win the race. Once all his investments pay off, Jack returns to England a rich man and claims his bride. The novel is episodic, and there is no real doubt that Jack will prove himself not only equal but superior to everyone he meets. Racing, in *The Second String*, has no negative moral connotations – like pearl diving, foiling native villains and discovering seams of gold, it is just something manly men do.[8]

Another racing novel set in Australia and England is *The Shearer's Colt*, by A.B. (Banjo) Paterson, born in New South Wales in 1864, and especially famous for his bush poetry, including 'Waltzing Matilda' and 'The Man From Snowy River'. *The Shearer's Colt* also concerns an Englishman who leaves England for Australia, but the 'nice boy' in question, Hilton Fitzroy, is primarily a mischief maker. When he loses his stake shortly after arriving in Australia, he joins the Queensland Mounted Police, where he is taken up by a rough-hewn older man, Red Fred, a former sheep shearer who has made a fortune, also in mining. Fitzroy's job is to teach the older man the ways of urbane society – as his employer says, 'If you go to England to race, you can go anywhere and meet anybody.' After several adventures, they buy a horse named Sensation and take him to England for a set of international races rather like a proto-Breeder's Cup. The night before the big race, two gamblers attempt to interfere with the horse, and Sensation does not hesitate to defend himself, though in the course of events he also injures Fitzroy, who is in his stall watching over him. Sensation does run his race (finishing in a near dead heat with the English and the French horse), and Fitzroy recovers, marries his beloved and uses the money he has earned to buy into a partnership with his father-in-law. Red Fred also achieves marital bliss. *The Shearer's Colt* has a loose structure, not unlike *The Second String*, but Paterson has a much more comic sensibility. Fitzroy and Red Fred are only two in a gallery of characters of all types and many nationalities who cluster around the horses (who are also given some personality). Several of them are troublemakers and scam artists, others are ambitious nouveaux riches or dedicated horsemen. Fitzroy's sweetheart is a straightforward girl with plenty of horsey skills of her own. Paterson nicely depicts the varying landscapes these characters find themselves in – unlike earlier novelists, he understands that that 'going anywhere and meeting anybody' means that on the race course, all classes and nationalities mix as equals – what really matters is whether the horse wins.[9]

The short story is in some ways made for racing because it is good at portraying both sudden twists of fate and intense feeling. Perhaps the most famous piece of popular fiction set in the racing world was for many years 'Silver Blaze', an Arthur Conan Doyle tale from 1892 in which Holmes is asked to solve the kidnapping of a favoured horse that also involves a murder by means of a blunt object. 'Silver Blaze' is a typical Holmesian puzzle in which several events that appear to be related cannot be understood until their logical sequence is revealed to Dr. Watson by Holmes. As with most Sherlock Holmes stories, the violence takes place off-stage and the pleasure is in the solution to the puzzle, not in the evocation of the scene of the crime, but other stories have excelled in capturing the feel of racing. Twenty-eight of these are anthologized in Dick Francis and John Welcome's *Complete Treasury of Great Racing Stories*, which includes 'Silver Blaze', but also 'The Dream' by Richard Findlay, 'The Tale of the Gypsy Horse' by Donn Byrne and 'Pullinstown' by Molly Keane. Edgar Wallace, who wrote *King Kong* as well as dozens of other books (eleven in 1926 alone), is represented by two good-humoured tales, 'The Coop' and 'The Man who Shot the Favorite'. Both explore the absurdities of racing investments, not the tragedy. J.P. Marquand, John Galsworthy, Beryl Markham and Sherwood Anderson are also represented, and the entire collection is remarkable for the sharpness of insight and variety of tone.[10]

My favourite of the stories is 'Harmony' by William Fain, first published in *The New Yorker* in 1955. John Stephens is an English jockey nearing the end of a successful career in France, who has a French wife and plenty of money. His dilemma is that his expertise in race-riding is making him more realistic and, as a result, more indifferent to winning. Stephens's sensitivity to the mental and physical idiosyncrasies of the horses he is riding is convincingly portrayed, as well as his understanding that his tact does not endear him to owners, trainers or younger jockeys. Fain's story is perhaps the first in what would become a standard trope of racing fiction – the jockey's point of view. Stephens is the expert, surrounded by different varieties of knaves and fools. His good fortune is in being able to connect with the animals; his ill-fortune is in knowingly abusing the animals for the sake of his obligations to the sport.

One story not included (perhaps for copyright reasons) is Ernest Hemingway's 'My Old Man', which was inspired by the career of Tod Sloan, the American jockey who rode in England at the turn of the century. The narrator of the story is a young man who knows that his father was once a great jockey in France, who now rides at smaller tracks in Italy and spends most of his days working to stay in condition and to sweat off weight. The young man is fond of his father, though he does remember a time at the races when his father won a large sum when a friend of his pulled the favourite. Father and son return to Paris, the father regains his license and rides in a few races over jumps. In the last of these, he is killed in a fall, and the son overhears two men discussing the death. One of them says, 'He had it coming to him on the stuff he's pulled.' The story is a beautifully sombre meshing of the ambiguities of filial love and of racing.[11]

In mid-twentieth-century America, the literary voice of horseracing was Damon Runyon. Perhaps his most famous racing story was 'Little Miss Marker', in which a bookie, Sorrowful Jones, accepts a little girl, 'Marky', as a guarantee for a bet. When she is abandoned, he and his disreputable friends care for her with great affection until she contracts pneumonia and dies just before the return of her father, who happens to have contracted amnesia after leaving her with Sorrowful. Runyon developed a witty and unique style based on, but not limited to, the patois of the New York demi-monde, full of colourful slang ('betsy' for gun, 'pimple' for head, 'giddyaps' for racehorses). Contractions and the past and future tenses are never used, and sentences often begin with 'Well', 'But', or 'Now', mimicking the oral delivery of a talkative raconteur. Runyon's narrator is, above all, an unsentimental fatalist, but his style is playful, making ironic fun out of death, danger, financial ruin or, indeed, the sudden reappearance, not only of Marky's father, but of the fact that Marky has just been left a large inheritance. Other well-known Runyon racing stories are 'All Horseplayers Die Broke', 'The Snatching of Bookie Bob' and 'The Lemon Drop Kid'. Runyon wrote thirty-one books and worked on several screenplays. He also wrote a baseball column for the Hearst newspapers.[12]

National Velvet, published in 1935, was made into a movie nine years later. It weds a child's fantasy story (running a piebald gelding of uncertain breeding in the Grand National and winning) to a naturalistic depiction of middle-class life in an English village. Velvet is one of five children of a butcher whose house adjoins the slaughterhouse. She wins the Pie in a lottery; Mi Taylor, Velvet's trainer, works primarily taking care of the cattle that come in for processing, but just happens to know how to train a stee-plechaser. That Velvet comes to own the Pie in the fall, and manages to learn to ride him well enough to go in the Grand National by March, profoundly tests the adult reader's willingness to suspend disbelief, but family life is ren-dered in such detail that the novel remains much more interesting than it might be. Each character, including the Pie, is not only convincing, but com-plex and idiosyncratic. Mi's scheme for getting Velvet into the race is desper-ate and clever, and the ensuing media fuss is far from the traditional happy ending. Bagnold is well aware of the different types of dangers her charac-ters find themselves in, and carefully considers their positive and negative merits. It is also the first of our racing fictions that incorporates the way that racing would use radio, movies and, eventually, television to become a more popular and lucrative enterprise.[13]

Most children's books about horseracing – fictionalised accounts of important horses – use the device of a child's attachment to the great horse. The most famous of these is *King of the Wind* by Marguerite Henry in which a mute stable boy accompanies the Godolphin Arab from North Africa to France and England. Both horse and child suffer many cruelties and indignities before the Earl of Godolphin recognises the horse's poten-tial as a stallion. Walter Farley's *Man O' War* (1962) operates on the same principle (which Farley admits in the preface is fictionalised). Because chil-dren's books are meant to be pedagogical, both novels give youthful readers a tour of worlds that are normally closed to them. A somewhat more daring book is *Black Gold* (1957), also by Henry, relating the career of one of the strangest horses ever to win the Kentucky Derby, son of a mare from what was then Indian Territory who had been sent to the best sire in Kentucky when her owners struck oil. Henry does not give Black Gold a child friend, nor does she downplay the tragicomic variations of Black Gold's story. She produces a book that is much more affecting than the standard racehorse biography.[14]

The most famous name in modern-day horseracing fiction is Dick Francis. His novels are thrillers – there is always a mystery to be solved, always con-siderable mayhem and always a villain who has perpetrated a crime. Francis wrote forty-three novels, thirteen short stories, two non-fiction books (his own autobiography and a biography of Lester Piggott) and, like many genre writers, collaborated on at least four of his novels. He has said that he never wrote more than a single draft, and that the violent content of his thrill-ers reflected 'life in general'. But Francis was a skilled writer and so knowl-edgeable about his chosen milieu that his plots and characters are almost always fresh and intriguing. He is so adept at mood that in many of his best works, mood becomes a form of philosophical inquiry. The short story,

'Carrot for A Chestnut', is told from the point of view of Chick, the disgruntled nineteen-year-old son of a successful trainer who agrees to dope one of his father's horses prior to an important race at Cheltenham. The jockey is to be his more personable and successful older brother, Toddy. Francis focuses on the moment-by-moment progress of Chick's state of mind, beginning in the middle of the night, when he feeds the horse the doped carrot, and ending some days after he himself is injured in a racing mishap later on the same day that the doped horse falls and breaks his shoulder. Francis skips from point of view to point of view – no one but Chick knows the whole story, and as a result, Chick is doomed to a life of solitary regret. Francis is playing with a trope of English racing fiction that we have seen many times, but the wrinkles of sibling rivalry and Chick's personality make 'Carrot for a Chestnut' a psychological study. Chick's fatal flaw is that he is shallow and thoughtless as well as ill-natured – he likes his brother; he only reflects that he might get hurt riding a doped horse as he is watching him mount for the race. The special genius of the story, however, comes during Chick's own race, when Chick is so preoccupied by thoughts of what he has done that he not only fails to heed the trainer; he fails to tighten his girths. His neatly drawn mental torment plays with the reader's empathy. When he jumps the fence where the chestnut had been killed, his eyes fill with tears, making him unable to guide his own inexperienced mount. The result is just, but painful.[15]

The protagonist of *Reflex* (1980), Philip Nore, is a jockey nearing the end of a moderately successful career, whose avocation is photography. Cheating is, once again, one of Francis's themes, because the principal owner that Philip rides for expects him to ride in accordance with whether he, the owner, has bet for or against his own horses, and the trainer who employs Philip expects him to go along with the owner's wishes. From the beginning of *Reflex*, Francis is depicting the world of racing as routinely corrupt, much more so than in, say, *Enquiry*, from 1969, in which the jockey who loses his license knows that he is innocent of wrongdoing. In *Reflex*, however, all appearances are intended to deceive, and one of Philip's talents as a jockey is that he can pull a horse without causing suspicion. His biggest dilemma is that, as his career comes to its quiet end, he has no idea what to do next. Francis neatly weaves the solution to this dilemma, once again, into the tale of Philip's various relationships. A jockey he is friendly toward has a father Philip dislikes, a man who apparently enjoys taking unflattering pictures of jockeys hitting the dirt, and, in addition, seems to be committing extortion and blackmail. This man is murdered, and Philip is drawn into the solution of the crime. The outcome neatly turns Philip's preconceptions inside out, not precisely exonerating English racing, but showing that the battle for honest racing is not entirely lost.[16]

While it should be noted that one indication of the wisdom of P.G. Wodehouse's character Jeeves is his successful history at betting the races (and one Wodehouse novel, *The Return of Jeeves*, has a racing plot), recent horseracing fiction in England has mostly followed Francis's model. Even *Jump!*, Jilly Cooper's vast elaboration of *National Velvet* (girl takes cast-off horse to Grand National) contains a mystery, as does D.J. Taylor's Victorian tableau vivant, *Derby Day*. Two jockeys who have taken up thriller writing in the tradition of Dick Francis are John Francome and Charlie Brooks. Francome has had a long career, publishing a novel per year since 1987. Brooks, eleven years younger, spent some time as a horse trainer before writing his first book, published in 2009. Both Francome's thriller, *Deadly Finish* (2009), and Brooks' thriller, *Citizen*, reflect the changes in racing wrought by late-twentieth-century globalization and the infusion of even vaster sums of money into an already gold-plated game. In *Deadly Finish*, the protagonist, Mariana, is a high-priced call girl from Brazil with an equestrian background who starts working as an exercise girl for a trainer just before he is murdered. The criminals who pursue her are mostly English, but there is the implication that money, sex and horseracing scams are now worldwide activities. *Citizen* posits that a Russian billionaire and former Soviet general enters the world of horseracing in a big way. Recognising that the real money is in breeding, he buys a winning mare in foal to a top stallion and takes her back to Russia, where he has built a huge indoor training facility. The Irish jockey hired to ride the colt (and who had previously ridden the mare) is mystified by the colt's resilience. His curiosity is somewhat satisfied by the revelation that the colt gets regular cryotherapy, but in the end he discovers that the Russians have in fact employed other, much stranger and more innovative technologies with the potential to transform horseracing as we know it.[17]

Although American authors have written plenty of racing thrillers (poet Stephen Dobyns wrote a ten-volume series set in Saratoga between 1976 and 1998, and *New Yorker* writer William Murray wrote nine books combining racing, magic and opera between 1985 and 1996), serious American racing fiction generally takes up different themes than English fiction. Hemingway's story 'My Old Man' is the precursor – although the story focuses on the boy and his relationship with his father, when the racing accident that kills the father takes place, Hemingway writes, 'Then Gilford rolled over to one side and got up and started to run on three legs with his front hoof dangling.'[18] While English authors (apart from Dick Francis) tend to focus on the implications of betting and scamming, American authors tend to focus on horses (part of Francis' greatness is that he leaves nothing out of his portrayal of the turf). William Fain's last novel, *A Sporting Life* (1961), also ends with a horse breaking his leg in a race, in spite of the honesty and care of his trainer and the great love of his owner. Fain seems to be asserting that no amount of effort can make a sporting life a happy one, and indeed, between delivery of the manuscript and publication, Fain, aged forty-four, committed suicide.[19]

When I conceived of *Horse Heaven* in the late 1990s, I wanted the novel to incorporate all literary forms – tragedy, comedy, romance, epic, realism and magical realism. I obliged myself to include accidents, death, chicanery, cruelty and despair, but also serendipity, pleasure, satisfaction and several happy endings. In one scene, horses die in a race when the horse in the lead suffers an aneurism and collapses. The trainer of the dead horse, witnessing the accident, gives up on racing and leaves the sport. One principal character, a trainer with a lifelong habit of cheating, is temporarily reformed when he finds Jesus, but he does not know how to train winners in an honest way. He goes back to cheating, only to gain a sinister new Satanic companion, a crooked veterinarian. But of the main horse characters, one wins the Breeder's Cup, one wins the Arc, one finds a new career in jump racing, one finds a loving child companion, one is rescued from slaughter and another old campaigner is returned to France.[20]

My horses are lucky – they race at Santa Anita, Pimlico, Belmont Park and Chantilly. Two recent American novels, Willy Vlautin's *Lean on Pete* (2010) and Jaimy Gordon's *Lord of Misrule* (which won the 2010 National Book Award), portray much more modest racing venues. *Lean on Pete*, set in Oregon, is a rewriting of *The Adventures of Huckleberry Finn*, in which Charley, the youthful protagonist, finds himself on his own when his affectionate but unreliable father dies. He goes to work for a crooked and profoundly cruel horse trainer and comes to love one of his charges, Lean on Pete. When it looks as though Pete will be sent to Mexico for slaughter, Charley steals him and escapes, hoping to get the horse to Wyoming and safety. If Charley's world is frightening, Lean on Pete's world is terrifying. Horses are routinely injured – Pete, who has had a little success, is damaged and worthless as a five-year-old. Vlautin's depiction of the underside of American life is relentlessly dystopian but rendered in hyper-realistic detail – this is a world we recognize, if we dare to do so. As in *The Duke's Children* or *Nana*, the world of racing is a metaphor for the larger nation. Unlike *Lean on Pete*, *Lord of Misrule* is set in the late 1960s, so the reader may imagine that conditions as they are portrayed at Indian Mound Downs have improved. Gordon's focuses so tightly on the characters and the horses that she seems to be making no larger claims for their symbolic meaning – what she is going for is a much more intense and darker Damon Runyon experience. From the beginning, she immerses the reader in the consciousnesses of different characters who each have different reasons for being at the track – 'the frizzly hair girl', Maggie, has followed her well-dressed boy-friend, Tommy, to this venue so that he can give the horses he trains a bit of experience before trying them elsewhere; Medicine Ed, a black groom, understands the probable fate of all the horses and people he sees around him, but sticks to his job, only trying a little magic when he has to. The horses, Pelter, Lord of Misrule, Mr. Boll Weevil and Little Spinoza, are strong characters in their own right, but in no way comparable to the long list of 'favourites' that racing literature usually portrays – these horses are lucky to be alive. Gordon does not make the connection between Maggie's world and the larger world explicit – it is enough that this corner of the racing world is unredeemed.[21]

From the beginning, racing fiction has been filled with moral ambiguity that grows out of the recognition that the combination of glamour, speed and money makes for powerful temptation. English fiction is largely formed by the nature of English betting – odds that shift over weeks and months supply a sharper motive and a lengthier opportunity to fix a race or damage a horse. English racing fiction, in the first decade of the 2000s, remains sociological and more or less even-handed – evil is present but can be contained, even if with difficulty. In the United States, writers have become more interested in equine personality, possibly owing in part to those children's novels and in part to the fact that a bet pays according to the odds when the horse leaves the post, and so realising an investment seems to depend on a horse's individuality. Perhaps as a result, American racing fiction, at least for now, sees evil as pervasive, represented by cruelty towards horses, whether intended or unintended, that seems to be in the very nature of horseracing. A survey of horseracing fiction brings us to the same conclusion as other studies of horseracing – the sport of kings tracks with the economy of capitalists. The outcome can be brutal or exhilarating, depending on the integrity of the participants and the willingness of those in charge to regulate the corruption that is the natural companion of temptation.

NOTES

1 M. Henry, *Black Gold* (Chicago: Rand McNally, 1957).
2 D. Defoe, *Robinson Crusoe* (London: W. Taylor, 1719), *Roxana* (London: T. Warner, 1724); S. Richardson, *Pamela* (London: Messrs Rivington & Osborn, 1740); H. Fielding, *Tom Jones* (London: A Millar, 1749); L. Sterne, *Tristram Shandy* (London: T. Becket and P.A. Dehondt, 1759–1767).
3 A. Reach, *Clement Lorimer, or, The Book with the Iron Clasps* (London: D. Bogue, 1849).
4 A. Trollope, *The Kellys and the O'Kellys* (London: London: Colborn, 1848).
5 A. Trollope, *The Duke's Children* (London: Chapman and Hall, 1880).

6 E. Zola, *Nana* (Paris: Charpentier, 1880); L. Tolstoy, *Anna Karenina* (Moscow: The Russian Messenger, 1880).

7 G. Moore, *Esther Waters* (London: Walter Scott, 1894).

8 N. Gould, *The Second String* (London: R. A. Everett and Co, 1904).

9 A. Paterson, *The Shearer's Colt* (Sydney: Angus and Robertson: 1936). Quote is from chapter 4.

10 Silver Blaze is one of twelve short stories in C. Doyle, *The Memoirs of Sherlock Holmes* (London: George Newnes, 1894); D. Francis and J. Welcome (eds.), *The New Treasury of Great Racing Stories* (New York: W. W. Norton & Company, 1992).

11 E. Hemingway, 'My Old Man' in *Three Stories and Ten Poems* (Paris: Contact Publishing, 1923).

12 D. Runyon, 'Little Miss Marker', *Collier's*, 89 (26 March 1932), pp. 7–9, p. 40, pp. 43–44.

13 E. Bagnold, *National Velvet* (London: William Morrow, 1935).

14 M. Henry, *King of the Wind* (New York: Rand McNally, 1948); W. Farley, *Man O' War* (New York: Random House, 1962); M. Henry, *Black Gold* (Chicago: Rand McNally, 1957).

15 Dick Francis quoted by M. Stasio, 'Dick Francis, jockey and writer, dies at 89', *New York Times*, 14 February 2010; D. Francis, 'Carrot for a Chestnut', *Sports Illustrated*, 5 January 1970.

16 D. Francis, *Reflex* (London: Michael Joseph, 1980); Dick Francis, *Enquiry* (London: Michael Joseph, 1969).

17 P.G. Wodehouse, *The Return of Jeeves* (New York: Simon and Schuster, 1954), published as *Ring for Jeeves* in the United Kingdom (London: Herbert Jenkins, 1953); J. Cooper, *Jump!* (London: Bantam Press, 2010); D.J. Taylor, *Derby Day* (London: Chatto and Windus, 2011); J. Francome, *Deadly Finish* (London: Headline, 2009); C. Brooks, *Citizen* (London: Harper, 2009).

18 Hemingway, 'My Old Man', p. 160.

19 S. Fain, *A Sporting Life* (New York: Crown, 1961).

20 J. Smiley, *Horse Heaven* (New York: Ballantine, 2001).

21 W. Vlautin, *Lean on Pete* (New York: Harper Perennial, 2010); J. Gordon, *Lord of Misrule* (New York: McPherson, 2010).

4

WRAY VAMPLEW

From Godolphin to Godolphin: The Turf Relaid

Track Record

When I wrote *The Turf* in 1976, there had been little academic research of horseracing. Previous works on racing had been non-academic and generally anecdotal rather than archival. It is fair to suggest that *The Turf* set the research agenda. Based, as much of it was, on secondary sources, it also left many topics awaiting investigation at the primary source level of race company records, diaries of breeders and day-books of owners.

Since the late 1970s, there has been much more research-based work on racing, published both in book form and in academic journals – something rarely, if ever, achieved prior to *The Turf*.[1] This research has challenged some aspects of *The Turf*, reinforced some of the other arguments, as well as taking racing history in new directions. Historians such as Mike Huggins and Roger Munting respectively produced book-length studies of flat-racing and National Hunt racing – the latter an area that I left alone in *The Turf* – and in tracing the origins of the Grand National, one of the premier jump races, John Pinfold demonstrated the detective work that historical research can be.[2] Mike Huggins challenged my downplaying of the role of the middle class in racing. I failed to note that many race committees were predominantly from that background. Mike took this further and developed an irresistible argument that the middle class had a major role in the development of racing not only as organisers and promoters, but also as owners, bettors and spectators.[3] Other scholars, not necessarily historians, have pushed the research boundaries. Christopher Hill, a politics lecturer, produced a serious review of racing's institutions in the post-war era.[4] Literature specialist Donna Landry took a cultural perspective in examining the change in human-equine interaction, one result of which was the development of the British thoroughbred racehorse.[5] Social anthropologists Rebecca Cassidy and Kate Fox respectively brought academic credence to the knowledge of the insider, one in the training and breeding establishments, the other at the track investigating a tribal subculture with its distinctive customs, rituals language and etiquette.[6] In the natural sciences, geneticists have revealed errors in the early entries to the *General Stud Book*.[7]

Of data, Mike Huggins has argued persuasively that the *Racing Calendar* in which I invested my research time is a flawed source.[8] However, Joyce Kay has revisited the *Calendar*, one of the longest continuous series of sporting records in the world, and suggested that it should not be abandoned as it enables an analysis to be made of the changing geography, extent and concentration of racing as well as giving glimpses into social aspects such as the role of women. Above all, 'its statistical evidence probably offers the most comprehensive view of British horseracing over a period of 200 years'.[9] Racecards remain a rather neglected source, with the potential to reveal much about societal and other changes.

Two dissertations that I supervised at De Montfort University (where I arrived in 1993 after eighteen years in Australia) led to publications expanding my views on early racing and changing my position on the role of the railways in the development of racing.[10] Iris Middleton's doctorate looked at the development of racing in Yorkshire. This was a follow-up to my argument that racing was Britain's first national sport, albeit one generally practised at the local and regional level, areas that I initially left to others to investigate. It was also an acceptance of the challenge by Huggins that my 'initial hypotheses' and 'generalisations' needed to be tested at the local level, away from the major meetings which, by virtue of their dominance, could present a different, even distorted, picture.[11] An article in 2003 developed this local argument further, by setting the pattern of Yorkshire horseracing into the work/leisure calendar of an agricultural society.[12] Using documented evidence from newspapers, early versions of racing calendars and diaries and correspondence of persons involved in racing, Middleton and I showed in detail that the timing of race meetings was influenced by holidays and fairs, the seasonal work patterns of a largely agrarian community and the dates of the Assizes. Wednesdays and Thursdays were the most popular racedays, primarily because they avoided settlement days and market days. Despite the work of Middleton, Wilkinson, Huggins and Moore-Colyer, the absence of local studies is still a deficiency in the academic literature.[13]

In *The Turf* I argued that 'it is no exaggeration to say that the railways revolutionised horseracing'.[14] But it was. John Tolson and I published an early paper on the topic in 1998 and a later one revisiting the subject after his thesis was completed.[15] What we demonstrated, with quantitative evidence, was that the railways had an important role in the transformation of British racing, but they were not the driving force. Although the speed and convenience of the railways eased travel for the distant spectator, thousands of whom took advantage of the racing specials, racing was a significant spectator sport before the railway network emerged. Indeed it was not until the 1930s that the railways carried as many passengers to the Derby as had attended a century before without the aid of the locomotive. In order to follow their occupation, jockeys too had to travel, but the increase in the miles they travelled over time owed more to the expansion of fixtures than to the railway. Using trains meant that horses could travel in a matter of hours what had previously taken them days or even weeks to walk, and by the end of the nineteenth century the railway was the standard method of transporting racehorses any distance. Yet there is no evidence that this led to horses racing more often or travelling greater distances to compete. As for railway company sponsorship of race meetings, even at its height it totalled less than 5 per cent of all sponsorship. Jockey Club regulations on prize money and restrictions on the opening of new courses were far more important in shaping the structure of the racing industry than anything to do with the railways.

Cantering On

In my later years at De Montfort I began to work with Scottish-based sports historian Joyce Kay, research that progressed when I moved to the University of Stirling in 2001. Our first joint piece was a chapter on Scottish racing which showed the historical paucity of the sport north of the border.[16] Our major undertaking was the writing of the *Encyclopedia of British Horseracing*, published as part of a Routledge sports reference series in 2005.[17] We resisted recycling old material and examined some previously neglected areas such as the link between racing and the arts, the church and alcohol. We looked at the social, economic and political forces that shaped the development of the sport and emphasised the historical duality of continuity and change. Like *The Turf* before it, the *Encyclopedia* was translated into Japanese.

One thing that was missing from *The Turf* was any real theoretical underpinning. I attempted to rectify this in *Pay Up and Play the Game: Professional Sport in Britain 1875–1914*, in which I applied the concepts of profit and utility maximisation, cartelisation and economic rent to several sports including racing.[18] Theory of course is not immutable and I have always argued that if the facts do not fit the theory, first check the facts and then, if they are correct, change the theory. This is what Joyce Kay and I suggested when we attempted to assess the relevance to horseracing of Allen Guttmann's famous seven-stage model of modernisation in sport.[19] By the 1830s, racing was a major British sport, organised at local level the length and breadth of the country; the Classics and other major races had been established; and large crowds were attracted, reputedly more than 100,000 at Doncaster, Epsom and a few other venues. However, using Guttmann's criteria, racing did not appear to be modernised at this time. While it undoubtedly operated in a *secular* environment and was highly *specialised*, it was only partly *rationalised* and *bureaucratised* and failed almost entirely to meet Guttmann's conditions of *quantification* and *records*. There was also little *equality* in terms of gender, ownership and the timing of events, but it could be argued that full equality could never be attained in the sport even today because of the financial costs of participation. We went on to suggest that Guttmann's model failed to give sufficient attention to the roles of gambling, professionalisation and commercialisation, all of which might change the view of the extent to which racing could be considered 'modernised' before Victoria became monarch.

Continuing to build on her specialised knowledge of racing north of the border, Joyce Kay has shown that the Royal Caledonian Hunt Club was not as influential in Scottish racing as previously thought. Even by the mid-1820s, when its affiliates had become more concerned with horseracing than carousing, the Club donated only 10 per cent of the prize money available at Scottish meetings and members comprised no more than a third of the owner-participants at elite Scottish meetings.[20] Similarly in Britain as a whole, there has been an assumption that the Jockey Club was in control of British racing from its foundation in the mid-eighteenth century.[21] There is no evidence that at the outset the Club had any interest in governing British racing; its raison d'être was to organise horse races at Newmarket for its members. When it first began to exert any control outside its own domain is unclear.[22] Apart from an isolated instance in 1757, when it was asked to adjudicate on a dispute arising from a meeting at the Curragh in Ireland, there is no other mention in either Jockey Club records or the *Racing Calendar* of the Club having – or seeking – any influence in the eighteenth century beyond its immediate jurisdiction.[23] By the early nineteenth century, however, the Club may have been seeking to formalise its influence in the wider racing world, but there was a limited take-up of its offer to adjudicate on disputes elsewhere in the country. The number of cases published in the *Racing Calendar* remained low – a total of eleven in 1826 had only risen to nineteen by 1833 – and most of these came from courses in the south of England. Up to the 1860s, outside Newmarket and a minority of elite courses, the Jockey Club was ineffective. It had some influence but little actual power.

As well as a chapter in *The Turf*, I have produced several pieces on both flat and jump jockeys.[24] One aspect I have examined in detail was the change in riding style forced on domestic riders at the turn of the nineteenth century by an influx of American jockeys who brought with them shorter stirrups, higher knees and a less erect position.[25] By cutting wind resistance and providing better weight distribution on the horse, these Americans gained an advantage over the Britons riding in their traditional style. In 1900, one of them was a champion jockey and three others were in the top ten. Although assisted by a concurrent immigration of American trainers who were not averse to using dope – not a turf offence at the time – the new riding style undoubtedly gave the diminutive Americans an advantage. Eventually, to safeguard their livelihoods, British jockeys began to adopt the American seat, and Tom Cannon, a highly successful teacher of apprentices, opted to instruct his young charges to ride more in the 'foreign' style.

My admiration for jockeys is unbounded. Not only do they risk life and limb every time they go to work, but they face the stress of public and private appraisal, constant weight-watching with its associated health risks, and the demeaning struggle to gain employment in an oversupplied labour market.[26] Were it not for the artificially low weights imposed on the industry, the supply situation would be even worse. Modern studies demonstrate that it is not just racing that is dangerous, but that about a third of all injuries reported by jockeys occurred during training activities, and there is no reason to believe that this would not apply historically.[27] We still know so little about jockeys. How, for example, did the barely literate Fred Archer manage to arrange 667 rides in 1885? And what of others in the racing labour market? For trainers, Huggins made use of the regional and local press to look at eighteenth- and nineteenth-century Yorkshire practitioners and examine their background, methods and finances. Some of these men were major local employers, but we know nothing of their workers as we have only two academic studies of stablehands and both of these are for the late twentieth century.[28]

Assessing the Odds

More than thirty-five years of research has convinced me that racing is different from other sports; that it has a long history of both commercialisation and internationalisation; and that it is conservative, irrational and, historically, certainly corrupt – partly because of its long association with gambling. In many respects horseracing is a unique sport. It is highly professionalised with little room for the amateur except in jump racing where National Hunt permits allow only the highly competent to participate and point-to-point is strictly amateur. It has no grass roots so, while many spectators at football and cricket games will have played those sports, few racegoers will have mounted a horse, let alone ridden one in a race. Another unusual aspect of racing is that it has large attendances but no real fan base. Spectators seldom follow particular horses or jockeys as they would a local team, and there is little shared, communal experience associated with winning or losing. Racing is largely for individuals, both at participant and spectator level. Nor is it for the sedentary viewer: in most other sports you take your seat and the event unfolds before you. In racing, to get most from the spectacle, you have to follow proceedings from stand to paddock, from paddock to rails, and from the rails to the winner's enclosure.

Race meetings have rarely been solely for watching horses compete. Even though eighteenth-century races did not have bookmakers, those who wished to gamble could find an outlet at the odds/even tables. Additionally there would be beer booths, refreshment tents, fortune tellers, musicians and other entertainers, and often cockfights, organised for the mornings and evenings with the races in the afternoon.[29] Where historians have to draw the distinction is between commercial activity associated with the races and commercialism of racing itself. Initially the races were only part of the amusement made available and, except for those who wished to patronise the grandstand and other exclusive areas, entry to watch the races was free. When racing became more serious, both commercially and in a sporting sense, gate-money was charged, but, in order to persuade spectators to pay for something that was previously available *gratis*, musical accompaniment by military bands and lawned areas for strolling were made available as part of the package.[30]

British racing has always been international, particularly in the development of bloodstock.[31] Britain exported the sport – including stallions, racenames, racing models and style of governance – to its formal and informal empires. As Andrew Lemon has noted, given that there have been other types of racing, from Roman chariot races to Sienna street racing, 'what is intriguing is the speed with which English thoroughbred racing took hold, particularly in the nineteenth century, and became the model that was followed across the globe'.[32] There is, however, a major research gap to be filled in looking at how Britain might have influenced racing in Europe. It had a significant presence in France and in Sweden (especially if harness racing is counted) but less so elsewhere. Where it did develop it seemed to adopt the English model; there was a plethora of 'Derbies' to race in and of Jockey Clubs to control the sport. Reasons for this are speculative. How much of a military presence did Britain have in Europe compared to its colonies? Did English ways become fashionable across a spectrum of activities, or did it have to do with wealthy and influential English touring abroad but looking for familiar recreations? In Britain it was argued that, by developing improved horseflesh, racing assisted agriculture, transport and the military. Were the needs of the forces, agriculture and transport the same in Europe as in Britain? Or – another potential research topic – was the British rationale a fiction, a rhetoric designed to give substance to an 'immoral' activity associated with gambling? Many continental countries appear to have shared Britain's regard for the ridden horse as a symbol of aristocratic status, power and influence. But whereas Britain's upper classes moved on to racehorse ownership, not all Europeans followed suit. A start has been made by Christiane Eisenberg who describes the cultural transfer of horseracing from Britain to Germany in the early nineteenth century and argues that, while in Britain horseracing was a gentlemanly sport embedded in a culture of betting and competition, in Germany it became part of the still feudal social hierarchy, with a special accent on posture and the 'heroic' virtues of the cavalry.[33]

Racing is inherently conservative: old measurements continue (but not for heritage reasons) and innovation has generally been slow. If, for example, we look at starting stalls, the photo finish, and all-weather surfaces, Britain has followed rather than led.[34] Additionally the sport was slow to acknowledge that women should have a vote in the running of the sport; not until 1977 were the first women elected to the Jockey Club. Racing also has an element of illogicality. In the eighteenth and nineteen centuries, geldings were eligible for Royal Plates, races supposedly organised to encourage breeding, and today, in contrast to agriculture, artificial insemination is outlawed, this despite one rationale of racing being to breed from the best.[35] Overall, the sport is economically irrational and is dependent on most owners treating it as a hobby, as consumption demanding expenditure rather than investment seeking a return. Although Moore-Colyer has argued that many Welsh gentlemen who engaged in the breeding business did so with profit as an important motive, Huggins has shown that only a minority of nineteenth-century Yorkshire breeders made a profit, although, to be fair, their deficient accounting procedure often presented them with a different picture.[36]

More than anything else, racing is associated with gambling.[37] Racing and betting have always gone hand in hand, from the simple wager on a match race in the eighteenth century to the millions spent on the Internet today. Other sports have betting but, Dubai apart, racing needs betting.[38] Gambling adds excitement to the races but almost inevitably leads to corruption. Mike Huggins' major re-examination of the 1844 Running Rein affair, in which the Derby of that year was won by a horse a year older than the rest of the field, showed the state of dishonesty at the highest level of British racing.[39] Yet an assessment needs to be made as to whether over time the problems of other sports with drugs, bribery and gambling scams have been any better than those of the turf, and whether the racing stables are as 'dirty' as some areas of business life, notably the financial services sector.

Betting has been the focus of several academic works usually concerned with the asymmetric legal position of the working-class and higher-class gambler.[40] Revisionist studies have also attempted to rehabilitate late-nine-teenth-century bookmakers as respectable small businessmen, albeit ones working in the black economy, rather than social parasites.[41] Huggins, how-ever, has argued, on the basis of a local study of Teesside that before the late 1880s, a majority of bookmakers displayed criminal characteristics, most often a recourse to violence.[42] Gambling is but one strand of the unholy trin-ity of long residuals associated with racing, the others being sex and alcohol. Certainly at the lower end of the social spectrum, working people histori-cally took advantage of the opportunity for getting drunk and gaining sex-ual license while at the races.[43] One aspect of crowd (mis)behaviour that has declined over time is violence. These days at British race meetings, the com-bination of alcohol and young men do not generally produce the endemic violence of earlier periods, although the Cheltenham Festival, the Kentucky Derby and the Melbourne Cup attract boisterous mixed crowds.[44]

Looking Forward

So what did I bring to the racing stables? I had two distinct approaches to racing history, first one of social science, particularly economics, and sec-ond a sense of quantification designed to give more precision to arguments. I have always had a reputation as a statistical historian, possibly stemming from my early training as an economic historian. Coincidently, in the years before either of us researched racing history, I was Mike Huggins' tutor on an Open University course on the use of statistics in history. Former colleague Mike Cronin has recalled that one of my first questions to any research student was 'what are you going to count?'[45]

I would explain the development of horseracing in economic terms along the lines that it originated from a combination of wealth, competitive instinct and lack of spending opportunities. It was a prime example of conspicuous consumption in which match races between two owners demonstrated an ability and willingness to risk money. Racing has been a dynamic prod-uct and clearly even by 1900 was a different sport from that of 1700. The pre-modern version was predominantly rural, highly localised and free to watch, but two centuries later it had national rules and many courses were enclosed and charging gate-money. What happened was a combination of commercial widening (more fixtures), commercial deepening (new revenue sources), product improvement (modifying the original sporting competition) and product development (changing the nature of racing).

As an economic product, how does horseracing fit into the conventional definition of a sports good? Like most sports goods, horseracing's output is non-predictable. Indeed uncertainty is absolutely vital to horseracing, a sport intimately associated with gambling: the greater the uncertainty of the result, the greater the likelihood of a betting market. Sports goods are non-durable: once played, a game or a match is over and cannot be stored for later consumption. However, in racing, perhaps there is an element of hoarding for future use in the intricacies of the breeding industry. Generally sport is regarded as a consumer good but sometimes it can be seen as an intermediate product. Clearly no one becomes a jockey to improve their health. However, the motivations of the spectators can vary. If they are at the racing for relaxation, then horseracing is a consumer good, but if they are there primarily to make money from betting, racing might be considered an intermediate good. Racing, like many sports, is often a complementary product that is rarely sold without being in a package with other goods and services: going to the races, for example, could also involve the travel product, the betting product, the catering product and the alcohol product. Racing, again like several other sports, exhibits some peculiar economics. Racecourses are underutilised; owners seek psychic income rather than economic rewards; and breeding can be influenced by conformation and pedigree, not just racecourse performance. That said, it also encompasses much conventional economic activity such as the employment of farriers and stablehands and the profit-seeking suppliers of catering facilities.

Unhappily the economic path has not attracted turf historians apart from Joyce Kay who looked at the state subsidy of some £5,000 per annum given to racing for nearly two centuries via Royal Plates.[46] Initially these races were important fixtures in the early racing calendar, offering prestige and substantial prize money. Kay argues that their original objective was the welfare of elite racing and that only later did the encouragement of breeding become their focus. However, there is no evidence that the 'muddled and misdirected policy' achieved this aim, and in 1888 the subsidy to racing ceased and the money was transferred to Queen's premiums for the purchase of twenty-two thoroughbred stallions to be placed at stud around the country. A similar approach could usefully be applied to contemporary institutions such as the European Breeders Fund.

Overall, my experiences as an author, researcher and consultant lead me to feel that many of those involved in racing have little interest in the history of their sport. Horseracing is one of the oldest sports on record and in the (British) *Racing Calendar* has the longest continuous sporting periodical in the world. Indeed we know more about the genealogy of eighteenth- and early-nineteenth-century thoroughbreds than of many of their owners and certainly most of their riders. Yet those involved in racing too often focus on the here and now and the production and prediction of winners for tomorrow to the neglect of history and heritage save for the form and more recent stud books. Like true gamblers, they prefer to look to the future in hope, rather than to the past.

NOTES

1 What follows is not intended as a comprehensive literature review, merely an acknowledgement of those works I feel have pushed racing research forward. It is also, notwithstanding the quality of some other work, restricted to academic studies.

2 M. Huggins, *Flat Racing and British Society 1790–1914* (London: Frank Cass, 2000); M. Huggins, *Horseracing and the British, 1919–1939* (Manchester: Manchester University Press, 2003); R. Munting, *Hedges and Hurdles* (London: J. A. Allen, 1987); J. Pinfold, 'Where the Champion Horses Run: The Origins of Aintree Racecourse and the Grand National', *International Journal of the History of Sport*, 15 (1998), 137–151.

3 M. Huggins, 'Culture, Class and Respectability: Racing and the English Middle Classes in the Nineteenth Century', *International Journal of the History of Sport*, 11 (1994), 19–41.

4 C. R. Hill, *Horse Power: The Politics of the Turf* (Manchester University Press, 1988).

5 D. Landry, *Noble Brutes: How Eastern Horses Transformed English Culture* (Baltimore: Johns Hopkins University Press, 2008).

6 R. Cassidy, *The Sport of Kings: Kinship Class and Thoroughbred Breeding in Newmarket* (Cambridge: Cambridge University Press, 2002); K. Fox, *The Racing Tribe* (London: Metro, 1999).

7 E. Hill and P. Cunningham, 'History and Integrity of Thoroughbred Dam Lines Revealed in Equine mt Variation', *Animal Genetics*, 33 (2002), 287–294.

8 Huggins, *Flat Racing*, pp. 65, 175.

9 J. Kay, 'Still Going After All These Years: Text, Truth and the *Racing Calendar*', *Sport in History*, 29 (2009), 353–366. [Quote on p. 359.]

10 I.M. Middleton, 'The Developing Pattern of Horse-Racing in Yorkshire 1700–1749: An Analysis of the People and the Places', PhD thesis, De Montfort University (2000); J. Tolson, 'The Railway myth: Flat Racing in Mainland Britain 1830–1914', PhD thesis, De Montfort University (2000).

11 M. Huggins, 'Horse-Racing on Teesside in the Nineteenth Century: Change and Continuity', *Northern History*, 23 (1987), 98–118.

12 I. Middleton and W. Vamplew, 'Horse-Racing and the Yorkshire Leisure Calendar in the Early Eighteenth Century', *Northern History*, 40 (2003), 259–276.

13 D. Wilkinson, *Early Horse Racing in Yorkshire and the Origins of the Thoroughbred* (York: Old Peg Publications, 2003); Huggins, 'Teesside'; R.J. Moore-Colyer, 'Gentlemen, Horses and the Turf in Nineteenth-Century Wales', *Welsh History Review*, 16 (1992), 47–62.

14 W. Vamplew, *The Turf* (London: Allen Lane, 1976), p. 33.

15 J. Tolson and W. Vamplew, 'Derailed: Railways and Horse-Racing Revisited', *The Sports Historian*, 18.2 (1998), 39–49; J. Tolson and W. Vamplew, 'Facilitation Not Revolution: Railways and British Flat Racing 1830–1914', *Sport in History*, 23 (2003), 89–106.

16 J. Kay and W. Vamplew, 'Horse-Racing' in G. Jarvie and J. Burnett (eds.), *Sport, Scotland and the Scots* (East Linton: Tuckwell, 2000), pp. 159–173.

17 W. Vamplew and J. Kay, *Encyclopedia of British Horseracing* (Abingdon: Routledge, 2005).

18 W. Vamplew, *Pay Up and Play the Game* (Cambridge: Cambridge University Press, 1988).

19 A. Guttmann, *From Ritual to Record: The Nature of Modern Sports* (New York: Columbia University Press, 1986); W. Vamplew and J. Kay, 'A Modern Sport? "From Ritual to Record" in British Horseracing', *Ludica*, 9 (2003), 125–139.

20 J. Kay, 'From Coarse to Course: The First Fifty Years of the Royal Caledonian Hunt, 1777–1826', *Review of Scottish Culture*, 13 (2000–01), 30–39.

21 Although the broadsheet press and even the *Racing Post* (12 February 2003) seem to believe that the Jockey Club has ruled racing since the mid-eighteenth century, this is patently untrue. Harvey and Wrigglesworth can be forgiven as they were not specialists in the area, but even racing historians have tended to accept that the Club was in charge much earlier than it actually was. Moore-Colyer, 'Gentlemen, Horses and the Turf', p. 47; A. Harvey, *The Beginnings of a Commercial Sporting Culture in Britain, 1793–1850* (Aldershot: Ashgate, 2004), pp. 117–118, 145; N. Wrigglesworth, *The Evolution of English Sport* (London: Cass, 1996), pp. 6–7; Huggins, *Flat Racing*, p. 175.

22 W. Vamplew, 'Reduced Horsepower: The Jockey Club and the Regulation of British Horseracing', *Journal of Entertainment Law*, 3 (2003), 94–111.

23 R. Mortimer, *The Jockey Club* (London: Cassell, 1958), p. 30.

24 These include W. Vamplew, 'Still Crazy after All Those Years: Continuity in a Changing Labour Market for Professional Jockeys', *Contemporary British History*, 14 (2000), 115–145; W. Vamplew and J. Kay, 'Captains Courageous: The Gentleman Rider in British Horseracing 1866–1914', *Sport in History*, 26 (2006), 370–385; W. Vamplew, 'Les sportifs professionnels: les jockeys' in C. Louveau and A. Waser (eds.), *Sport et Cité: Pratiques Urbaines, Spectacles Sportifs* (University of Rouen Press, 1999), pp. 113–132.

25 W. Vamplew, 'Sporting Innovation: The American Invasion of the British Turf and Links 1895–1905', *Sport History Review*, 35 (2004), 122–137.

26 W. Vamplew, 'Riding for a Fall: The Health Hazards of Professional Jockeys in Nineteenth and Twentieth Century British Horseracing' in T. Terrey (ed.), *Sport and Health in History* (Berlin: ISHPES, 1999), pp. 118–126.

27 S. Cowley, B. Bowman and M. Lawrance, 'Injuries in the Victorian Thoroughbred Racing Industry', *British Journal of Sports Medicine*, 41 (2007), 639–643.

28 M. Huggins, *Kings of the Moor: Yorkshire Racehorse Trainers 1760–1900* (Teesside University Papers in North Eastern History, 1991); M.P. Filby, 'The Newmarket Racing Lad: Tradition and Change in a Marginal Occupation', *Work, Employment and Society*, 1 (1987), 205–224; J. Winter, 'Industrial Relations-Lite? The Management of Industrial Relations in the United Kingdom Thoroughbred Racehorse Training Industry' in C. McConville (ed.), *A Global*

Racecourse: Work, Culture and Horse Sports (Melbourne: ASSH, 2008), pp. 87–100.

29 I. Middleton, 'Cockfighting in Yorkshire during the Early Eighteenth Century', *Northern History*, 40 (2003), 129–146.

30 Vamplew and Kay, 'A Modern Sport?', pp. 125–139.

31 M. Huggins, 'The Proto-globalisation of Horseracing, 1730–1900: Anglo-American Interconnections', *Sport in History*, 29 (2009), 367–391.

32 A. Lemon, 'Horse Racing: An English or an International Sport' in McConville (ed.), *Global Racecourse*, p. 2.

33 C. Eisenberg, 'Pferderennen zwischen "Händler" und "Heldenkultur". Verlauf und Dynamik einer englisch-deutschen Kulturbegegnung' in: H. Berghoff and D. Ziegler (eds.), *Pionier und Nachzügler? Vergleichende Studien zur Geschichte Englands und Deutschlands im Zeitalter der Industrialisierung* (Bochum: Geburtstag, 1995), pp. 235–258.

34 See Wayne Peake, Chapter 9 in this volume.

35 J. Kay, 'Closing the Stable Door and the Public Purse: The Rise and Fall of the Royal Plates', *Sports Historian*, 20 (2000), 21–22.

36 Moore-Colyer, 'Gentlemen, Horses and the Turf', 53; M. Huggins, 'Thoroughbred Breeding in the North and East Ridings of Yorkshire in the Nineteenth Century', *Agricultural History Review*, 42 (1994), 115–125.

37 W. Vamplew, 'Taking a Gamble or a Racing Certainty: Sports Museums and Public Sports History', *Journal of Sport History*, 31 (2004), 177–191.

38 See Rachel Pagones, Chapter 11 in this volume.

39 M. Huggins, 'Lord Bentinck, the Jockey Club and Racing Morality in Mid Nineteenth-Century England: The "Running Rein" Derby Revisited', *International Journal of the History of Sport*, 13 (1996), 432–444.

40 These include D. Dixon, *From Prohibition to Regulation* (Oxford: Oxford University Press, 1991) and M. Huggins, 'The Manchester Betting World', *Manchester Regional History Review*, 20 (2009), 24–45.

41 D.C. Itzkowitz, 'Victorian Bookmakers and Their Customers', *Victorian Studies*, 32 (1988), 7–30; C. Chinn, *Better Betting with a Decent Feller* (Hemel Hempstead: Aurum, 1991); M. Clapson, *A Bit of a Flutter* (Manchester: Manchester University Press, 1992).

42 M. Huggins, "The First Generation of Street Bookmakers in Victorian England: Demonic Fiends or 'Decent Fellers'?" *Northern History*, 36 (2000), 129–145.

43 Moore-Colyer, 'Gentlemen, Horses and the Turf', 51; Huggins, 'Teesside'.

44 Fox, *Racing Tribe*, pp. 17–18; Vamplew, *Turf*, pp. 137–142. Wayne Peake, Sean Magee (Chapter 5), this volume.

45 M.J. Cronin, 'What Went Wrong with Counting? Thinking about Sport and Class in Britain and Ireland', *Sport in History*, 29 (2009), 392–404.

46 J. Kay, 'Closing the Stable Door', 18–32.

5

SEAN MAGEE

Festivals

In Chester in 1856, the nonconformist William Wilson complained to the local Watch Committee that the city's race week had 'robbed many an inexperienced youth of his better principles, and many an unguarded female of her purity'. According to Wilson, racing produced 'Brawling, drunkenness, gambling, theft, fornication, suicide, and every vice denounced by the divine authority'.[1] Slightly later, Father Storm, in the influential book *The Christian* (1897), describes racecourses as 'reservoirs of avarice and drunkenness and prostitution'.[2] Concerns about racecourse morality are not confined to nineteenth-century reformists. In 2011, the right-wing commentator Amanda Platell wrote that a drunken brawl at Royal Ascot and the presence of a well-known prostitute, 'parading around like a Duchess', marked 'the death of civility and the rise of the vulgarians'.[3]

Numerous artistic and literary representations suggest that racecourse etiquette is more varied and complex than this implies. Festivals in particular are the most socially fluid racing format and share with the French tradition of La Fête Des Rois (King's Day) a deliberate suspension or inversion of the usual social divisions and standards of behaviour. In the nineteenth century, 'travelling shows, gaming booths, beer tents, cock fights, boxing and wrestling matches, open-air dancing, and, for a privileged few, balls and dinner parties' were part of a good days racing – what Vamplew refers to as 'the catharsis of escaping from worldly cares'.[4] When Doncaster solicitor Robert Baxter went before the House of Commons Select Committee on Gaming in 1844, he was asked whether 'the lower classes' attending the sport on Town Moor came 'for the pleasure they derive from seeing the races'. He replied: 'A little more than that, the mass of them. There is a great percentage who come for the other sensual gratifications provided for them.'[5]

Festivals – in contrast to race meetings with aristocratic or royal beginnings, as at Newmarket and Ascot – were often rooted in the Christian calendar. They provoked anxiety amongst reformers because they exposed the working class to dangerous distractions and could, as Richard Nash relates in Chapter 1 of this volume, provide a potential rallying point for the opposition. Despite the disapproval of the governing classes, however, racing festivals have survived and even flourished.

Festival Arts: Alcohol, Sex and Dressing Up

The fourteenth-century metrical romance *Bevis of Hampton* refers to races being run 'In summer about Whitsuntide', whereas Chester races were traditionally held on Shrove Tuesday. In Ireland, according to Welcome, early horseracing took place 'at the public assemblies or fairs, whose origins went back to pagan times'.[6] The September meeting at Listowel in County Kerry, for example, enabled the local farming community to celebrate the end of the harvest. Fairs marking seasonal rhythms were an opportunity to conduct business of all kinds: political, legal and familial. As Welcome notes, 'marriages were celebrated, deaths recorded, laws debated and defined, methods of defence agreed'.[7] Business was followed by sport, and particularly racing. At the core of the festival is the idea that a race meeting can provide an opportunity for people from many different walks of life to come together. This coming together has the potential to reduce differences that exist outside the racecourse, as when winning punters of all backgrounds cheer home a winner. However, these levelling experiences are often temporary and fragile. When the lower orders got too big for their boots at one of the intersectional match races held at Jerome Park in New York in 1842, for example, distinguished members of the course joined hands and walked the length of the track, punching in the face anyone who refused to leave.[8]

Festivals, and the intense but temporary unity they generate, are lubricated by alcohol. In *Nicholas Nickleby* (1839), Dickens describes how, after 'the great race of the day had been run', the people who had been lining the rails dispersed to their various gastronomic activities:

> Drinking-tents were full, glasses began to clink in carriages, hampers to be unpacked, tempting provisions to be set forth, knives and forks to rattle, champagne corks to fly, eyes to brighten that were not dull before, and pickpockets to count their gains during the last heat. The attention so recently strained on one object of interest, was now divided among a hundred; and look where you would, was a motley assemblage off feasting, laughing, talking, begging, gambling, and mummery.

Dickens produced two set pieces about Derby Day – for *Household Words* and *All the Year Round* – and also wrote about other racing occasions. In 1857, he and Wilkie Collins visited Doncaster during Race Week (that is, St Leger week) as the final leg of the *Lazy Tour of Two Idle Apprentices* – which was a journalistic assignment used by Dickens as a mask for his pursuit of Nelly Ternan, the actress soon to become his mistress. Struck by the maelstrom of Doncaster during the St Leger meeting, Dickens, in the character of 'Mr Francis Goodchild', divided the horde of people filling the town into Lunatics, whom he described as 'horse-mad, betting-mad, drunken-mad', and the 'designing' Keepers who were 'always after them'.[9]

The minimalist diary of Thomas Smales, written in 1731, provides an even more eloquent description of the relationship between racing and alcohol:

June 12 To Newcastle races. Very drunk.
June 13 Sunday. At ditto. Drinking day and night.
June 14 Won the Plate. Drinking day and night.
June 15 To Durham. So to Aldbrough. Drinking all night.
June 16 To Gilling, with Plates; so home very drunk.
June 17 At home very ill.
June 18 Ditto. Extreme ill. Note: in this journey spent £5 17s 6d.[10]

Smales's experience was mirrored a few years later at the other end of England. Thomas Turner, a shopkeeper in Sussex, kept a modest diary in which he recorded his fondness for racing and for the bottle:

5 August 1758: Mr Blake's rider called on me, and he and I rode together to Lewes, when I think I see the finest horse-race that ever I see run on that down or any other. There was four horses started for the purse of £50. There was a numerous, but I think not brilliant, company. I came home in company with Mr Francis Elliss, about ten; but, to my shame do I say it, very much in liquor.

23 August 1764: Mr Banister dined with me on some hashed venison, and after dinner we set out for Lewes races.... Came home about three o'clock; but happy should I be if I could say sober. Oh, my unhappy, nay I may say, unfortunate disposition! – that am so irresolute, and cannot refrain from what my soul detests. See several London riders upon the downs, with whom I drank a glass or two of punch.[11]

A more recent racecourse toper was Jeffrey Bernard, who chronicled a life of betting and drinking with a touch unparalleled by any other writer. One particular binge found him under a tree at Windsor, drunk and moneyless when a white Rolls Royce approached:

The owner as suave as a film star, asked what he could do for me. I said, 'I'm pissed and potless. Will you please take me to the Dorchester immediately and buy me a drink.' I'd never seen him before and I've never seen him since, but he was absolutely charming. He recognised someone who'd done their bollocks and was feeling thirsty. He drove me straight to the American Bar and stood me a huge one. We never introduced ourselves. He just filled me up and then gave me the taxi fare to get back to Soho.

Sex, and particularly prostitution, was commonly bracketed with drunkenness as one of the principal evils of the races. In 1857, the journalist Hugh Shimmin wrote of 'coaches filled with harlots' making their way to the Grand National meeting at Aintree, and described a system for selecting women based on the distribution of cards and the descriptions of 'colours', a process which resembled that of picking a horse in a race:

> The great event being over, lazy-looking and fashionable attired men cross the course and entered the ploughed gallop, drawing from their pockets the cards they have received in order that they more easily distinguish their favourites. The girls, flushed with wine, waited on by bullies and pimps, watched keenly by their keepers, who are hovering about, are thus decorated to captivate the turfites.

This scene was echoed by the late Sir Clement Freud in 2006:

> I once mentioned to the head man at Ascot that I much admired the white stretch limo in No. 3 car park that regularly bounced up and down when the engine was off, and from which I had heard a pleasant female voice say, 'It has been a business doing pleasure with you,' as an elderly man crept out the rear door. Was it, I asked, part of the service at the royal meeting, or had a private enterprise stolen a march? Also, was I, as a boxholder for many years, eligible for a discount?[12]

'The head man at Ascot' gave Sir Clement short shrift.

Prostitution is less visible at most modern race meetings, while fashion has become increasingly important. Festivals provide opportunities for displays of wealth, status, taste – including fashion sense – and, of course, nonsense. At the very first Ascot meeting in 1711, Miss Forester, described by eyewitness Jonathan Swift as 'a silly true maid of honour' to Queen Anne, caused a stir by appearing at the sports wearing 'a long white riding coat over a full-flapped waistcoat and a habit skirt; on her head, over a white-powdered periwig, a small three-cornered cocked hat, bound with gold lace, the point placed exactly in front'.[13] This was the precedent for the weird and wonderful millineries that appear at Ascot each year. As a fixture bound by protocol and a strict dress code with all of the potential for division that implies, Royal Ascot does not meet the conditions to be considered a true 'festival' meeting. However, there are signs that it has been appropriated by the masses. It is certainly no longer sufficiently exclusive to be taken seriously by the establishment. Perhaps Ascot is a festival in waiting.

'Ladies' Day' – a term first used of Ascot in the 1820s when a poem referred to Gold Cup day as 'Ladies' Day, when the women, like angels, look sweetly divine'[14] – is a tradition that has been exported to many other race-courses. Participating in Ladies' Day fashion face-offs has become a serious business. With cash prizes and, at the biggest meetings, expensive cars to be won, racecourse fashion is no longer a question of turning up at the racecourse suitably attired, as some racecourses have been quick to appreciate. Fashionistas need their pit stops as much as any Formula 1 driver, and shortly before the Grand National Festival at Aintree in 2009, the *Liverpool Echo* described, 'A crack team of stylists is on hand at Aintree to help race-goers deal with fashion disasters, including smudged make-up, snapped heels and windswept hair. A fashion first-aid tent, prepared for any weather, is being run by Matalan.'[15] Not long before the 2012 Cheltenham Festival, the course announced that the Racing With Style restaurant – an 'exclusive Ladies' Day Dining and Pampering Experience' – 'will have award-winning hairdressers on hand to offer quick fix solutions to keep hair looking great throughout the day – whatever the weather. A beauty therapist will also be offering mini manicures to keep hands and nails in peak condition.' A bargain at £200 a head.[16] Although these kinds of attractions infuriate some racing purists, they are a return to the broad range of facilities and entertainment that was provided at the original festivals. Instead of cockfighting and boxing matches, punters are treated to inflatable Sumo wrestlers and mini manicures.

Derby Day: 'Temporary Saturnalia of Social Equality'

Derby Day provides the historical template for racing festivals.[17] The proximity of Epsom racecourse (13 miles from Charing Cross in the centre of London) made the race accessible to everyone who had shoes. Before it was moved to Saturday from Wednesday in 1995, many businesses were closed for the afternoon of the race – for much of the nineteenth century, House of Commons business was suspended on Derby Day – and it was said that the entire population of London migrated to Epsom. Descriptions of Derby Day emphasise the suspension of class division, some in order to protest at what they regard as an outrageous flouting of social order, others to revel in the carnivalesque spirit of the occasion.

Exactly when and how the running of the Derby shifted from a horse race dreamed up by the local aristocracy – first run in 1780 – to a jamboree described disapprovingly by the nineteenth-century politician Wilfred Lawson as a 'Cockney carnival and suburban saturnalia' is impossible to chart accurately.[18] However it reached its unique position, the Derby Day scene has been painted by Degas, Dufy, Millais ('Such tragic scenes I saw on the course!'[19]) and Doré as well as, more predictably, Alken, Herring and

Munnings, and most famously by William Powell Frith, whose panoramic *Derby Day* caused a sensation when first exhibited at the Royal Academy in 1858. Frith recalled his first visit to Epsom in 1856:

> My first Derby had no interest for me as a race, but as giving me the opportunity of studying life and character, it is ever to be gratefully remembered. ...
> The more I considered the kaleidoscopic aspect of the crowd on Epsom Downs, the more firm became my attempt to reproduce it.[20]

The same sentiments could have come from the pens of most of the great Victorian novelists. Amongst those whose novels include Derby Day scenes are Trollope, Disraeli, Thackeray – who wrote 'of the shouting millions of people assembled to view that magnificent scene'[21] – and George Moore. Moore's great racing-based novel, *Esther Waters* (1894), discussed by Smiley in this volume, contained a highly atmospheric Derby Day scene:

> Drags and carriages continued to arrive. The sweating horses were unyoked, and grooms and helpers rolled the vehicles into position along the rails. Lackeys drew forth cases of wine and provisions, and the flutter of table-cloths had begun to attract vagrants, itinerant musicians, fortune-tellers, begging children. All these plied their trades round the fashion of grey frock-coats and silk sunshades. All along the rails rough fellows lay asleep with their hats over their faces, clay pipes sticking from under the brims, their brown-red hands upon the grey grass.

Henry James is one of several foreign authors to suggest that something essential about the English people can be learned from studying the Derby scene. The Derby was one of two 'English excursions' taken by James in 1877, the other was to Commemoration at Oxford. Both are described in his *Collected Travel Writings*, beautifully illustrated by Joseph Pennell. James found Derby Day 'extremely low and rowdyish', but added that 'a stranger of even the most refined taste might be glad to have a glimpse of the popular revel, for it would make him feel he was learning something more about the English people.'[22]

Dickens – who in *Great Expectations* discloses that Magwitch and Compeyson had met at Epsom races – wrote two pieces about Derby Day. The first, for *Household Words* in 1851 with W.H. Wills, is a tour de force of reportage, the literary equivalent of Frith's painting. The Derby is about to start, but not everyone is concentrating on the race, as the piece exclaims: 'And now, Heavens! all the hampers fly wide open, and the green Downs burst into a blossom of lobster salad.' A cornucopia is unveiled: 'All around me there are table-cloths, pies, chickens, hams, tongues, rolls, lettuces, radishes, shell-fish, broad-bottomed bottles, clinking glasses, and carriages turned inside out.' The race competes with this feast, and loses:

Amidst the hum of voices a bell rings. What's that? What's the matter? They are clearing the course. Never mind. Try the pigeon-pie. A roar. What's the matter? It's only the dog upon the course. Is that all? Glass of wine. Another roar. What's that? It's only the man who want to cross the course, and is intercepted, and brought back. Is that all? I wonder whether it is always the same dog and the same man, year after year! A great roar. What's the matter? By Jupiter, they are going to start.[23]

Dickens's second major Derby piece describes the 'The Dirty Derby' in 1863, which the novelist attended with his Irish friend, Mr O'Hone. Again, competition between the various appetites created and sated by the Derby festival are a central theme. Dickens tells the apocryphal sounding story of an American who, 'seized with the pangs of hunger at about half-past two on the Derby Day, entered Mr Careless's booth, and began amusing himself with some edible "fixings" in the way of lunch'. Thus occupied, he missed the Derby itself, and, 'finding that the race had been run and was over, burst into the piercing lamentation: "Oh, Je – -rusalem! To come three thousand miles to eat cold lamb and salad."'[24]

As well as great literature, the Derby has been the subject of music hall songs (such as 'Going to the Derby in my Donkey Cart'), films and plays. The simple juxtaposition of two pieces of drama sums up the changing nature – and perception – of Derby Day in the twentieth century. *Derby Day: A Comic Opera in Three Acts* was written by A.P. Herbert in the spring of 1931 and, with music by Alfred Reynolds, staged later that year. Early in act two, a mass of racegoers from all strata of society – including the 'toffs' in their large car and a group of Cockney 'pearlies' in a donkey cart – arrive at Epsom racecourse in full voice:

> High-cock-a-lorum! We're off to the races!
> We've all got a winner, just look at our faces!
> > Costers and countesses,
> > Parsons and publicans,
> > Barmaids and baronets,
> > > Hip, hip, hooray!
> Rich man and poor man, today we're all one
> For we'll all be much richer before the day's done –
> > We're off to the Durby –
> > We're off to the Durby –
> > > Hip, hip, hooray![25]

By contrast, Howard Brenton's play *Epsom Downs*, centred on the 1977 Derby won by Lester Piggott on The Minstrel and first staged at the Round House in 1977, provides a more complex reflection on the Derby crowd and the emotions it stirs. Margaret is queuing for the bathroom, reflecting on her love for and hatred of, the Derby:

> I hate the little men in pretty colours, who go by on the horses, with their mean, hard little heads and mean, hard little bums. I hate the penguins in the grandstand we gawk at through binoculars. I hate the race officials whizzing along the other side of the rail in their yellow car, chinless wonder masks behind the glass. I hate the jolly boys on the tops of the buses, roaring pissed, stripped to their navels, showing off their lovely tummies in the sun. I hate the coach party lovers. The totties that are pulled. The marriages that are made beneath the great wheel at the fair. Oooooh I begin to hate my fellow men and women.[26]

American writer Bill Bryson visited Epsom in 1990. After the pitch-perfect opening observation that 'The Derby is a little like your first experience of sex – hectic, strenuous, memorably pleasant and over before you know it,' he echoes Henry James as an outsider glimpsing an exotic world of Englishness:

> Racing is only a small part of Derby Day. There is also the gambling and drinking, the vast funfair, the gipsies with their baskets of heather, the fortune-tellers, the wandering crowds, the noise, the tumult, the sense of being part of one of the great rituals of summer. It is impossible not to be captivated by it all. One of the first things that strikes you about the Derby is that there are no normal, everyday people there.... Everyone looks like either an aristocrat or one of the Krays.[27]

Sadly, the fair at Tattenham Corner was cancelled in 2009 in order to make room for more car parking, a decision which prompted gloom amongst the large group of people who went to the Derby to get drunk, be spun around on a large and badly maintained piece of machinery, eat candy floss and throw up. The closure of the fair is not in the festival spirit, and Epsom may have passed its torch to other meetings like Cheltenham and Aintree.

The Epsom Derby may not even be the most festive of Derbies world-wide. 'Until you go to Kentucky and with your own eyes behold the Derby', wrote local humorist Irwin S. Cobb, 'you ain't never been nowheres and you ain't never seen nothin'!'[28] The difficulty comes in being able to recall what you did see, for the most ingrained tradition of the Kentucky Derby is the reckless consumption of the day's lethal bespoke drink, the Mint Julep – a concoction of bourbon, iced water, sugar and mint leaf. That combination fuels all manner of depravity among race fans, making the first Saturday in May at Churchill Downs an annual bacchanalia of proportions unmatched at Epsom or Cheltenham. It also puts the revellers in good voice for the spine-tingling communal rendition of 'My Old Kentucky Home' as the runners for the big race come out onto the track.

The Kentucky Derby, now the opening leg of the U.S. Triple Crown, was first run in 1875. It earned its soubriquet of 'The Run for the Roses' in 1833 when E. Berry Wall presented red roses to women attending a post-Derby party: roses have been draped on the winner since 1896. Just as the Derby at Epsom proved irresistible to a variety of writers, so the Kentucky Derby has been chronicled by some of the best writers in the United States. In 1955, William Faulkner used a visit to Churchill Downs to ruminate on the special place that horses enjoy in the hearts of humans, describing racing as 'a sublimation, a transference: man, with his admiration for speed and strength, physical power far beyond what he himself is capable of, projects his own desire for physical supremacy, victory, onto the agent'.[29] A year later John Steinbeck, attending the Derby for the first time, found the experience exhausting but exhilarating. At the end of the afternoon he wrote:

> I am fulfilled and weary. This Kentucky Derby, whatever it is – a race, an emotion, a turbulence, an explosion – is one of the most beautiful and violent and satisfying things I have ever experienced. And I suspect that, as with other wonders, the people one by one have taken away from it exactly as much good or evil as they brought to it.[30]

The Kentucky Derby excels in revelry. The other two legs of the U.S. Triple Crown – the Preakness at Pimlico in Baltimore and the Belmont Stakes at Belmont Park in New York – are an excuse for a good day out, but not remotely in the same league as their Kentucky sibling. The same applies to the Breeders' Cup, the end-of-season international fixture which draws horses from all over the world to a series of championship races, usually staged at a different track each year. The Breeders' Cup lacks the populism and localism of the Kentucky Derby, perhaps because it has no home track and brings together horses that may not be familiar to North American race fans, but also because it lacks a history around which it can invent traditions. It has yet to decide upon a trademark drink, song or floral tribute. The Derby also attracts a far larger number of complaints about behaviour in the Churchill Downs infield, suggesting that it has preserved more of the anarchic impulses that were so thoroughly exercised on the Epsom downs.

The Cheltenham Festival

For all the Derby's historic credentials as racing's greatest communal gathering, nowadays the one meeting which is known amongst British racing aficionados simply as 'The Festival' is the four-day jumping extravaganza held in mid-March at the foot of Cleeve Hill, on the edge of Cheltenham. What is now called the Cheltenham Festival was formerly known as the National Hunt Meeting, which, before settling at Cheltenham in 1911, was a peripatetic fixture that moved around the country with the National Hunt Steeplechase. This historic race – which still forms part of the Festival programme – was first run at Market Harborough in 1860, and for the next half-century enjoyed a nomadic existence, being run at such places as Melton Mowbray, Bristol, Bedford and Crewkerne, as well as at courses more familiar to the modern racegoer such as Sandown Park and Kempton Park – and, just once, at Newmarket. But wherever it was staged, the National Hunt Steeplechase was the centrepiece of two days of sport which, as the National Hunt Meeting, formed an annual gathering of steeplechasing enthusiasts from around the country. This was the festival as a once-a-year travelling circus rather than a meeting like Chester, rooted in a particular place.

The National Hunt Meeting was hugely popular long before the founding of its two main races in the 1920s: the Cheltenham Gold Cup in 1924 and Champion Hurdle three years later. That popularity was evident when Cheltenham resumed racing after the Second World War, and the March meeting was already being referred to informally in festive terms. In 1948, *Cope's Racegoers' Encyclopaedia* described how the fierce winter of 1946–47 had disrupted racing and reported that 'record entries had been received for the National Hunt Festival at Cheltenham'.[31] And in 1950, the short-lived series *British Racecourses Illustrated* referred to 'the exceptional richness of the Festival programme' at Cheltenham.[32]

The late 1940s was a pivotal point in the history of the National Hunt Meeting, which was transformed by the first hints of what today gives the fixture its incomparable mood: the involvement of the Irish. Prince Regent, trained near Dublin airport by Tom Dreaper (later trainer of Arkle), won the first post-war Gold Cup in 1946, and in his wake came a stream of Irish big-race winners, an extraordinary number of which were trained by Vincent O'Brien. Before concentrating on an astoundingly successful career on the Flat, O'Brien won four Cheltenham Gold Cups (three with Cottage Rake, one with Knock Hard) and three Champion Hurdles (all with Hatton's Grace), but his most remarkable Cheltenham achievement came in the Gloucestershire Hurdle (now the Supreme Novices' Hurdle). Between 1952 and 1959, he had twelve runners in the race: ten won, and the other two finished runner-up.

Horses trained by O'Brien, Dreaper and a select band of other Irish trainers became 'bankers' – horses whose certain victory on the track could underpin three days of profitable betting, and thus support the trip. Add sideshows such as all-night poker schools in the Queen's Hotel and the traditional festival fuel – principally but not exclusively Guinness – and Cheltenham was soon distilling the *craic* in its purest form. Alongside the Irish factor, what makes Cheltenham so special is that the racing is of the highest class – to the extent that for the majority of owners, trainers and jockeys, the Festival dominates the entire season. For horses as well as partisan humans, all roads lead to Cheltenham. As recently as 2004, the fixture, while universally known as 'The Festival', was still strictly called the National Hunt Meeting, but when in 2005 the programme was expanded to a fourth day – Tuesday to Friday – 'The Cheltenham Festival' became formally adopted as the meeting's name in the fixture list, as in popular parlance.

Even Cheltenham cannot please everybody. Journalist Matthew Engel, a gifted social observer, allowed his dyspepsia to get the better of him when previewing the Festival in 1993. He declared that 'Cheltenham has become too popular', resulting in traffic snarl-ups, packed bars and stands full of drunks: 'Very few of those present who are in a fit state to watch the racing can actually get into position to do so.... By the fifth race each day, the place stinks of fried onions and puke. The idea of Cheltenham is glorious; the reality is always vile.'[33] Grumpy – but this is an early example of a view that has taken root amongst those who believe that racing should be more important than competitive drinking. It reflects a more general problem. If racing is no longer the raison d'être of a festival it risks becoming an inauthentic piss-up. Like Royal Ascot, Cheltenham has become a victim of its own success. As the appeal of *the* festival has widened and the crowd has changed, some racing supporters have looked elsewhere, and particularly to Ireland, for their fix.

Most Irish race meetings have a festival feel to them, but two stand out from the others: Punchestown in County Kildare, five days of top-class jump racing in late April and/or early May; and Galway, in late July and/or early August and now (like its County Kerry equivalent Listowel) a liver-testing seven days long. Of the two, Punchestown has the more serious racing, coming as it does only weeks after the Cheltenham Festival and thus forming a natural target for Cheltenham runners, while Galway has the more serious revelry. Punchestown had racing at its current location just outside Naas since 1850 – when the potato famine was coming to an end (though Kildare was not as badly affected by the Great Hunger as other parts of Ireland). The first two-day meeting took place in 1854, and by the 1860s the course was attracting huge crowds and the April fixture had become something of a national carnival. In 1868, the Prince of Wales – Bertie, a fervent racing fan, later Edward VII – travelled to Punchestown races with Princess Louise. Bertie's attendance attracted the disapproval of his mother, Queen Victoria, who wrote to him that going to the races 'naturally strengthens the belief, already too prevalent, that your chief object is amusement' – to which the Prince replied that his mother 'should fully understand that I do not go there for my amusement, but as a duty'.[34] The same year, the *Irish Times* complained that with the races being 'held in a wild and inhospitable district, at some distance from a railway station and with but the small town of Naas to afford the accommodation so urgently required for a gathering of such calibre, it would be the last place to select for a festival so truly national.'[35]

Despite its relatively remote setting, in the twentieth century, Punchestown went from strength to strength. The big meeting was extended to three days in 1963 (when Arkle won the John Jameson Cup without breaking a sweat) and the opening of a new Grandstand complex in 1998 heralded a new era. Finance minister Charlie McCreevy, who performed the opening ceremony and had been coming to the course since childhood days, declared: 'I associate Punchestown to this day with the smell of chips – chips like you got them nowhere else. It was a time when freedom – the freedom of open spaces – sang in our hearts, and it was a world we would not have exchanged for anything.'[36]

Galway – immortalised in the W.B. Yeats poem 'At Galway Races', which celebrated a time of 'horsemen for companions, / Before the merchant and the clerk / Breathed on the world with timid breath'[37] – has twin racing peaks in the Galway Plate (a handicap steeplechase first run in 1869) and Galway Hurdle and attracts massive crowds to the course at Ballybrit. Journalist Donn McClean wrote of Galway in 1994: 'This is not just another race meeting. It is not just another festival. Here is a different world. An abstract. It is a frame of mind. An ideal. A sane madness.'[38] This suggests a return to the original festival values, the suspension of disbelief, the creation of a community sharing an alternate, temporary reality. In 2008, former jockey Richie Forristal summed up the meeting, but could have been summing up the festival spirit more generally over the centuries, when he wrote: 'For these seven days in the west of Ireland, work, recession and political controversy will be but dots on the horizon of the collective merriment. In their united states of oblivion, the hordes escape to a blithe existence.'[39]

NOTES

1 Quoted in R.M. Bevan, *The Roodee: 450 Years of Racing in Chester* (Chester: Cheshire Country Publishing, 1989), p. 31.
2 H. Caine, *The Christian* (London: D. Appleton and Co, 1897), p. 689.
3 A. Platell, 'Death of civility and the rise of the vulgarians', *The Daily Mail*, 20 February 2012.

4 W. Vamplew, *The Turf: A Social and Economic History of Horse Racing* (London: Allen Lan, 1976), p. 131.

5 House of Commons, *Report from the Select Committee on Gaming* (London: House of Commons, 1844), p. 297.

6 J. Welcome, *Irish Horse-Racing: An Illustrated History*, (London: Macmillan, 1982), p. 1.

7 Welcome, *Irish Horse-Racing*, p. 1.

8 S. Reiss, *The Sport of Kings and the Kings of Crime: Horse Racing, Politics and Organised Crime in New York 1865–1913* (Syracuse, NY: Syracuse University Press, 2011), p. 12.

9 M. Slater (ed.), *Dickens' Journalism*, volume 3, (London: J.M. Dent, 1998), p. 467.

10 Quoted in J. Gill, *Racecourses of Great Britain* (London: Barrie and Jenkins, 1975), p. 143.

11 T. Turner, *The Diary of a Georgian Shopkeeper*, ed. G.H. Jennings (Oxford: Oxford University Press, 1979), p. 31, 68–69.

12 C. Freud, 'Sex and racing – it's the way forward', *The Racing Post*, 1 March 2006; reprinted in Sean Magee (ed.), *Freud on Course* (Compton: Racing Post Books, 2009), pp. 230–32.

13 S. Magee, *Ascot: The History* (London: Methuen, 2002), p. 15.

14 P. Egan, *Pierce Egan's Anecdotes of the Turf, the Chase, the Ring, and the Stage* (London: Knight & Lacey, 1827), p. 148.

15 V. Kellaway, 'Style experts will help Grand National racegoers with fashion emergencies at Aintree', *Liverpool Echo*, 1 April 2009.

16 Information about the Racing with Style offer can be found at: www.chelten-ham.co.uk/dining-and-hospitality/restaurants/the-festival-racing-with-style-r estaurant/. Accessed 8 March 2012.

17 *Illustrated London News'* comment on Frith's painting *Derby Day*, quoted by M. Cowling, 'Frith and His Followers: Painters and Illustrators of London Life', in M. Bills and V. Knight (eds.), *William Powell Frith: painting the Victorian age* (New Haven, CT: Yale University Press, 2006), p. 39.

18 Two days before the Derby in 1875, Sir Wilfred put a motion to the House of Commons suggesting that business should continue as usual on race day. According to the *Sydney Mail*, he lost by 'an overwhelming majority'. 'Sport in England: the Derby and Oaks', *The Sydney Mail*, 31 July 1875.

19 Quote is taken from a letter to Charles Collins dated 31 May 1853, reproduced in J.G. Millais, *The Life and Letters of Sir John Everett Millais, President of the Royal Academy* (London: Methuen, 1905).

20 W.P. Frith, *My Autobiography and Reminiscences* (New York: Harper and Bros, 1888), p. 191. These words recall those of David Milch, creator of *Luck*, quoted in the Introduction to this volume.

21 W.M. Thackeray, *The History of Pendennis* (London: Bradbury and Evans, 1850), p. 195.

22 H. James, *Collected Travel Writings: England and America, English Hours, the American Scene, Other Travel* (New York: Library of America, 1993), p. 157.

23 'Epsom' *Household Words*, Vol. 3, No. 63, 7 June 1861. Reprinted in C. Dickens the younger (ed.), *Reprinted Pieces* (London: Macmillan, 1896), p. 125.

24 C. Dickens, 'The Dirty Derby', *All the Year Round*, Vol. IX, 13 June 1863, p. 369.

25 'Pearlies' is an abbreviation used to refer to Pearly Kings and Queens, men and women drawn from the working-class cultures of London who dress up in clothes decorated with pearl buttons and take part in parades in order to raise money for charities, particularly local hospitals. A.P. Herbert, *Derby Day, A Comic Opera in Three Acts* (London: Methuen, 1931), p. 16.

26 H. Brenton, *Plays: One* (London: Methuen, 1986), p. 319.

27 B. Bryson, 'The sport of gipsies and kings', *The Sunday Correspondent*, 10 June 1990.

28 Quoted by J. Bolus, *Derby Fever* (Gretna, LA: Pelican Publishing, 1995), p. 23.

29 W. Faulkner, 'Kentucky: May: Saturday – Three days to the afternoon', *Sports Illustrated*, 16 May 1955.

30 J. Steinbeck, 'Needles – Derby Day choice for President?', Louisville *Courier-Journal*, 6 May 1956.

31 A. Cope (ed.), *Cope's Racing Encyclopaedia* (London: David Cope Ltd., 1948), p. 117.

32 F.N. Johnston (ed.), *Cheltenham and West Country Meetings: British Racecourses (Illustrated) Vol. 1* (London: F. Johnston's Sporting Pub., 1950), p. x.

33 M. Engel, 'And they're off!' *The Guardian*, 16 March 1993.

34 Quoted in R. Smith and C. Costello, *Peerless Punchestown* (Dublin: Sporting Books Publishers, 2000), p. 29.

35 Quoted in Smith and Costello, *Peerless Punchestown*, p. 29.

36 Quoted in Smith and Costello, *Peerless Punchestown*, p. 4.

37 Full text of the poem is available at: www.poetry-archive.com/y/at_galway_races.html. Accessed 8 March 2012.

38 D. McLean, 'A sane madness', *Sunday Independent* [Dublin], 31 July 1994.

39 R. Forristal, 'A shared sense of abandon', *The Racing Post*, 28 July 2008.

6

JOHN MAYNARD

Bodies on the Line: The Social and Physical Capital of Race Riding

Like champion boxers, successful jockeys are feted by the press and courted by kings, queens, politicians and the rich and famous. The rise and fall from the top can be equally quick: easy money, accolades and winners can disappear overnight and with them the backslappers they attract. In a recent interview, three-time Melbourne Cup–winning jockey Glen Boss highlights the adrenalin rush that comes with being a top-flight jockey, saying, 'I'm 41 now and the buzz, the thrill, is stronger than ever after a big win. It's like you're Robbie Williams on stage, every one's looking at you and you're like a rock star.... it's electric.'[1] Addiction to the limelight leads many jockeys to stay too long, and hard-earned wealth is quickly consumed: the lifestyle produced by success is not easily given up. This chapter examines the impact of such a high-risk occupation on jockeys and their families. It is based on my experience of growing up as the son of a jockey and thus provides a personal insight from the track – a perspective that is currently underrepresented in the academic literature.[2]

On reflection, being born the son of a jockey was exciting, colourful, and meant a lot of travelling. My family stories go that by the time I was twelve months old, I had been in every town in New South Wales, Australia – at least all of those with a racetrack, and there are not too many towns in NSW without. As I grew, the travelling continued and included overseas trips, chasing rides for my father. When I was four, we lived in New Zealand; when I was eight, we were in Singapore and Malaysia. Some of my earliest memories are being awakened by the glow and buzz from the doorway of my parent's room as my father's Goblin Teasmade alarm went off at three-thirty in the morning, waking him in time for trackwork. Sometimes I would get up with him and he would make hot toast and tea for a sleepy-eyed kid before heading out the door. Early mornings were also to be feared. Occasionally, my mother would wake me in the dark and we would set off in the car to a hospital, as my father had crashed before racing had begun, in the morning training session. Trackwork holds its own dangers as horses converge to exercise, some of them 'green' – inexperienced and unpredictable. A recent study showed that 30 per cent of accidents reported by jockeys in Victoria occurred during training, in the dawn light before the crowds arrive.[3] I have also seen my father fall in races and sustain broken collarbones, ribs and punctured lungs. I can clearly remember the anxiety of visits to intensive care where he would sometimes spend weeks at a time.

The public, even those who are regular racegoers, is completely detached from these routine parts of the jockey's life, the ritual early rises, the falls and the breaks, the hospital stays. I can recall a discussion with my mother some years back and asking the question, 'Did you worry when pop rode?' She answered in the way of those who are most closely connected to these events, saying, 'You never think about it, you can't allow it to affect you. It always happens to someone else.' That is the truth of it; one never thinks it can happen to your own family. I have known of many jockeys and their families over the years that have suffered tragic losses at the track. People like Cecil 'Skeeter' Kelly who lived next door to us for a while when I was a kid. Stan Cassidy, Bob Baker and Neville Sellwood were others tragically killed. Sellwood was a champion jockey whom my father rode against many times. Born in Brisbane in 1922, he defied the wishes of his mother in order to ride racehorses. She wanted him to become a solicitor, a future he ruled out by deliberately flunking his schoolwork. After a successful career in Australia, the United States and Britain, he was killed in France on 7 November 1962, when a filly named *Lucky Seven* rolled on top of him at Maisons-Laffitte racecourse near Paris. It is typical of the proclivities of race riding that he should have enjoyed perhaps his most high-profile success earlier that year, on Larkspur in the Epsom Derby. As a writer in a recent Australian article observed, the general public remains largely unconcerned or perhaps unaware of the dangers of race riding and training to jockeys' health: 'So many jockeys – like their steeds – risk riding to an early grave. Investors wager heavily to develop and groom horseflesh, yet such largesse is not extended to the health and welfare of jockeys. Have punters forgotten the high personal cost and risk involved?'[4]

My family is steeped in racing tradition: two of my maternal grandmother's brothers were jockeys, her son was a jockey, her son-in-law also. My maternal grandfather had two cousins both of whom were top-class jockeys: Harold Badger and Jim Pike, the legendary jockey of Phar Lap. One of my grandmother's brothers, Wallace, was killed at Caulfield going over the steeple jumps on Caulfield Cup day in 1926 (Figure 6.1). A journalist friend penned a short note on a funeral card, which sums up the jockey's life:

Figure 6.1. Jockey Wallace Hibberd, John Maynard's grandmother's brother, who died from a fall on Caulfied Cup day in 1926.

At Caulfield last Saturday, the cross-country jockey, W. Hibberd received a fatal fall off a 'goat' named Guy Fawkes. Hibberd has often shown his skill in the saddle, and was a friend of the writer, but, like everything else in life, his battle for recognition was a tough one![5]

In Wallace's memory, the writer posted a short verse to remind the punter of the high price the jockey pays to enable his wager:

> Young and hopeful like all true men,
> Who take to the steeple game,
> Rode he hard to win – and, then
> As patiently waited for fame.
> The risk he took – they all must take,
> Experience makes the head;
> A 'battling' rider for practice sake,
> And the price of his daily bread.

> Safe and sound in our grandstand seat,
> We 'cuss' at a riderless horse;
> Little we know what brings defeat
> In a 'Chas O'er the two mile course!
> With riders flying twixt earth and sky
> And your fancy jumps like a 'hack'
> Don't do a weep or cowardly sigh
> Just smile and straighten your back. [6]

Wallace Hibberd left behind a young wife and son.

My father, Mervyn Maynard, did not come from a racing family. His entry into the racing world was one of chance, luck or fate. When Mervyn was twelve, his father died, leaving his mother to care for four very young children, with limited financial backing. Mervyn was sent to live for a short time with family members in the city of Newcastle, about 160 km north of Sydney. At the time, Newcastle was a heavy industrial city with a great sporting history. Racing had begun in the city in 1848 in an area known as Wallaby Flat. By the time my father arrived in Newcastle, Broadmeadow racecourse was well established, benefiting from the proximity of the Hunter Valley and the influence of the progressive Newcastle Jockey Club which formed in 1901. It must have seemed very exciting to my homesick father, who was living very close to the track. He began to spend a lot of time watching the horses, riders and trainers. A small lad, weighing less than five stone, leaning on the fence watching with such rapt attention, he caught the eye of the racing fraternity. Keith Tinson had been training since 1928, having learned his trade from his uncle, Jack Hartigan. He had trained at Newcastle since 1941 and was talented and successful, topping the leading trainer tables in the north on four occasions. He recognised the interest and suitability of the young boy and quickly had him assisting around his stables. Sadly, my father was recalled to Sydney by his mother. But his interest and passion had been set alight with dreams of the track.

My father nurtured this dream when he returned to Sydney, watching track gallops at Canterbury racecourse most mornings. He also began to frequent the course on racedays, peering through cracks in the fence to watch the races. On one of these regular trips to gaze through the fence at the action within, my father spotted a familiar face: Keith Tinson had travelled horses to compete at Canterbury. He called out 'Mr Tinson, get me in and I will look after your horses.' Tinson arranged for the boy to come onto the course where he spent the day. Tinson, to his credit, recognised my father's unbridled passion for horses. He subsequently spoke to my grandmother, and it was arranged that her son would return to Newcastle to be apprenticed to Tinson as a jockey.

Life as an apprentice in the 1940s was tough. Bound by contract to a particular trainer, apprentices had few privileges and were expected to work long hours for pocket money. They were entirely dependent on trainers and owners for their chance to ride. My father lived in a small room attached to the stables, with few furnishings. An old family friend Laurie Howe recalled that when he started he had no decent clothes to wear on the day of his first ride in 1948:

> We all pitched in with some clothing a hat, a small coat and pair of trousers with a belt that had to hold them up. He was so tiny it was virtually impossible to get anything to fit him. We got a pair of ladies golf shoes, brown and white and knocked the sprigs off them. They were the only shoes small enough we could find to fit him.

Despite sartorial challenges and women's shoes, my father was an immediate success, riding eight winners in his debut season and hundreds of winners throughout his apprenticeship. Newspapers began to call him 'Keith Tinson's little goldmine'. Australia is divided into three distinct regions for racing: country, provincial and the city. Newcastle, despite being Australia's sixth-largest city, was still a provincial track. My father's success quickly had him riding, winning and making an impact at the city metropolitan meetings in prestigious Sydney, Melbourne and Brisbane.

In 1952, at the age of eighteen, my father won the first Queen's Cup at Randwick on a 50-to-1 outsider, Salamanca. This victory was to serve as a marker throughout his life and a reference point to which he regularly returned. The race had formerly been known as the King's Cup, and I can recall today my father's disappointment as he reflected that 'only for the King dying I would have met the Queen'. At the time, the newly married Princess Elizabeth was in South Africa, bound for Australia, on her honeymoon. She was engaged to present the Cup at Randwick but en route she received news of her father's death and returned to England. Thus my father lost his chance to meet the monarch, something that he regretted very much. The story was revived forty years later, when Queen Elizabeth was returning to Australia to perform duties which included opening a new grandstand at Randwick. Without notice, my parents received a late-night call from someone who informed my mother that 'the Queen has requested to meet Mervyn Maynard at Randwick racecourse during her visit'. My mother hung up the phone thinking that someone was playing a prank. Minutes later, family friend and Australian Jockey Club Chairman Bob Charley rang and informed my mother that the call had come from the Premier's Department in New South Wales. They were dead serious: the Queen wished to meet the jockey who won the first Queen's Cup, which would be held again on

Figure 6.2. Queen Elizabeth II congratulating Mervyn Maynard on 22 February 1992, forty years after his victory in the Queen's Vase.

the day. My father, who was still riding at the time at the age of sixty, went to Randwick and was introduced to the Monarch: a great moment for him personally. He rode on for another two years and retired at the age of sixty-two (Figure 6.2).

I was destined not to follow the jockey tradition. At around the age of thirteen, my father said, 'Son if you want to be a jockey you best pack your bags for India and ride elephants'. I decided to write, not ride. In 2002, I published a book about the history of Australian Aboriginal jockeys, titled *Aboriginal Stars of the Turf*. This history was largely missing from Australian horseracing.[7] As part of my research I interviewed Leigh-Anne Goodwin, a talented young Indigenous female jockey. She was full of life, and brimming with ambition to make her impact at the track. Despite riding mostly in the bush, she had recently broken through at the metropolitan courses in Brisbane: she was the first Indigenous female jockey to ride a metropolitan winner. It seemed highly likely that trainers in the city would soon recognize Leigh-Anne's talent. In our interview she expressed her hopes and dreams for the future. As a single young mother, she had the added responsibility of raising her young son. Goodwin acknowledged that she had the dual barriers of race and gender to overcome to make her mark on the 'Sport of Kings'. She had already overcome parental disapproval. Both Goodwin's mother Barbara and father Mark were from racing backgrounds, and they recognized the dangers and also the heartache of trying to make it in racing. At first, she buckled under the weight of trying to break through and at the age of nineteen gave up riding for a while. But the bug was quickly reignited, and this time her father Mark realised that his daughter's passion was not to be dismissed and relented, saying, 'Well if you're going to do it you've got to ride like a man. You're in a man's game and you've got to be able to ride like one.'[8]

By late 1998, when I interviewed Leigh-Anne, she had clocked up 127 career winners. In September of that year she achieved her greatest thrill when she piloted Getelion at Brisbane's Eagle Farm course. It was a family affair as the horse was owned and trained by her parents and both her mum and dad were on hand to share the celebrations. Despite being a long-priced outsider, Goodwin punched Getelion home for a convincing victory. 'That was my ambition, to win a race in the city with the whole family involved,' she said at the time.[9] Sadly, the victory would mark Leigh-Anne Goodwin's career's high point. Shortly after this, and only two weeks after our interview, she suffered severe head and internal injuries in a race fall at Roma, a Queensland country track. The horse she was riding fractured his leg whilst sharing the lead about 200 m after the start. Goodwin was catapulted head first into the track, and horses following also struck her. Two days later her distraught parents were left with no alternative than to advise the medical staff at the hospital to switch off her life support system. Her father Mark stated that it was his daughter's wish that if she were ever involved in a fall and was severely injured, she did not want to remain in an unresponsive state. She had made them both promise they would stick with her decision. As Mark said, 'Leigh-Anne had seen a few other jockeys like Billy Barnes and Merv Marion go on for ages even though they had serious brain injuries. She didn't have a premonition about having an accident. She was just being realistic.'[10]

More than a hundred people attended Leigh-Anne Goodwin's funeral in Toowoomba. Her memory and legacy remains with those who knew her. The man with the record of the most winners in Australian racing history, Robert Thompson, who has attended nine or ten funerals of jockeys, reflected, 'When somebody's been hurt, it's a tragedy and you really feel for them, but you just have to accept it and get on with the job.'[11] By 2010, in just slightly more than 200 years of racing, 308 jockeys had been killed on Australian tracks.[12]

But death or injury from a fall is not the only risk faced by jockeys and apprentices. Historically, alcohol and weight loss have contributed to the early deaths of many riders who battle the pressure and the high stress of their chosen profession.[13] The leading jockey of the nineteenth century, Fred

Archer, known as 'The Tinman', shot himself while grieving for his wife, in a bout of depression to which wasting is said to have contributed. Recently, in the United Kingdom, where the minimum weight is eight stone four pounds, leading international jockey Frankie Dettori told the *Independent* that 'weight rules are ruining jockey's health'.[14] Some cope and others use diuretics to lose weight and stimulants to ease the pressure. As well as a preoccupation with weight, fear and loss of nerve is also part of everyday life. My father has reflected that when he was a young rider, some of the older jockeys needed a shot or two of whisky to build up the courage to be legged up in the mounting enclosure. Close shaves and living in the fast lane accentuates those fears. Recently, a number of jockeys have tested positive for recreational drug use and suffered lengthy suspensions from the track as a result. Insiders speculate that in some cases, tension and fear, a dreaded loss of confidence, may contribute to drug use: clearly, these riders risk harming themselves or others. Champion Australian jockey Glenn Boss reflected on the importance of instinctive confidence in race riding in 2010:

> If you're out there thinking you're going to fall or expecting it or second-guessing yourself, that's the time you should give riding away. You become a dangerous person – not just to yourself but to the guys behind you. You're doing stupid things in races because you don't like being tightened up. Race riding is about instincts and you can't make instinctive decisions when you're not relaxed, you just don't function the same. I guess the thought process is slowed down by the simple fact that you're worrying about something else.[15]

During the last decade, several promising young jockeys have taken their own lives. In her suicide note, twenty-eight-year-old Korean jockey Park Jin-hee, who had recorded 38 winners in 651 rides, said that the racecourse had reduced her self-esteem 'to rock bottom'.[16] Twenty-four-year-old Michael Baze was found dead in his car at Churchill Downs in 2011, the day before he was due to attend a court hearing on cocaine charges.[17] In Australia, Keith Mahoney, Ray Setches, Rodney Smyth, Arron Kennedy, Ray Kliese and Neil Williams reflect a tragic trend. These riders 'suffered the indignity of their careers stagnating after reaching great heights. They had a few personal problems but they had no one to turn to.'[18] The climb to the top can be too fast to enable jockeys to acclimatise to their new lives. Josh Adams, a leading Sydney apprentice jockey who recently served a five-month suspension for drug use, highlights how quickly a run of winners can transform into an avalanche of cash:

> You feel like it's almost never going to end. That there's no stop to this flow of money coming in. You get your pay every two weeks – there's always ten, eleven, twelve grand there on a slow week.... I was eighteen and I was making

fourteen grand a fortnight, at least ... I remember one fortnight I was having a good run and I made twenty-four grand. [19]

The end of this seemingly never-ending flow of money, and the additional sudden loss of attention, seems to cause the greatest difficulty for leading jockeys. Neil Williams was a champion rider and exposed to the limelight from a very early age. He was the number-one rider in Queensland and regarded as one of the best in the country during the 1980s. By age thirty-five, however, Williams had fallen from the top; he gassed himself in his car on the Gold Coast in 1999. He had been deeply shaken by the loss of a close friend, Ken Russell, in a fall at Canterbury in 1993. A week before his death, his old friend Ray Setches killed himself in rural Victoria. Williams was also said to be having marital problems. All these things undoubtedly contributed to his death, and each suicide is a tragic response to the unique circumstances faced by a particular individual. However, certain shared, structural problems emerge from these cases.

Daniel Ganderton, the champion apprentice jockey in Sydney in the 2008–2009 season, recently walked away from racing with no regrets. Much of the money he made during his short career he spent maintaining a certain lifestyle and being generous to those around him. Like Ganderton, Josh Adams commented that he was the one who would shout the bar rounds of drinks and shots. He recalled going out with friends from his school days 'who go out with 200 bucks, and you go out with your keycard.... You'll stand there and punch $200 through a pokie. Your mates will go, "What are you doing? How can you spend that much money?" You just think "I don't care. I'll make that in two minutes."'[20] When he finally had the courage to walk away, Ganderton confessed that for the previous six months he was sick every morning before the races. It was, he said, in the end 'like a weight was lifted off my shoulders'.[21] Following these high-profile cases and attention in the media, racing authorities are beginning to realise that they will need to take steps to protect the emotional well-being of young jockeys and offer support and guidance for their futures.

Horseracing remains the 'Sport of Kings', and the rich and famous are attracted to the colour and excitement of the racecourse. With the premium that racing sets on light weights, jockeys have traditionally come from humble beginnings. Many apprentices fail in their chosen trade, growing too large or losing their nerve. A few become suddenly and unexpectedly wealthy, often temporarily. They are prone to dismiss that it all can be taken away very quickly, and many fail to prepare for life after racing and find it difficult to cope. What can retirement hold for someone who is accustomed to the adrenalin rush of race riding, when galloping alongside the girth buckle is the ever-present danger of death? How do athletes accustomed to taking such great risks return to the parochial grind of ordinary life? I recall visiting the jockey's room with my father many times as a small boy, sitting with him amongst the other riders on raceday. Those memories are brought back by Ernest Hemingway's description of the jockey's room in France during the 1920s:

> I followed him over to the jock's dressing room back in the trees and there was a big crowd around there, too, but the man at the door in a derby nodded to my old man and we got in everybody was sitting around and getting dressed and pulling shirts over their heads and pulling boots on and it all smelled hot and sweaty and linimenty and outside the crowd was looking in.[22]

NOTES

1 *The Sydney Morning Herald*, 30–31 October 2010.
2 Wray Vamplew is one of the few historians to have written about the lives of jockeys in, for example, 'Still Crazy after All Those Years: Continuity in a Changing Labour Market for Professional Jockeys', *Contemporary British History*, 14 (2000), 115–145; W. Vamplew, 'Les sportifs professionnels: les jockeys' in C. Louveau and A. Waser (eds.), *Sport et Cité: Pratiques Urbaines, Spectacles Sportifs* (University of Rouen Press, 1999), pp. 113–132; and with Joyce Kay in W. Vamplew and J. Kay, 'Captains Courageous: The Gentleman Rider in British Horseracing 1866–1914', *Sport in History*, 26 (2006), 370–385.
3 S. Cowley, B. Bowman and M. Lawrance, 'Injuries in the Victorian Thoroughbred Racing Industry', *British Journal of Sports Medicine*, 41 (2007), 639–643.
4 *The Weekend Australian*, 12–13 February 2011.
5 Part of family collection.
6 *Ibid.*
7 Hotaling has unearthed an equally important and untold story in North America where the greatest jockeys of the first national sport were 'slaves and sons of slaves'. See E. Hotaling, *The Great Black Jockeys: The Lives and Times of the Men Who Dominated America's First National Sport* (New York: Prima, 1999).
8 J. Maynard, *Aboriginal Stars of the Turf* (Canberra: Aboriginal Studies Press, 2007), p. 128.
9 Maynard, 2007, p. 129.
10 *Ibid.*, s131.
11 *The Sydney Morning Herald*, 30–31 October 2010, p. 33.
12 *Ibid.*
13 E. Dolan, H. O'Connor, A. McGoldrick, G. O'Loughlin, D. Lyons and G. Warrington, 'Nutritional, Lifestyle and Weight Control Practices of Professional Jockeys', *Journal of Sports Sciences*, 29 (2011), 791–799.
14 C. McGrath, 'Weight rules are ruining jockey's health says Dettori', *The Independent*, 12 April 2006.
15 *The Sydney Morning Herald*, 30–31 October 2010.

16 J. Cho, 'Jockeys suicide opens ugly side of horseracing', *The Korea Times*, 17 March 2010.

17 M. McGee, 'Michael Baze autopsy inconclusive: jockey was facing cocaine charge', *Daily Racing Form*, 15 May 2011.

18 R. Guilliat, 'The Dark Side of the Track', *The Weekend Australian Magazine*, 29–30 January 2011.

19 *The Sunday Telegraph*, 12 June 2011.

20 *The Sunday Telegraph*, 12 June 2011.

21 *Ibid.*

22 E. Hemingway, *The Complete Short Stories of Ernest Hemingway* (New York: Scribner's, 1987), p. 155.

7

JAMES HELMER

Life in the Backstretch

In the community surrounding Orchard Downs,[1] the harness racetrack in the northeastern United States where I began fieldwork in the 1980s, 'track people' were clearly regarded as different. Outsiders saw fragments of their lives: horsehair and grit in washing machines at the coin laundry; a barroom fight reported in the newspaper; kids who started school in September then disappeared in October or November and reappeared in April, when the track reopened. A teacher who worked summers at the track remarked to me on the odd boots they wore, which were often caked with stone dust, the chief constituent of almost every surface on which they worked. Some arrived and left in the horse compartments of huge vans with carts and sulkies, stable equipment and beds strapped on top. Others lived in the area year-round, in the village or on farms or in trailer homes on the racetrack grounds. The locals gave little thought to how these people produced the racing spectacle that kept hundreds of others at least seasonally employed and radiated economic benefits throughout the local community.

This chapter is about the men and women who live and work in the backstretch, the area behind the racetracks of the United States, described in the 1980s by the sociologist John Rosecrance as 'invisible horsemen'.[2] They have been brought more fully into view recently in the work of a small number of social scientists and writers.[3] Drawing on these authors and my own fieldwork during the 1980s and more recently, this essay describes some of the key features of backstretch life today. Participant observation – the core method of social anthropology – is a particularly effective means of studying communities who are wary of outsiders. It involves spending long periods of time alongside research subjects, encouraging them to talk about their everyday lives and experiences, their responsibilities, fears and hopes for the future. As such, it provides a picture of track life that is not immediately obvious from questionnaires or interviews. At Orchard Downs, as I show, much has changed over the past twenty-five years, but horse people continue to devote themselves to an uncertain enterprise, full of risks and challenges, that often returns little financial reward, prestige or security.

Place and Community

The backstretch as it existed at many U.S. tracks twenty-five years ago was much like a small town. At Orchard Downs it contained thirty-six barns, two harness shops selling equipment and supplies, six blacksmith shops, a small eatery known as the track kitchen, two dormitories offering a total of one hundred rooms and seventy-five spaces for mobile homes. At the track kitchen, people could buy not only meals and snacks but also toiletries, tobacco products and beer, and even cash a cheque. There was usually someone around who could give a good haircut, and the veterinarians carried medicines that, with a little adjustment in dosage, worked on humans. Consequently, there was little need to leave the backstretch for any of the basic services. While not everyone who worked with the horses lived on the grounds, so many people spent so much time there every day that the place had the *feel* of a small town. People talked while working around the barns and while jogging horses on the track. As they went about the grounds on foot, on bicycles or in golf carts, they would stop and talk at the barns or on the pavement between the kitchen and the blacksmiths' shops. Inside the kitchen, most people would find someone to sit with, so except during the slowest periods, a person rarely ate alone. The harness shops and the blacksmiths' shops across the way were social centres, too, where people not only did business but also gossiped, shared concerns, joked and told stories.

Cassidy observed that, in contrast with the community that produces racing in the United Kingdom, where people see themselves as exclusively associated with a town – Newmarket or Lambourn, for instance – in the United States, 'racetrackers identify less with a single place and emphasize links between people'.[4] My informants in the 1980s characterised the community as 'a fraternity' and 'a close-knit clan' that transcended the boundaries of any one racetrack. 'I could go to any racetrack in any state and I'd find people I know', a trainer told me. 'People handle their relationships as if they are going to run into each other later. You better treat people right because somewhere down the road you *are* gonna run into them again.' Another horseman recalls that 'pretty much everybody was friends even if they weren't friends, if something drastic happened', like an accident or a serious illness, 'there'd be people over there helping him jog his horses'. He continued, 'Back then … if somebody was having financial difficulty, [a better-off trainer would] either loan them money or send them a couple of horses [to train] to help them get by…. It wasn't so much the bottom line as how you got there. It wasn't all about profit…. It was more the sport of harness racing than the business side.'

Racetrack workers routinely describe a change in the morality of their community, from one based on core values of mutual aid and care to that of competition. As with many trades, this perceived change can be investigated as a form of nostalgia – examples of mutual aid can still be found on the track – but also as a reflection of changes in the structure of horseracing in the state, and particularly in the relationship between betting income, prize money and race conditions. Today, 'things have changed', says a trainer's wife. 'The people have changed. They used to be more friendly…. [Now] the big guys move in on you. It's so dog-eat-dog now.' 'Big guys' refers to upper-echelon trainers, typically stabled at training centres rather than racetracks and racing some of the best horses, often owned by syndicates – essentially corporate structures of investors who buy racehorses not for fun, as wealthy individuals once did and sometimes still do, but to make money. 'It used to be one guy owned ten horses', said one trainer, 'Now ten guys own one horse. They're in it for money and they want their horses to race wherever the money is.' Race secretaries – the racetrack officials who write the race conditions – used to 'take care of their own' by writing conditions tailored to the horses on the grounds, a trainer explained. But state rules do not allow that any more. So 'everybody's shipping all over'.

The geography of the backstretch has also changed as some tracks have eliminated amenities to save money and headaches, or sold or converted property for higher value uses, such as residential development, shopping or casinos. After a fire destroyed the grandstand at New Jersey's Freehold Raceway in 1984, new owners rebuilt the grandstand but closed down most of the barn area, retaining only raceday holding stables.[5] This made available some fifty acres, on which they built the Freehold Raceway Mall, an upscale shopping centre. Horsemen interpret this change as further evidence of the change in priorities in the industry from people to profit. 'Now they've got a ship-in barn and a racetrack and a shopping mall', says a horseman familiar with the place: 'The backstretch is Macy's. Used to be a community of people; now it's like the backstretch of a corporation – a parking lot.' At Orchard Downs, trailer spaces were eliminated several years ago, so families no longer live on the grounds as they once did. One of the two dormitories has been closed, and the track kitchen, once a lively gathering place, is now a maintenance shed. A sixty-five-year-old trainer who opened his stable here when he was twenty says, 'There isn't a backstretch. Backstretch is just go in and take care of your horses. Not like when I was young.'

Roles, Power and Stratification

The top tier of U.S. harness racing stables began leaving the largely asphalt environments of eastern urban racetracks more than twenty years ago in favour of training centres offering complete facilities, including grassy paddocks and full-size tracks. Though costly at up to $400 per stall per month, their locations in southern New York, eastern Pennsylvania, New Jersey and Delaware put horsemen within a three-hour drive of more than a half-dozen racetracks with some of the highest purses in the nation. Most racetracks charge only a modest fee or nothing at all to rent stalls during the race meet so long as the horses race at that track. The stables most commonly housed on racetracks today are small operations, some as large as a few dozen horses, but many of a size that can be handled by a couple or a family. For some people, small scale is a choice freely made in consideration of their other employment, aspirations or other factors. For others, according to informants who spoke with me in early 2011, shrinking size is an effect of or an adaptation to a generally weak and uncertain economy. 'I think people are scared', says a woman in her seventies who has had both knees replaced but still helps her husband run their stable at Orchard Downs. In a shaky economy, she says, '[people] don't need racehorses' – an observation echoed by a thirty-year-old trainer at a Florida track: 'It's hard to find owners who want to invest in racehorses with the economy the way it is.' His fifty-four-year-old father, also a trainer, says they cannot charge enough to offset the expenses. So they have adapted in two ways: the dad holds a regular job at the racetrack eight months of the year and they have gone from what was a stable of twenty-five horses a few years ago to one of four-to-eight horses now. 'We found we make more money', his wife says, 'if we have fewer horses and just do the work ourselves.'

Work roles within the stables, while to some extent prescribed by custom and licensing practices, are quite flexible. Grooms perform most of the routine work of stall cleaning, horse care and equipment cleaning. Trainers oversee and direct the work of grooms, drive the horses for their training 'trips' – fast miles that develop speed – and in some cases do the race driving. They manage relationships with horse owners and make virtually all decisions regarding general stable management and the horses themselves, including their conditioning and training programmes, veterinary care and racing schedules. But in many of the smaller stables, particularly the many that are family operations, roles blur as the work is often divided up based on expediency, individuals' physical capacities, skills or habit. Job descriptions in the conventional sense are virtually non-existent here. Instead, what emerges is a 'negotiated order' in which the individual strengths and preferences of grooms and trainers are expressed and coordinated.[6] To the extent that this occurs, backstretch workers generate a division of labour and power which is a function of interaction rather than the product of a formal hierarchy. As Case observed, lines of authority in the backstretch are unclear, and no one, save racetrack management, has unilateral power over others.[7] Between trainer and groom there may be no contractual agreement, although the trainer does hold the power of wages. The trainer, however, does not hold all the aces even in relationships with his or her own grooms. As everyone knows, somebody has to take care of those horses.

The accounts of two experienced grooms suggest how formal roles, individual personalities, communication styles and contextual factors interact in the working out of authority and responsibility. According to one groom, some trainers 'will tell you to do something and if you ask them why, it's "because I told you to!" It depends on how much they like you, how much they want you to learn. Some of them may not want you to know because they don't want you to know as much as they do.' But if some trainers do not try very hard to teach their grooms, it may be 'because they get idiot help and they've gotten sour on trying to teach them anything, or they know they're going to quit and be gone in two weeks and figure, "why bother?"' On the other hand, some grooms do not want to make major decisions about the horses in their care. As another groom explained, 'I would rather have a trainer come to me and say "paint his hocks with this, paint his legs with that". I'll do the rubbing, I'll do the painting, but let me know what he needs to have. *You're* the one that's training him, *you're* the one that sits behind him when he's going. *You* tell *me* where he's off. I don't want to take the responsibility for diagnosing his lameness, where [it] is or why it's happening.'

Although trainers and drivers have always included a few women, harness racing traditionally has been dominated by men. By the 1980s, while there were nearly as many female grooms as male ones, there were few women trainers and still fewer women drivers. Some men doubted women's ability to maintain an even keel emotionally. 'You get a woman with a filly or a mare', one man said, 'they have a bad week about once a month.' 'The woman or the horse?', I asked, innocently. 'The woman *and* the horse.' Today some still doubt whether women have sufficient upper body strength to control a pulling horse, although there is no question that they can carry a loaded manure basket. Larsen heard other reasons offered by men to explain why there were not more women drivers: 'They're not aggressive enough', 'they're not comfortable in tight quarters' and their eyesight 'isn't as keen at a short distance going at speed'.[8] Larsen's research on self-employed women trainers revealed that, while comparable to men in terms of knowledge and experience, women have a harder time achieving success because they lack key resources: good horses, because owners of expensive horses are biased against them; a winning reputation that good horses could produce; and access to top-tier male trainers, who could help them learn but whose 'big-guy' networks tend to be closed to 'little guys' of both sexes. Women who aspire to greater visibility and success in racing are left with three unattractive options: buy their own horses, likely cheaper ones that will do little to enhance their reputation; hire good male drivers, who will still get most of the attention if the horses do well but also will provide a buffer for the woman's reputation if they do not; or settle for 'literal invisibility' as a trainer's wife.[9] Despite the obstacles described by Larsen, attitudes are in practice fluid, and exceptional women regularly overcome their apparent disadvantage to excel. In 2010, the top two trainers at Orchard Downs were women, with 125 wins and more than $675,000 in purses between them. Another dozen U.S. tracks listed one or more women amongst their top trainers.[10] Young women at Orchard Downs were familiar with gendered ideas about strength, eyesight and emotional fortitude but pointed to their champion trainers and told me that they can achieve anything they set their minds to.

Workforce

'Nothing about this is hard', a groom called Kitch once told me. 'A monkey could learn to do what I do in three days.' Nevertheless, another groom who knew Kitch called him 'a professional groom'. Through his responsibility, attentiveness and skill, Kitch exemplified what one horseman called 'good, honest career grooms'. These days, one more often hears how hard it is to find good grooms. A young trainer recently told me that he once had hopes of having a forty-horse stable, 'but you can't get the help you need to run a forty horse barn'. A married couple in their early fifties, who do operate a forty-horse stable, were having a tough time recently breaking in two men they had just hired. The men had worked with another stable for several months but evidently had not learned as much as their new bosses had hoped. Although they were Americans and native speakers of English, the men did not seem to understand what she and her husband were trying to tell them. 'You have to babysit so much now', the trainer told me. All they need to do is 'shut up and listen.... You don't gotta kiss my ass. You don't gotta even like me. Just take care of my horse ... I was a good groom. I groomed horses for eight fucking years. I loved being a groom.' But today, 'nobody wants to work'. He had much kinder words, however, for the six undocumented workers from Guatemala, Honduras and Mexico that he and his wife employ. 'They take such pride in their horses', he said, and his wife praised their dedication, especially that of the thirty-three-year-old Mexican woman, whom she calls 'my second-in-command'. She is paid to care for five horses, but 'she knows what every one of forty-four horses wears. She can tell you everything that goes on in the barn. She's the only one who can set up feed', which includes for some of the horses not just grain and nutritional supplements but also a bottle of beer – 'helps regulate their sweat', the trainer says – and thirty cc of yellow mustard that 'gets them eating'.

A seventy-year-old trainer put his hiring policy succinctly: 'I hire all Guatemalans because Americans don't want to do the work.' Clarifying that they actually employ two Americans and two Guatemalans, his son said that the two nationalities have a different work ethic. The Americans 'have a list of what *they* want', whereas the Guatemalans 'do what *you* want'. Are the Guatemalans legal? I asked. 'They've got social security cards', he replied. To get temporary visas to hire workers from foreign countries, employers have to prove they cannot fill the positions with Americans. The Hispanic services coordinator for the Kentucky Horsemen's Benevolent and Protective Association argues that case every year as he tries to get workers into Kentucky and other states. He told a journalist in 2009, 'When we applied to the Maryland Department of Labor [for stable workers], we needed fifty guys. We got forty-six responses from Americans interested in the job. As soon as we told them what the job [required] them to do, out of forty-six, only seven remained. Out of those seven, only two agreed to work.'[11]

At a seven-horse stable, the woman who runs the operation with her husband and son tells me that when they had twenty-five horses a few years ago, they had some good Mexican and Guatemalan help, 'but it always left a knot in my stomach to have to pay them cash' because they are illegal. They buy social security numbers so they can get licensed and they sometimes get caught, which can result in a substantial fine for the employer. But what is the alternative, I ask, if you have a big stable and need the help? 'Well that's it', she says. She, like others, sees the Americans that will take the job as unambitious, unreliable and drunks or drug addicts. That is why they do not stick around in the afternoon. 'Like those guys over there', she says gesturing to the barn across the way. 'If they're not out of here by eleven o'clock they get the shakes.'

Grooms have long been characterised as drunks and addicts, even by other grooms. 'A lot of the people in this business are misfits', a groom told me years ago. 'Alcoholics, potheads, people who couldn't hold a regular job.' Recently, another groom said the same thing: 'Some are real good and some aren't worth a damn. Most of them would sooner do drugs and drink than work.' Cassidy saw 'men and women who were addicts of various kinds'.[12] Schefstad and colleagues reported that 'alcohol and drug use patterns in the thoroughbred racing industry [are] not an anomaly.'[13] Data they collected at a mid-Atlantic racetrack were consistent with findings of the National Household Survey of Drug Abuse, which measures patterns in the general population. But while alcohol and drug use may not be worse inside the backstretch than outside it, the fact that it is so taken for granted and visible tends to promote it and may keep people from seeking treatment. Schefstad and colleagues emphasise that a successful treatment program must be not only effectively designed in terms of structural matters such as staffing and funding but also adapted to the unique conditions of racetrack employment and backstretch culture.[14]

Schefstad and colleagues suggest that many of these workers bring these problems with them when they enter the backstretch: 'Due to poor or non-existent employee screening methods, the backstretch attracts marginal employees, many of whom have pre-existing psychiatric, medical, criminal or other problems.'[15] Horsemen suggest that they cannot be too selective in any case, and that part of the attraction of the backstretch may be that it is a more tolerant place than the world outside. Indeed, Schefstad and colleagues note that 'the backstretch may be an improvement for many'.[16] At least half of the grooms I spoke with seem to have come to the racetrack to get away from something – abuse, betrayal, prejudice, injustice or lack of other opportunities. A black man I met in 1986 told me why he went to work with racehorses in 1958: 'In those days, if you were black, the best thing you could do was pack a brown bag and hop a horse truck.' Like some of the gay men I met in the 1980s and the undocumented Hispanics today, some people, says one horseman, 'may just feel more comfortable inside the gate than outside it'.

The Horse in Backstretch Experience

'A horse', Mead observed, 'is not simply something that must be ridden. It is an animal that must eat, that belongs to somebody. It has economic values.'[17] In the backstretch, the horse also has social, psychological and political values. As a focus for both activity and contemplation, the horse functions both materially and symbolically in helping to produce life in the backstretch.[18] Through its needs as an animal, the horse provides much of the structure of daily life, which often seems an endless cycle of stall cleaning, feeding and grooming. And for virtually everything related to its job as an athlete, the horse requires the presence of the groom – harnessing, exercising, shoeing, shipping, waiting in the paddock. The horse thus influences when the groom gets up in the morning, when he can go to bed, where and how much he travels, whom he meets and how pleasant his day will be.

As the primary commodity, the horse is fundamental to the backstretch economy. A trainer told me about a filly that appealed to him despite her alleged unmanageability. He and a partner bought her for $900. The trainer sorted out her issues and she went on to earn more than $80,000 in a year. Six months later he sold his share in her for $30,000. His wife asks with a smile, 'How often can you turn a $450 investment into $70,000 in eighteen months?' For grooms, too, the horse has economic value, though that may be forgotten sometimes. On a day in August, a groom who was not getting his work done as quickly as he had hoped complained about the filly he was caring for: 'Look what she's done for me – screwed up my whole day.' 'Look what else she's done for you', another groom pointed out: 'kept you fed all summer.' Perceptions of horses – as 'good', 'common' or 'classy' – often get worked into the self-concepts of the people associated with them. 'If your horse races well,' one groom said, 'of course you feel like *you're* doing a good job.' Horses imbue human experiences with poignant meanings. 'Anticipation' is the springtime, when hopes are high as young horses get started and older ones come back rested and healed. 'Reality' is the summer, when it becomes clear that many horses are not going to live up to spring's great expectations. 'Desperation' sets in sometime in August, as horsemen realise they are 'running out of tomorrows and next weeks'. These three metaphors create and sustain the sense that progress or movement in one's life is a function not only of time and money but also of horses and their performance.

Horses, Politics and the Public

Horses are essential to racing, but it is no longer clear that horseracing is the main business of North American racetracks. The 'racino' business model that has been spreading over the past decade, while providing a lifeline for racing, has brought concerns that, coupled with states' economic troubles, waning public interest in the sport and activism over animal welfare, continue to produce uncertainty about whether horseracing will retain its traditional place in the sporting and gambling landscape. A combination racetrack and casino operation, the racino was developed in response to declining racetrack attendance and wagering, as a way to preserve horseracing and its benefits to agriculture, employment and state treasuries. A report on racing in the state of Indiana, which opened a combined pari-mutuel racetrack and casino in 1994 and legalised electronic gaming at its two pari-mutuel racetracks in 2007, concluded that 'the State of Indiana is generating extraordinary economic activity from its design of and ongoing investment in the state['s] horse racing and breeding industry.' While a 2005 study had reported a total economic impact of $294 million, 'the findings of this study five years later indicate … over $1 billion total impact for the [Indiana] racing industry'.[19] Where the earlier study had helped to secure legalisation of racetrack gaming, the more recent one was instrumental in protecting horseracing from a proposed 50 per cent cut in casino subsidies. The data persuaded Indiana lawmakers to reduce by only 5 per cent the casino subsidies going to the Thoroughbred and Standardbred racing industries in the two-year budget adopted in early 2011.[20]

Horsemen in states where racinos have produced robust growth – such as Delaware, New York and Pennsylvania – are enjoying the present but worry about the future. Pointing to purses for 'overnight' races that rival those for stakes races, a trainer at a New York harness track said, 'Things are good' as long as the slot machine revenue continues, 'but is it gonna stay?' Another New Yorker said, 'Gotta wonder how long before the state takes a look at it and says, hmm, how come we're giving them forty-five per cent when we could put that into health care?' Horsemen's concerns about the casino-racetrack marriage are driven not only by uncertainty over whether, when and by how much states will reduce racing's share of gaming money but also by questions about which part of the operation dominates decisions made by racino management. One man succinctly described the contrast in management priorities at different racetracks. At one Midwestern track, management assures everybody 'this is a racetrack with a casino. But you come here [to this southern track] and it's a casino with a racetrack.' Those who see the racetrack as secondary, he says, 'forget how they got the casino' – a reference to the advocacy of agriculture and horse interests that helped to pass laws to permit gaming.

The extent to which racetrack management is horse- or casino-oriented is a concern to others beside horsemen. The American Association of Equine Practitioners (AAEP), founded in 1954 by eleven racetrack veterinarians and now serving nearly 10,000 members worldwide who represent all equine breeds and disciplines, released a white paper in 2010 scrutinising standardbred racehorse welfare. They concluded that 'a concerning trend in the spread of the racino business model is an increasing number of racing executives that do not have experience in horse racing or horse care. We believe it is imperative that senior racetrack management become knowledgeable about issues and business practices that directly affect the welfare and safety of the horses that race at their tracks.'[21] As welcome as the casino revenue has been, some horsemen see the casinos as 'a Band-Aid on a sport that needs surgery'. It is not about the horses anymore, they say;

it is all about money. Several successful Illinois trainers readily admit that the reason behind their recent moves to the racinos of the east coast was 'strictly money'.[22] In the eyes of some horsemen, the primacy of money in the new economics of harness racing is implicated in two worrisome trends: a decline in horsemanship and an increase in the use of medication and illicit substances.

There are echoes here of things I heard twenty-five years ago, particularly from older horsemen, who often said 'this business has changed' and 'it's not like it used to be'. A blacksmith at that time explained: 'They used to take better care of the horses.... Used to be more *horsemen* in the business.... Years ago they wanted to work with the horses. Now they want to make big bucks.' Training, one man said, 'used to be an art form' that involved paying close attention to each horse, carefully observing how he was going, how his feet hit the ground, whether he was hitting himself, and any number of other cues that would help the trainer to figure out how to make him go better. Similarly, shoeing and balancing 'was so intricate', what one esteemed horseman called 'a delicate science of inches and ounces'.[23] Today there is a perception that there is less concern for each horse as an individual. The horses are seen as 'more of a herd', I was told. 'Shoe them all the same way and they'll either make it or they won't.' If a horse is lame, 'they can't take the time to have a groom work on rubbing and wrapping legs when each groom might be caring for as many as eight horses, and owners don't want to hear that their horse is laid up for three weeks. It's just "call the vet" and he'll give an injection that will keep the horse sound for a couple of weeks.' 'They forget these horses are athletes', says a trainer's wife. 'Nobody conditions anymore.' 'That used to be the game', her husband says, ' – get 'em conditioned, feed 'em right. Now it's who's got the "gas". They give [the horse] half training and shoot him with steroids to tighten the muscles.' Another trainer laments the attitude that he sees as all too prevalent today: 'Horses are expendable.' For him, 'the horseman part of it is gone'. Not everyone agrees with this assessment. Some say the breed has become so much better and the sciences of conditioning and nutrition so advanced that the old ways are not necessarily the best anymore. Some say drugs are not such a big problem. 'There's always someone who wants to blame drugs for another's hard work or good luck', says one woman.

One thing horsemen do agree on is that 'people just don't go to the races'. And public perceptions that horses are misused would not bring them back. The AAEP urges the racing industry to make 'a sincere industry-wide commitment to equine welfare', noting in their 2010 report the recent elimination of dog racing in the state of Massachusetts as 'a bellwether event that serves as a stark warning to all animal spectator sports'.[24] The AAEP recommends structural and procedural changes that address a wide range of issues, including training and racing schedules, racing surfaces and equipment, pre- and post-race veterinary examinations, the conduct of claiming races, the use of medication, the future of horses that can no longer race and the reliance on ever-faster race times as the 'gold standard' in standardbred racing, which eventually is likely to threaten the structural limitations of the horse. The AAEP report concludes by affirming the belief that the effort to reform policies and practices 'in order to enhance the safety and welfare of the horse … will also be the key to restoring public confidence in the racing industry. Simply put, what is good for the horse is good for racing.'[25]

NOTES

1 This is a pseudonym intended to protect the identities of my research participants.

2 J. Rosecrance, 'The Invisible Horsemen: The Social World of the Backstretch', *Qualitative Sociology*, 8 (1985), 248–265.

3 C. Case, *Down the Backstretch: Racing and the American Dream* (Philadelphia: Temple University Press, 1991); R. Cassidy, *Horse People: Thoroughbred Culture in Lexington and Newmarket* (Baltimore: Johns Hopkins University Press, 2007); H. Castañeda, N. Kline and N. Dickey, 'Health Concerns of Migrant Backstretch Workers at Horse Racetracks', *Journal of Health Care for the Poor and Underserved*, 21 (2010), 489–503; J. Helmer, 'The Horse in Backstretch Culture', *Qualitative Sociology*, 14 (1991), 175–195; A. Schefstad, 'An Invisible Population and Its Visible Problem: Alcohol and Substance Abuse among Horsecare Workers', *Alcoholism Treatment Quarterly*, 15 (1997), 1–16; A. Schefstad, S. Tiegel and A. Jones, 'Treating a Visible Problem within a Hidden Population', *Employee Assistance Quarterly*, 14 (1999), 17–32.

4 Cassidy, *Horse People*, p. 122.

5 B. Pepe, *Freehold: A Hometown History* (Charleston, SC: Arcadia Publishing, 2003), p. 86.

6 A. Strauss, L. Schatzman, D. Ehrlich, R. Bucher and M. Sabshin, 'The hospital and its negotiated order' in E. Friedson (ed.), *The Hospital in Modern Society*. (New York: Free Press, 1963), pp. 147–169.

7 Case, *Down the Backstretch*, p. 44.

8 E. Larsen, 'A Vicious Oval: Why Women Seldom Reach the Top in American Harness Racing', *Journal of Contemporary Ethnography*, 35 (2006), 119–147, 133.

9 E. Larsen, 'A Vicious Oval', p. 139.

10 J. Pawlak (ed.), 'Tracks', *The Trotting & Pacing Guide: The Official Handbook of Harness Racing* 65th edn (Columbus, OH: United States Trotting Association, 2011), pp. 6–62.

11 P. Lavigne, 'Immigration issues impact workers', *ESPN Sports*, 15 September 2009. http://sports.espn.go.com/espn/hispanicheritage2009/news/story?id=4465735 (last accessed 4 February 2012).

12 Cassidy, *Horse People*, p. 142.

13 Schefstad et al., 'Treating a Visible Problem within a Hidden Population', p. 19.

14 *Ibid.*, pp. 28–30.

15 *Ibid.*, p. 22.

16 *Ibid.*, p. 30.

17 G. Mead, *Mind, Self and Society* (Chicago: University of Chicago Press, 1934), p. 12.

18 Helmer, 'The Horse in Backstretch Culture'.

19 S. Conners, J. Furdek, L. Couetil and G. Preston, 'The Impact of Indiana Horse Racing on the Indiana Economy: A Preliminary Study', *Proceedings of the Academy for Economics and Economic Studies*, 14 (2011), 3–8.

20 J. Pawlak, 'Indiana horsemen avert major subsidy cuts in state budget', *United States Trotting Association News*, 4 May 2011. http://xwebapp.ustrotting.com (last accessed 4 February 2012).

21 American Association of Equine Practitioners (AAEP), *Putting the Horse First: Veterinary Recommendations for the Safety and Welfare of the Standardbred Racehorse* (Lexington, KY: AAEP, 2010). www.aaep.org/images/files/AAEP%20Standardbred%20White%20Paper%202010.pdf (last accessed 4 February 2012), p. 4.

22 M. Martinez, 'Shrinking purses drive harness racers out of Illinois', *State Journal-Register*, 13 August 2010. www.sj-r.com (last accessed 4 February 2012).

23 J. F. Simpson Sr., 1968. 'The Theory of Shoeing and Balancing', in J.C. Harrison, *Care & Training of the Trotter & Pacer* (Columbus, OH: United States Trotting Association, 1968), pp. 292–373; p. 293.

24 AAEP, 'Putting the Horse First', p. 3.

25 *Ibid.*, p. 11.

8

MICHAEL HINDS

Irish Racing's Peaceable Kingdoms

In his description of the events of the spring of 1945, historian S.J. Watson wrote that 'After Punchestown, the war in Europe moved rapidly to its end.'[1] The Irish Racing Calendar persists, even as the rest of the world goes up in flames. This essay explores the unique and incredible place of racing in Ireland where horses frequently bear more than a jockey on their backs. When Orby became the first Irish-trained horse to win the English Derby in 1907, he also became emblematic of the united drive towards Irish independence.[2] Both a force of nature and ideology, Orby was famously toasted by the Protestant students of Trinity College, but also anointed hero of Irish Catholicism, running with a rosary tied onto his bridle. Other Irish horse stories contrarily affirm the power of the union with Britain, like that of the Byerley Turk winning a race in Ulster on his way to serving on the Williamite side at the Battle of the Boyne, before becoming a foundation stallion of the English thoroughbred.[3]

War stories aside, horseracing has allowed Irish Protestants and Catholics to co-participate in a sporting activity without killing each other – not an insignificant achievement. In this way, Irish racing signifies the possibility of a transhistorical harmony, surviving war, famine and disease; in other words, a vicariously alternate reality. Despite its detailed coverage of the international scene, *The Irish Field* reads like a parish newsletter, effectively representing racing as a choric network of dedicated families rather than an industry, a complacently pastoral domain in which people are unified by their love of the horse. Carrying more advertising from studs and feed mills than bookmakers, *The Irish Field* also incorporates *The Irish Horse World*, federating racing with equestrianism, farming and hunting (there is also a regular column by a vet). This suggests that while betting is evidently important in Ireland, it takes its place alongside other concerns, namely the country's traditional economic interests in agriculture and the countryside.

Racing everywhere allows for all sorts of social constellating or clustering; in Ireland, however, it is also a sufficiently complex phenomenon to generate a diversity of parochial subcultures that rarely interact. All of these parishes generate distinctive discourses that nevertheless contribute to the general assumption that a love of the turf is somehow fundamental to Irish nationhood, something reified by political actuality. For example, Irish festival meetings have traditionally been events that are woven into the political life of the country, but this has become particularly significant in recent years. As racing in most countries has become just another source of entertaining distraction, in Ireland it has remained a means of doing serious business. The Fianna Fáil fundraising tent at the Galway Races was notorious as the most intense deal-making and cronyistic environment in pork-barrel Ireland, so much so that it became a source of embarrassment for this usually unrepentant party and was closed in 2008 when Brian Cowen became Taoiseach (Prime Minister).[4] Racing and government had become increasingly complicit with one another in the emergence of the Celtic Tiger (and its subsequent debacle).[5] During Ireland's economic 'miracle', trips to the races became increasingly hazardous for its reliably voluptuary political class, perhaps most notoriously when the former minister Jim McDaid was arrested as he drove home drunk from the Punchestown festival on the wrong side of a motorway, only coming to a halt when a truck blocked the road.[6] Less haplessly and much more adroitly, at the Mahon Tribunal into institutionalised bribery and corruption, the former Taoiseach, Bertie Ahern, explained away with characteristic braggadocio any embarrassment about the substantial sums of sterling in his possession by proclaiming to his serial good luck on the horses in England.[7] Conversely, at the onset of the 2008 banking crisis, when money was nowhere to be found, and the head of the European Central Bank telephoned the Irish Minister of Finance, he was at Gowran Park races, not returning the call until the following day.[8] If there was an official state ideology in this purportedly non-ideological country, it turns out to have been punterism.

In keeping with the *turfiste* predilections of its engineers, the Celtic Tiger was like an overlong and orgiastic day at the races, and its ultimate disaster also finds perfect symbolic expression in the shape of a racehorse, a hubris machine unlike any other. Just about the most successful Irish business of the twenty-first century, indeed, specialized in the trading of these chancy wares: the Tipperary-based Coolmore operation, a stud business so globalised and media-savvy that it managed to harness a Hollywood film as part of its marketing operations, and completely demoralise even the princes of Dubai, whose Godolphin brand plummeted in value as Coolmore's stables and stallions came to dominance in the late 1990s.[9] Even the stupefying prosperity of Coolmore could not insure it against The Green Monkey, a two-year-old with a name straight out of H. Rider Haggard. Bought at a breeze-up sale in Florida for a record price of $16 million after recording some spectacular times, The Green Monkey raced three times in the United States, never finishing better than third.[10]

The significance of the Irish racehorse as both a dignifying symbol of the state and as its most saleable commodity in the global market was given acute emphasis during the four-day visit of Queen Elizabeth II to Ireland in May 2011. Her public trip to the National Stud in Kildare was particularly significant in terms of the history of Anglo-Irish relationships, in that it remained the English National Stud until 1948, long after independence, proving that racing operates in a different legislative continuum. Subsequently, the queen took in a private visit to Gilltown Stud, the Aga Khan's Irish base, which prompted a wretched memory of the Provisional IRA's kidnapping in 1983 of Shergar from his then HQ at Ballymany Stud, the owner having been declared a legitimate target as an 'absentee landlord'. The queen also took in the Tipperary redoubt of Coolmore and its training centre at Aidan O'Brien's Ballydoyle stables. These three different stud operations each represent a distinctive form of political economy, while being engaged in the same business: if The National Stud promotes a timeless image of horse culture, and identifies itself primarily through its relationship to the great horses of the sometimes distant past, it also exemplifies the beleaguered state sector; the Aga Khan is typical of the figure of the feudal owner-breeder that has often patronised Irish racing; and late-capitalist and globalised Coolmore is expert at generating good horses but equally adept at PR. The National Stud is a museum and educational facility that is not especially good at doing business, which has led to proposals that it be sold.[11] It is valuable, but not in the way that late capitalism likes to define value. Through its long-term presence in Ireland, the Aga's operation brands itself ('Success Breeds Success') as an inevitable presence, fostering a royal line and the maintenance of blue-bloodedness. By contrast, Coolmore is hyper-dynamic and highly profitable; its value is not sentimental but viewable on a balance sheet. Coolmore could be said to be Ireland's flagship business, and has been encouraged in its radical internationalism by a system of tax credits for horse breeders that confirmed the status of the industry in national politics. It has fashioned itself into a phenomenon that respects no borders, with stallions shuttling back and forth between continents and hemispheres around the year as part of its programme of hegemonic insemination: Coolmore is an absentee landlord on every continent. This is a perversity typical of the twenty-first century; Coolmore is protected by the state even as it gives nothing back to it, the implication being that it does enough for Ireland by way of its reputation for excellence. If you go to the races at one of Tipperary's three courses, however, it is visible that Coolmore is of more than symbolic importance. Half of the crowd seems to be wearing a baseball cap with the name of a Coolmore stallion on it; they literally are covering the heads of their local community.

It is possible to exaggerate the enthusiasm of the Irish public for racing. James Joyce in *Ulysses* probably had it right when he showed a portion, but not all, of Dublin's menfolk communicating inferentially about who would win the Ascot Gold Cup.[12] When the barhound Bantam Lyons asks Joyce's benignly insouciant protagonist Leopold Bloom for a loan of his paper so he might 'see about that French horse that's running today', Bloom offers him the whole paper:

> – I was just going to throw it away, Mr Bloom said.
> Bantam Lyons raised his eyes suddenly and leered weakly.
> – What's that? his sharp voice said.
> – I say you can keep it, Mr Bloom answered. I was going to throw it away that moment.
> Bantam Lyons doubted an instant, leering: then thrust the outspread sheets back on Mr Bloom's arms.
> – I'll risk it, he said. Here, thanks.[13]

Bloom has no interest in the horses but has heuristically tipped the winner to Lyons; throwaway remarks are construed as a tip for Throwaway, the outsider that did indeed take the race in 1904. This receives further misconstruction in the barroom discourse of the city, in particular a misconception that Bloom has won big on Throwaway, but is not buying any drinks: 'He had a few bob on *Throwaway* and he's gone to gather in the shekels' (321). In part, this is a reminder of the lonely plight of the punter who wins on a long shot, even if Bloom did not back it; but the Cyclopean patriot, The Citizen, also places horse-betting in a nationalist-racist discourse. Backing horses is decidedly a pastime for patriots, not Jewish *deracinés* like Bloom: 'Is it that white-eyed kaffir?' says the Citizen, 'that never backed a horse in anger in his life?' (321). A later curiosity is how the catechetical chapter of the novel erroneously classifies the Gold Cup:

> What reminiscences temporarily corrugated his brow?
>
> Reminiscences of coincidences, truth stranger than fiction, preindicative of the result of the Gold Cup flat handicap, the official and definitive result of which he had read in the *Evening Telegraph*, late pink edition, in the cabman's shelter at Butt Bridge. (628)

Either Joyce had confused the Ascot Gold Cup with the Ascot Stakes, a handicap over the same distance, which means this most finicky of writers had not done his research, or he did not care (likely enough), or he wanted to confirm Bloom's ignorance, or he was satirising the inability of catechetics to provide accurate answers to complicated questions.

Throughout all of this slippage, Joyce understands very well the Irish tendency to turn conspiratorial at the races, daringly or desperately attaching significance to the most arbitrary of utterances. This phenomenon manifests itself in the reality of the Irish racetrack and not just the imagination of Joyce; Irish betting rings are lively but furtive environments. The races that generate most track betting income are often not graded races or big handicaps, but the 'bumper' races that conclude most days of racing in Ireland. Unlike the versions of these two-mile flat races for National Hunt–bred horses recently introduced into Britain as pre-schools for jumpers, Irish 'bumpers' permit no professional jockeys to ride. In Ireland they are more of a serious end in themselves, practically a sport within a sport, and the relative obscurity of some of the jockeys is intrinsic to their popularity. Bumpers are beloved because they are based on so many unknowns, and the only relevant form guide is hearsay. *The Racing Post* only began to publish time figures for Irish races in 2009, as such scientific measures are apparently irrelevant; there is nothing empirical about picking an Irish winner.

If Irish racing might be defined by its particular emphasis on the value of privileged information, it is not so concerned with the ostentatious assertion of privilege in other ways. In the past, Ireland fulfilled the servant's role of being Britain's stables. Even the country's greatest animal, Arkle, was owned by Anne, Duchess of Westminster. It has now become the stables of the world, but it still also supports the idea of 'class' as something that is played out mainly on the racecourses of England rather than at home, something best indicated by the fact that many top Irish trainers aim to win races in England above anywhere else (although Dermot Weld's extraordinary achievements show a far greater reach).[14] Ireland does not eradicate complex class difference entirely, but rather attaches amnesia to it, fostering an aura that nobody cares who or where you are from when you are at the track. This is further indicated by the lack of respect for keeping the two codes of racing apart, as they conventionally are in Britain; throughout the Irish summer, codes are often intermingled, disconnecting the flat and steeplechasing from the social complexes attached to them; indeed, the particular association of Ireland with steeplechasing also reflects this collective, deliberate amnesia. This form of racing was invented with the race between the parish churches of Buttevant and Doneraile in Cork in 1752, and has traditionally permitted runners that are not entirely thoroughbred. Although less commonly than before, you may yet glimpse the forlorn term 'Sire Unknown' or 'Unregistered Mare' in a jumping pedigree. Furthermore, steeplechasing provided racing for discrete groups of people at times (races for farmers, officers or gentlemen), but it also held Open races for all.

If the crudely expressed nuances of socio-economic class are visible in the English racecourse's subdivisions of spectators (Silver Ring, Tattersalls, Grandstand, Members and Royal Enclosures), the Irish system communicates something more simple but equally robust. Ireland divides more simplistically into have and have-not, and so racecourses often have either two sections or increasingly none at all, as it has become a spectator sport only for 'haves'. The one big exception to this is the Irish Derby meeting at The Curragh, when punters have paid double or treble the usual fee to enter into an unfamiliar hierarchy that parodies the English experience. This is the pleasure of horseracing at its most vicarious, particularly as the track clientele is not much different from the usual; for all the best-dressed lady entrants, the race crowd looks very familiar, if a little bit more out of pocket. At The Curragh, the more the people have paid, the more they remain the same. Despite its attempted stratifications (although there has perhaps been less effort to divide in recent years), the enclosures at the Irish Derby tend to be quite lively, particularly in the years during Budweiser's sponsorship, when stands brimmed with cowboy-hatted punters fostering a genially beery disorder. Jeffrey Bernard was a keen observer (even orchestrator) of such misrule, as his account of his initiation into the heart of punterism on a trip to the Irish St. Leger meeting exemplifies:

> At The Curragh I was treated like visiting royalty in the way that the Irish always treat nonentities. I was taken to the oak-lined, champagne-filled private rooms occupied by the men that ran the course. Compared to England it was an unbelievable scene. They wouldn't even let the Stewards of the course in the place it was so posh and yet there was I drinking what they called shampoo with the director of the course, Joe McGrath, and his brother the director of the Irish Hospital Sweeps, Paddy McGrath, who was reputed to have one hundred and fifty million in his current account. He turned to me half way through the afternoon and said, 'I can't understand why they call us the McGrafia'. Then he told me he couldn't buy or sell shares without the knowledge of it sending firms broke or ridiculously upmarket.[15]

While Bernard appears delighted, he also communicates a sense of being somewhat appalled. He voices a familiar notion that Ireland is England's other, parodying it but also menacing it: 'There are things and people that can only happen over there and the place was still the friendly madhouse it has always been' (42). The image of the Irish punter as mad and wild has been around in the English imagination for a long time, as Webster's *The White Devil* attests:

An Irish gamester that will play himself naked, and then wage all downward, at hazard, is not more venturous.[16]

The idea that the Irish play with a particular desperation has found regular expression in relationship to racing, but not just in terms of gambling. Irish riders have often been objects of awe, such as the reverence that has been accorded in the English media to the will to win of the champion jump jockey in every year since 1995–96, Ulsterman A.P. McCoy. On the other hand, they have also been vilified, notably at the Cheltenham Festival, as in 1980 when Irish champion Joe Byrne and Tommy Ryan were banned from riding in Britain for three months after a series of offences relating to misuse of the whip. The bans were unprecedented in their duration and were partly the product of a sustained media campaign that had been calling attention to whip abuse in the lead-up to Cheltenham. The language used to indict the 'desperate' and 'brutal' jockeys echoed directly that used to describe the IRA in this period immediately prior to the Maze Hunger strikes, and Ryan's excuse for his ride – 'with the money our lads had on this one, I'd have been lynched if we'd got beat' – confirms that terror was in the air.[17] The horse was a legitimate target, war is war, and winners are winners.

The postcolonial line that Cheltenham is the exemplary Irish racing experience because it allows for an opportunity to stick it to the English might hold some truth, but the level to which nationalism influences betting there is negligible. The tallying of Irish winners versus British is largely dismissible as another media-generated exercise, not least because the Irish diaspora is so thoroughly enmeshed in English racing that the distinction between Irish and British is almost arbitrary.[18]

If the performance of Irish horses at the Festival has provided an index for the state of the Irish economy, then this came into horribly sharp focus in the slump years of the late 1980s, when only one Irish horse managed to win a race in 1987 and 1988, the champion staying hurdler Galmoy. Of course, this did not necessarily mean that everyone in the Irish racing industry was suffering. Good Irish horses were still winning at the Festival, as they always have, but they were trained in Berkshire, although bred, born and broken in Cork. In a country with almost no mineral wealth, horses have always been king-sized commodities, ready for export.[19]

Cheltenham is also an imaginary event, a state of apprehension; in part this comes from the mythic narratives it attracts, something encouraged by the meeting's timing in mid-March, an unholy triangulation of Carnival, Lent and St. Patrick's Day. One story presents Irish horse people as pilgrims, performing a necessary national rite;[20] on the other hand, Irish punters are seen as simply drinking and betting to forget. The Cheltenham imaginary is so powerful partly because it offers a mass of races for horses to be prepared for (laying a horse out for a race is effectively a matter for powerful imagining); nearly all jump racing in Ireland and the United Kingdom now subordinates itself to the grand denouement that is Cheltenham, making most of the season one big preparation race, perhaps to the detriment of the sport.[21] One could argue that the actuality is inevitably something of an anticlimax.

Irish steeplechasing *is* an exemplarily postcolonial phenomenon, in that it reflects back to England a cherished ideal of itself as a pre-industrial place in which nationality was immanent in nature. Britain's National Hunt heartlands of the West Country, North Yorkshire and the Scottish-English borders are presented in racing as hyper-authentic spaces, exemplary 'countrysides'; as such, these places are mini-Irelands, where racecourses generally demonstrate a form of primitive style that is the antithesis of what you would find at Ascot, Sandown or Auteuil. The contrast with France is probably most instructive; if you go to almost any provincial French course that has steeplechasing, apart from the industrial centre of the sport in Paris at Auteuil, you will see an impossibly intricate system of fences, banks and ramps. This corresponds to a fairy-tale imagining of nature in which the racecourse signifies an old dream of luxury, an abundance that exceeds even the natural abundance that tends to surround a provincial French course.[22] So if Pompadour in the Limousin country offers something between Arcadia and Disneyland, Thurles in Tipperary gives us the blasted heath. An Irish course is typically embedded in the fields that surround it, to the extent that the racecourse is practically indistinguishable from them. The perfect statement of this Irish vernacular is Fairyhouse, home of the Irish Grand National: one un-distinctive but unyielding fence after another, practically black with months of accumulated moisture, a testing hill (Ballyhack) and a steady grind of a finishing straight that allows for rapid changes of fortune. Of course, there are plenty of exceptions to this, such as Downpatrick, which finishes on a hill so sheer that the runners go out of view a furlong and a half out, only to emerge, heads bobbing, about one hundred yards from the post.[23] Although steeplechasing is often seen as more rooted, open and authentic than other forms of racing, this should not disguise that from its inception it was for people who rode around the country as if they owned it, which they effectively did.[24] Steeplechasing is not classless; rather, it is more embedded in the culture of privilege and entitlement that class implies, when class becomes something more than money.

The record number of Irish winners at Cheltenham 2011 demolishes claims for the Festival as a facile index to national prosperity; a more meaningful statistic might be gleaned from the BBC news Web site, which reported that a significant number of racehorses had been casualties of the economic crisis:

> Abattoirs, where horses are slaughtered for their meat for human consumption, have become a growth industry. In 2008, there was just one in the Republic of Ireland, but today there are five. Last year, 9,790 horses were killed in them. Of these, the BBC has learnt that 4,618 were thoroughbreds. But this is not the whole picture. Figures are not available for the number of horses that have ended up in Ireland's 40 registered knacker's yards.[25]

Such vivid wastage may yet leave a permanent mark on the bloodstock industry and on the breed, as a swollen crop of youngsters is culled according to calculations of efficiency that have been mediated by sentiment and imagination in previous generations. Overproduction has created other peculiar problems. Nearly all races run in Ireland, whether over jumps or on the flat, and particularly its maiden races and handicaps, are now oversubscribed. Part of the legacy of the Celtic Tiger was the absurd ratio of races to runners; a balloting system had to be introduced for the most modest of contests, and even now, in the middle of the economic slough of all sloughs, no handicap ever appears to have less than eighteen to twenty runners. The still-generous prize money available in Ireland makes racing there very attractive, but often owners cannot get a run for their massive outlay. One consequence of this has been an increase in visits by Irish trainers (particularly Northern ones) to Scottish tracks, both to get a run but also to participate in races that usually do not have more than a dozen runners (as opposed to the twenty-five opponents they may face at Navan or Fairyhouse). The one glaring exception is when Irish flat racing moves beyond handicapping, where runners become scarce, and most grievously, group races are dominated by Coolmore horses to the extent that they can approximate wanly uncompetitive private gallops. Always good for a quote, the Australian master trainer Bart Cummings delivered this verdict on Irish group racing in *The Racing Post*: 'I wouldn't stay up at night for it. The racing over there isn't worth two bob.'[26]

Where Ireland stands in relation to flat racing is made clear even from this report on the opening day of the flat season in 2011, where the hostility is palpable:

> There is no greater evidence of the post-Cheltenham lull than the start of the 2011 Irish flat season at the Curragh tomorrow.... Back to its traditional kick-off date on turf, the new flat campaign invariably suffers in terms of profile, being sandwiched between Cheltenham and the coming Grand National.[27]

Nobody seems to like it, but it has to exist, because the breeding industry needs the shop window; yet despite this affectionate preference for steeplechasing in Ireland, trainers often regard jumps training as a stepping-stone to the flat. Aidan O'Brien's achievements as a National Hunt trainer are practically forgotten, despite the greatness of Istabraq, his triple Champion Hurdle winner. Vincent O'Brien would always have been feted for his range of incredible achievements at Cheltenham and Aintree in the 1940s and early 1950s, but it took Nijinsky, Sir Ivor and other flat champions to secure his legend.

The master trainer O'Briens are not related: Ireland does not have a racing tribe, but tribes, and these tribes pay less attention to one another than might be assumed. Even as the postmodern punter bets indiscriminately on a three-year-old gelding called No Pekans at Moonee Valley, a colt called Kierkegaard at Sligo or a jumble of pixels called Baba O'Reilly at the virtual track, there are fans of point-to-pointing who never go to a 'proper' race meeting, even though many point meetings now take place at racetracks rather than in farmers' fields.[28] Similarly, you will meet punters at a 'flapper' meeting in the otherwise racetrack-deprived North-West who would not be seen dead at an official racetrack. Countercultural forms of racing have acquired further popularity, as owners struggle to get a 'legitimate' run; the races at Dingle beach in Kerry are not run under rules, but they attract crowds that can exceed those found in that county's official festivals.

For my father, these worlds came into unusual collision in the early 1990s as he set off on the three-hour drive home north from Dublin, where he had been at the Irish Champion Hurdle. As he progressed up the dual-carriageway, he was confronted suddenly by three horses running loose but quickly and directly towards his car. He attempted to avoid them, but one took a glancing blow, while another mounted the bonnet and crashed its front legs through the windscreen on the front passenger's side. Even for someone on his way back from a thorough 'cleaning' at the track, my father claimed that he had been more instinctively worried about the horses than himself. The police told him that their loosing in this way was commonplace, that the horses (robust specimens, usually skewbald with great shaggy hooves) were kept for racing, but let go if they were either too slow or in need of expensive care, and sometimes they did indeed just get loose by themselves. My father inclined to the latter explanation, mostly because he did not like to admit of the viciousness inherent in the other explanation. The question of how and where these horses raced seemed practically unfathomable; horses are still visible in most working-class areas of Dublin and other Irish cities, but they are normally runty animals being ridden by eight-year-olds to no obvious purpose. Poor people in Ireland keep horses because they love horses as much as anyone else.[29] Sometimes, riding on my bike in Dublin, however, I saw what appeared like ghost horses materialise in the traffic, pausing only for traffic lights; not quite the vengeful spirits that assaulted my father, but highly decorated animals in multicoloured racing regalia (hood, blinkers, blue sheepskin noseband). This is not just purposeless bling, and the sentimental characterisation of Ireland as one great big multicultural pony club does not really convince once you realise that Irish street horses are kept for work, not pleasure, and that work is road-racing.

If you search on YouTube with an apt set of words, you will come upon footage of harness races on Irish motorways and public roads in what looks like the early morning.[30] Usually these races take place on public holidays, when normal traffic and policing is at a low ebb, adding to the sinister quiet of these events. Races are always matches, and the races take place usually over a distance of around two-to-three miles. To ensure that no vehicles accelerate to interfere with the race, a phalanx of jeeps drives, LAPD-style, just a couple of metres behind the horses to ensure that nobody can overtake, while a car in front of the horses films the event. This racing probably has the oldest origins of all, yet it also expresses a peculiarly modern violence of spectacle, and even watching it online prompts a vicarious criminality; the jeeps shield the horses but they also remorselessly drive the horses on. This scene confirms powerfully that while racing horses has an atavistic allure for the Irish, this does not necessarily mean that they care for horses any more than people who may eat them.[31] This paradox of the hatefully horse-loving Irish finds a voice in Yeats's 'At the Galway Races'. Written in the pre-revolutionary moment of 1910, he hears at the track a savage cadence of a heroic past even as he sees evidence of a venal present where 'the merchant and the clerk / Breathed on the world with timid breath':

> Sing on: somewhere at some new moon,
> We'll learn that sleeping is not death,
> Hearing the whole earth change its tune,
> Its flesh being wild, and it again
> Crying aloud as the racecourse is,
> And we find hearteners among men
> That ride upon horses.[32]

Yeats captures an abiding truth: that Ireland puts its talent into brutality and its genius into hedonism, and you can find them both at the races.

NOTES

1 S. J. Watson, *Between the Flags: A History of Irish Steeplechasing* (Allen Figgis: Dublin, 1969), p. 249.

2 M. Hinds and M. Wilson, 'Horse Racing' in *The ABC-CLIO Encyclopaedia of Irish-American Relations* (Santa Barbara, CA: ABC-Clio, 2008), pp. 421–22.

3 For discussions of the origin stories of the three 'founding fathers' of the breed, see D. Landry, *Noble Brutes* (Baltimore: Johns Hopkins University Press, 2008);

R. Nash, '"Honest English Breed": The Thoroughbred as Cultural Metaphor', in K. Raber and T. Tucker (eds.), *The Culture of the Horse: Status, Discipline, and Identity in the Early Modern World* (Palgrave, 2004), pp. 245–72; and R. Nash, Chapter 1 in this volume.

4 S. Ross, *The Bankers* (Dublin: Penguin Ireland, 2009), pp. 114–117.

5 It is also remarkable (and characteristic) that the Irish government should have attempted to raise revenue for the state in a prior economic depression after World War II with the purchase of a stallion for the National Stud. In 1952, the Irish National Stud paid a then world record sum of £250,000 for the Aga Khan's Tulyar, winner of the Epsom Derby and St. Leger. This punt on behalf of the nation was not a great success; Tulyar was sold to the American breeder Arthur 'Bull' Hancock for £240,000 in 1955, without having sired a horse anywhere remotely as good as himself. On the other hand, Ireland is also unique in having paid for a great deal of its infrastructural development from the 1930s through a lottery related to horse races, namely The Irish Hospitals Sweepstake, which effectively raised revenue by selling tickets not only in Ireland but to the massive expatriate Irish communities in the United States and Britain.

6 Few nations have had a minister of state like Ivan Yates, Minister of Agriculture, Food and Forestry in the Fine Gael government of 1994–97, whose day job was as a bookmaker.

7 S. Molony and D. McDonald, 'Ahern: I won my sterling backing horses', *The Irish Independent*, 5 June 2008.

8 Ross, *The Bankers*, pp. 190–91.

9 *Dreamer*, Dreamworks Pictures, 2005.

10 D. Biles, 'The Green Monkey retired', *The Blood-Horse*, 13 February 2008.

11 *Report of the Review of the State Assets and Liabilities*, April 2011. www.finance.gov.ie/viewdoc.asp?DocID=6802. Accessed 4 February 2012.

12 It is not an accident that this takes place in the section of the novel known as 'the lotus eaters', wherein Joyce explores a variety of opiates for the masses.

13 *Ulysses: The 1922 Text* (Oxford: World's Classics, 1993), p. 82.

14 Weld has not only won numerous Group One races in Europe, but is unrivalled in having trained the winners of a Belmont Stakes (Go and Go, 1990) and two Melbourne Cups (Vintage Crop in 1993 and Media Puzzle in 2002).

15 *Talking Horses* (London: Fourth Estate, 1987).

16 *The White Devil*, Act I, Scene ii.

17 Quoted in 'Whipping up a storm', *The Sunday Tribune*, 1 March 2009. The Provisional IRA bomb scare that postponed the English Grand National in 1997 reactivated the imagining of the racecourse as a war zone, prompting the headline in *The Daily Record* 'We'll fight them on the Becher's: Merseyside Blitz spirit rescues race refugees', 7 April 1997.

18 The bogus assumption that Ireland cheers every Irish winner was exposed brutally when Tom Hogan's Silver Jaro won the County Hurdle in 2008 at 50-to-1.

19 Ireland conventionally envisions horses as two things at once: commodities to be raced and commodities to be sold. Arguably, it tends aggressively towards the latter. Compared to many of their peers in England, Irish horses are often relatively lightly raced, principally because unexposed horses are more marketable.

20 It is interesting to note how traditional Irish Catholicism asserts itself at Cheltenham unlike any other race meeting, with multiple references made to

racing priests (such as the late Father Sean Breen) and jockeys reaching for imagined totems: 'I blessed myself because I dropped my stick going to the last' – Ruby Walsh interviewed in *The Evening Herald*, 18 March 2011.

21 Bill Barich's *A Fine Place to Daydream* (London: Collins Willow, 2007) demonstrates brilliantly how a besotted outsider can be swamped by Cheltenham speculation.

22 Contrasting radically with the madcap chicanery of French cross-country courses, the flat courses that often encircle them are almost always the same, effectively modelled on the *Circus Maximus*.

23 Jockey Tommy McGivern once jumped the last fence at Downpatrick to discover a bull calf grazing on the other side.

24 The fiction of Sommerville and Ross is particularly good at evoking this world. See, for example, *Some Experiences of an Irish RM* (London: Longmans, Green & Co., 1899).

25 R. Morelle, 'Irish racehorses led to slaughter as recession bites', *BBC News Europe*, 17 March 2011. www.bbc.co.uk/news/world-europe-12682680. (Last accessed 4 February 2012).

26 Cummings added: 'When I was last over there ... there were 18 bookmakers in parliament,' *The Racing Post*, 24 May 2011.

27 B. O'Connor, 'Flat returns with Murtagh gone from Ballydoyle', *The Irish Times*, 19 March 2011.

28 Pointing's quest for authenticity took a bizarre turn in the 1980s, when the Fermanagh Harriers held their meeting on either side of the landing strip of a small airport.

29 If the queen were driven along the relevant stretch of the M50 motorway that circles Dublin, she would have seen Ireland's truly 'national' stud, where the road horses of Ireland are reared.

30 A regular poster of such videos on YouTube is *antociara*. See also the documentary film 'Sulky', by Paul Kelly.

31 Bloodsports remain popular in Ireland. The Annual National Coursing Meeting, held at Clonmel racecourse in early February 2011, attracted more than 20,000 people. A competitive National Hunt card the following day drew only about 1,000.

32 *The Green Helmet and Other Poems* (London: Macmillan, 1910).

9

WAYNE PEAKE

'Sydney or the Bush': Adaptation, Centrality and Periphery in Australian Horseracing

Racing in Australia changed significantly as it emerged from the shadow of British influence and remains different even from racing in physically and culturally 'close' New Zealand. Historically, moreover, it has been as complex as it is unique, predicated, appropriately enough for Dorothea McKellar's land of 'droughts and flooding rains', on dichotomies and polarisations. The idiomatic phrase 'Sydney or the bush', with its notion of the all-or-nothing gamble, of urban sophistication versus backblocks 'make-do', has no more appropriate application than to Australian horseracing. Traditionally, this unique interpretation of racing, with its emphasis on risk taking, whether from the picnic blanket or the grandstand, has been a key element in the Austral-Anglo male imaginary. However, racing is losing the centrality once acknowledged by both local and international commentators. If the once-a-year phenomenon of the Melbourne Cup is excluded, what resonance does horseracing now have? What function do racecourses, from venues of Promethean architecture like Melbourne's Flemington to the 'bush carpentry' infrastructure of once-a-year picnic meetings, serve? Who goes to them, when and for what purpose? What effect is economic rationalism, privatisation and other change having on the ubiquity of Australian racing?

The Australian Obsession with Horseracing

Two parables are often cited in works on Australian horseracing. The author of the anthematic '*Waltzing Matilda*', A.B. 'Banjo' Paterson – balladeer, amateur jockey, racing journalist – conceived the first: that, 'Before the North Pole was discovered, some cynic said that it would be discovered easily enough by advertising a race meeting there, when a couple of dozen Australians would infallibly turn up with their horses.'[1] And possibly the second as well: 'I recall the story about the establishment of country towns in the nineteenth century. They would erect a church, a school, a pub and a racecourse – though not necessarily in that order of priority.'[2] The first quotation satirises the historical pervasiveness of horseracing in Australian culture. The second says something about the patterns of settlement, and the priorities of the white pioneers. Any self-respecting town established in the wake of pastoralist expansion in the 1830s, the 1850s gold rush or the spread of free land selection from 1861 would soon build a racecourse, although some venues, certainly, were flattered by that nomenclature. As a result, many country racecourses are now located close to the centres of towns amidst housing or industrial parks, rather than on downs, as is common in Britain.

Racing quickly gained a central place in Australian popular culture, commanding space in daily newspapers and, in the late nineteenth century, sporting weeklies dedicated primarily to the turf. *The Referee* published the early racing novels of Nat Gould, who became one of the best-selling fiction writers of all time. In 1895, Gould, having returned to Britain, reflected that 'in no other part of the world can be found more enthusiastic followers of the turf than in Australia'.[3] The Melbourne Cup amazed Mark Twain: 'I can call to mind no specialised annual day, in any country, whose approach fires the whole land with a conflagration of conversation and preparation and jubilation.'[4] Another American observer wrote in 1905 that 'horseracing is a mania – perhaps a monomania – with the generality of the Australian people'.[5] Racing's pre-eminence continued until the 1950s at least, when the *Australian Encyclopaedia* could still describe it as the national sport.[6]

A national passion, horseracing in the early twentieth century generated a number of durable idioms. All Australians knew a *drongo* was a clueless person. The term derived from the racehorse Drongo, now thought of as a 'no-hoper', but good enough to almost win a Victoria Derby. It was his propensity for finishing second that led to his eponymous fame. A large amount of currency was a 'pile of notes Jack Rice couldn't jump over'; Jack Rice was a famous steeplechaser of the 1930s. Someone in a seemingly hopeless position was 'further behind than Walla Walla', a reference to a champion pacer required to concede enormous handicap starts. Politics borrowed freely from racing-related expressions. 'First past the post' referred to a vote without preferences, an upset election result became a 'turn-up for the books'; a front runner in a campaign was said to be 'making every post a winner' or 'holding the rails running'.

The men instrumental in popularising the racing argot, the race callers, were worshipped by the racing public like the emissaries of the racing god. In the 1950s, thanks to his broadcasts and numerous radio commercials, the twangy cadence of Ken Howard was almost universally recognised within his home state (New South Wales). Films and television made in Australia until the 1970s – *The Sundowners, They're a Weird Mob, My Name's McGooley* among them – frequently featured a scene in which a race call by Howard unfolding in the background was used to create the unique ambience of a Saturday afternoon in a tiled city or country pub.[7] Melbourne caller Bert Bryant might have performed a similar function. Racing in Australia reached the peak of its appeal after each world war. Few pleasures compared with an afternoon at the track, especially after the trenches, or rationing. A racing journalist captured the exquisite anticipation of a trip out to a pony race meeting at Sydney's old Ascot track in a poem published in the *Sydney Sportsman*:

> My cobbers talked of nought but horse–
> Of horse at Redfern, horse at Mascot,
> Nor ceased they till we reached the course,
> To revel in the joys of Ascot.[8]

Not all of Australia endorsed these pleasures equally. John O'Hara has shown that there were sections of the middle class in the late nineteenth century that opposed racing and its twin evil, gambling.[9] There were, however, broad sections of the middle class that followed it with avidity and, as in the United Kingdom, horseracing's appeal crossed class barriers.[10]

A British Tradition

The British occupied Sydney in 1788 and the first fully sanctioned race meeting followed quickly, given the straitened frontier town circumstances, in 1810, though there were races of a more impromptu nature – road match races – earlier. There is no evidence of side betting on the outcomes of this first meeting, and it seems that, in the British tradition of the eighteenth century, sideshow activities were of more interest to the commonfolk than the racing.[11] The most remarkable feature of nineteenth-century racing is how quickly after developments in Britain came their equivalents in Australia: the replacement of heat races by sweepstakes handicaps as the staple format; the appearance of fully fenced and railed racecourses; general admission charges and the establishment of differentially priced enclosures and grandstands; the ascent of principal clubs into the role of regulators and administrators of racing; the creation of betting rings; and the advent of taxation and legislation affecting racing. Within a few decades of their establishment, the infrastructure of major courses like Flemington and Randwick challenged anything in Britain. By the twentieth century, Australian racing had overtaken the mother country in the innovative *conduct* of racing in such matters as starting barriers, stipendiary stewards, on-course communications and totalisators. Often the lead was taken in these by the various registered and unregistered proprietary clubs that had begun to appear in the 1880s.[12] In these ways, and others, Australian horsemen proved themselves to be innovators, not just imitators.

Australia followed Britain's lead, however, in the creation of the modern racecourse bookmaker, and it was a Briton, Robert Sievier, who, on a working holiday to the Antipodes, introduced the practice. In the 1860s, the majority of bookmaking was, as in the United Kingdom, 'ante-post', conducted off-course, on credit, and settled on the first working day after the meeting. Racecourse bookmakers were itinerant opportunists, moving from place to place, soliciting business. Sievier set up business at one location, betting in cash and paying on the declaration of correct weight. Bookmakers took to wearing garish clothing to attract attention, and to 'calling the odds'. The 'betting ring' became a vibrant, compelling place into which unencumbered male racegoers were drawn as into a vortex. Women, generally, were not welcome.[13]

By 1914, when A.B. Paterson wrote his treatise on Australian racing, its modern format and features, with the exception of the betting boards that appeared in 1947, were fully evolved.[14] His treatise analysed every facet of racing in that era, from the breeding and buying of horses to a typology of its various practitioners and adherents (such as 'knowledge boxes' – the *cognoscenti* of the racecourse).[15] Despite his stated hostility to excessive gambling, Paterson undertook a complex study of bookmaking. He was not enthusiastic about the totalisator, which he dismissed as 'the machine'. He preferred the masculine, hand-to-hand combat of the betting ring. Paterson was writing three years before the introduction of the totalisator at Sydney's pony racecourses. Australian Jockey Club (AJC) tracks followed suit soon afterwards. All-totalisator meetings had been held in New Zealand from 1910, and were the subject of a protracted Royal Commission in New South Wales. Despite the rise of the 'machine', bookmakers survived, and indeed flourished, perhaps because of attitudes like those expressed by Paterson.[16]

In Paterson's era, betting was much more a sine qua non than it is now, when eating, drinking and socialising may be equally important motivations to go racing. Virtually all participants bet; even, allegedly, some stewards.[17] Some trainers were more enthusiastic participants than others: 'Bob [Skelton, a leading trainer] was so keen to have a bet when he felt lucky that on one occasion, when Rufe Naylor refused to bet him an even thousand on the favourite, he offered to bet the bookmaker the same amount to the same odds that the favourite *wouldn't* win.'[18] Even conservative trainers described betting as a necessary evil and acknowledged that only betting stables were viable in the long term. Stories such as these contribute to the maintenance of a national stereotype that Australians would bet on 'two flies crawling up a wall'. It fitted well the self-image of risk taker the Australian Imperial Force had brought home from the war, and built on similar ideas created by the gold rush and frontier phases in Australian history discussed at length by Ward, amongst others.[19] Australians might have loved to gamble but not all venerated bookmakers, and there were periodic calls to ban them from tracks.[20] In the 1950s, the Sydney Turf Club experimented with all-totalisator meetings, forty years after the Totalisator Royal Commission had considered barring bookmakers. Raceday attendances plummeted. In true Paterson fashion, racegoers accustomed to the jungle of the betting ring found dealing exclusively with reserved totalisator clerks rather insipid and perhaps even emasculating. Bookmakers returned a few weeks later.[21]

Except in Adelaide, Australia did not adopt arcane British betting fractions. Bettors were not asked to deal with brainteasers like a price of 100/12. Betting with bookmakers, and also initially with the totalisator, provided few options. It was dominated by win and doubles betting. Place betting, considered an acceptable diversion for females by racing administrators, was accommodated by the tote. The quinella totalisator pool was not introduced until 1952. Bookmakers began to bet 'each way' in Sydney in 1957. Later in the decade, New South Wales race clubs offered a jackpot dividend, for picking the winner of several races, but it was discontinued when it was realised that the pool was proving a benefit match for professional punters. It was reintroduced in the early 1970s by the Australian Capital Territory Totalizator Agency Board (ACT TAB) but was soon discontinued for similar reasons. More successful was the trifecta, pioneered on course in 1977, to be joined later by still more complex options. These 'exotic' betting forms were influential in totalisator pools eventually matching and then exceeding bookmakers' turnover.[22]

Australia, like North America, declined to follow the British example of undulating downs courses and figure eights. With a few exceptions, such as Ballarat, Randwick and the dog-legged Mount Gambier, the major courses are flat and regular in shape. The majority of the few Australian courses opened in recent years, such as Melbourne's Sandown, Caloundra in Queensland and Goulburn in New South Wales, are based on the North American oval track, albeit on a larger scale. And Australian tracks rely on a solitary winning post, unlike, for example, Newmarket. Most of the major centres now have a least one synthetic track intended to take some of the wear and tear from the turf circuits, and to host meetings that would otherwise be lost to bad weather. Nor did Australian racing follow the British tradition of reserving particular racecourses for jumps racing. In the more utilitarian Australian paradigm, it is conducted on flat-racing racecourses adapted for the purpose. Usually a jumps track lay inside the course proper, or a steeple lane left and rejoined it in the back straight. Thus at Randwick, which is built on a flat below a steep rise to high ground above the eastern suburbs beaches, the steeple course went up and over a hill that was only a few degrees shy of qualifying as a cliff. Not surprisingly it was noted for being a tough test and for the number of falls that occurred on it. Only a small number of steeple courses, such as Warrnambool and Colac in Victoria, are truly cross-country.[23]

Flat racing took place all year round in Australia, uninterrupted by a winter jumping season. In general, jumps racing failed to reproduce the popularity it enjoyed in the United Kingdom and some other racing countries, despite its relative popularity in the colder southern colonies. It struggled for relevance in Sydney and had been abolished by the 1930s (in the case of steeplechasing) and 1940s (hurdling).[24] It was unknown on Brisbane tracks in the twentieth century. Nevertheless, champion jumpers like Jack Rice, Greenseas, Redditch and Crisp, the Liverpool Grand National runner-up, became household names. Today, jumps racing is under constant threat from animal rights groups and may not survive the decade.[25]

The Australian racing calendar differed markedly from Britain and the United States. Meetings took place in each capital every Saturday from the 1880s, on one racecourse, then two, then a multitude, once proprietary racing emerged. Proprietary racing was an enormous factor in Australian racing from the 1880s. Some proprietary clubs were registered with the principal clubs and raced under their rules, but others were something akin to rugby and cricket breakaways, racing in opposition to the Establishment, and often drawing the bigger crowds to their so called pony meetings – a misleading and pejorative label, as most of the races were open to thoroughbreds of any height. The popularity of the pony racecourses and their significant place in the culture of the cities has been greatly underestimated by later commentators.[26] By 1906, Sydney, with a population of less than half a million, staged more race meetings (236) annually on the flat than in all of the United Kingdom, with a population of around forty million. By the end of the Edwardian decade, in Sydney there were nine racecourses for thoroughbred and 'pony' racing within forty miles of the city, despite six having closed in that decade. Between 1906 and 1914, six more opened just outside this boundary, imposed in 1906 to limit further proliferation of metropolitan racecourses. There were even more racecourses in and around Melbourne. Constant racing was yet another departure from the British model, where large cities and towns might see no racing for weeks on end. It was further still from the American arrangement, in which a dirt racetrack might race for thirty days straight, then close for the rest of the year. The number of Australian metropolitan racecourses began to decrease in the 1940s, when state governments legislated against proprietary racing. There are now four in Melbourne and Sydney, two in Brisbane and Perth and one in Adelaide, Hobart, Darwin and Canberra.[27]

Polarisations and Dichotomies

Australian racing exhibits many dichotomies and polarisations: the greatest of all is between city and country racing. Bush racing is mythologised as the heart of the Australian turf; 'real' racing in its proper bucolic setting, though landscapes rarely resemble the English countryside. Within country racing there is a further division, between once-a-year 'picnic' racing and the clubs that race regularly. The latter are part of a network that feeds through the near-city provincial clubs (in most states) to the city clubs. Most of their racecourses are well maintained, have good grandstands and complete turf courses. The jockeys are paid professionals. Picnic racing operates in a separate orbit to this network. The infrastructure of its racecourses consists of rough bush carpentry. Many lack a grandstand and boast a running rail in the home straight only. Trees on the infield may obscure views of much of the track. Until recently the prizes were horse equipment rather than cash; amateur jockeys, some tall enough to play Australian Rules, ride (until the 1970s they also mustered to ride in a 'Corinthians' race at Randwick on Bank Holiday). At some picnic races a set of coin-operated scales, stationed the rest of the year outside the pharmacy in the main street of town, is pressed into service by the clerk of scales.

The Tirranna races near Goulburn were the first picnic meeting. In the 1830s, sons of the owner of the Tirranna property hacked a track out of the scrub. Days were set aside for racing, and the station's mistress began to invite the district's far-flung settlers, laying on a famous spread of food and drink. By 1871, the meeting had grown so much that it was necessary for a committee to take over, and racegoers began to bring their own provisions. So celebrated were the Tirranna picnics by the 1920s that George Lambert, the famed Gallipoli war artist, sought to capture its spirit in oils (Figure 9.1). Picnic racing was a major part of the fabric of life in the bush, particularly in the big pastoralist states, New South Wales and Queensland, where distances between neighbours could be vast. Weddings aside, the annual race meeting was the main social event of the year, the mandatory race-eve ball at least as anticipated as the racing. *The Australian Women's*

Figure 9.1. George Lambert, *Untitled* (The Tirranna Picnic Race Meeting), 1929.
The University of Melbourne Art Collection. Gift of the Russell and
Mab Grimwade Bequest 1973 0036.

Weekly, Australia's leading journal of the social, regularly ran pictorials of
these meetings, concentrating on the people and the fashions rather than
the horses and the racing. Occasionally, however, photographs reveal strong
rings. Betting on the rough bush product was well catered for.[28]

The number of picnic race meetings has declined greatly. The safety of
horses and jockeys, once hardly a concern, has caused the closure and dis-
continuation of some courses and meetings. Others, including The Bong
Bong Cup meeting held on a Saturday in Bowral, south of Sydney, became
victims of their own success. Attendance reached five figures by the 1970s,
swollen by busloads of revellers from the city intent more on sinking 'tinnies'
than the traditional tea and scones. Upsetting occupied portable lavatories
and other riotous behaviour became such a problem that before the decade's
end the meeting was banned. After a respectable hiatus it returned, but on a
workday, with attendance limited to members. Despite these setbacks, picnic racing officials assert that their product is the healthiest in rural racing.[29]
The bigger meetings are iconic and some, such as Birdsville and Louth, have
inherited the 'party hard' crown. Despite Bong Bong, many picnic meetings
still allow racegoers to bring alcoholic drinks in 'eskies' – a privilege that
was lost on city tracks in the 1980s.[30]

If country racing is an aspect of the imagined Australia of old, metropolitan racing is the activity's political frontline and economic powerhouse.
The twin seats of power are Sydney and Melbourne and, as in so many
aspects of Australian culture since the rise of 'marvellous Melbourne' in

the wake of the 1850s gold rush, the title of 'leading racing city' is hotly
contested. Sydney racing enjoyed a head-start of thirty years, but this handicap was quickly made up by Melbourne. By the 1880s, the Melbourne Cup
and the Spring Carnival were unquestionably the acme of Australian racing.
At times Sydney racing officials tried wholeheartedly to undo Melbourne's
hegemony; at others they seemed resigned to it. In 1900, before the Racing
Association Bill Select Committee, AJC officials rather lamely suggested that
more people went to the races in Melbourne than in Sydney because there
was nothing much else to do in Melbourne, whereas Sydney had the harbour and the beaches and a multitude of other attractions. But all was not
lost for the premier state; the AJC remained the most prestigious club and
Sydney racing the most competitive and economically vital. Throughout the
twentieth century the Hunter Valley studs near Sydney were the equivalent
of the Kentucky bluegrass: the country's unrivalled breeding capital.[31] They
remain pre-eminent in bloodstock terms to this day.

On some matters rapprochement of a sort was achieved. There was a
tacit agreement that the Spring Carnival was the showcase of Victorian racing, while the autumn belonged to Sydney (or rather, the AJC). There were
carnivals run at the 'away' venue, but they did not seek to challenge the
seasonal 'main event'. Melbourne's autumn features races usually ended
several weeks before the Sydney carnival began, allowing time for a refo-
cus on Sydney and the movement of horses to the north. From the 1980s,
this gentlemen's agreement tottered, then fell. The Melbourne autumn carnival sprawled closer to Easter and new feature races, like the Australian
Guineas, kept horses in Melbourne longer, thus weakening the AJC carnival.
However, Melbourne may not have been first to violate parole. The Sydney
Turf Club, created to take over the courses and racing dates of the old proprietary clubs, grew tired of being the provider of restricted-class racing and
little else. It desired a signature race and came up with the concept of the
Golden Slipper, a rich six-furlong race for two-year-olds run some weeks
before the AJC carnival. The Slipper and its lead-up races encroached upon
the Melbourne autumn, ultimately causing the southern clubs to break the
uneasy truce.

Not only did the Golden Slipper cause a disturbance of the racing hemispheres; it created a paradox between breeding practices and the prize money
allocated to feature races. Traditionally, as in Britain, the richest Australian
prizes were for races run over a 'distance', as a champion racehorse was
expected to possess stamina. So strong was the distaste for 'speedy squibs'
that the principal clubs for many years did not program races of less than
six furlongs for horses older than two years. But the success of the Golden
Slipper (after a shaky start) led breeders to turn increasingly to speed sires.

Consequently, longer Australian races are now often contested by horse with no staying blood, and the features often fall to horses bred overseas.[32] Some clubs, with a sensibility not in keeping with Australia's claims to egalitarianism, have begun converting premium races from their traditional handicap formats to weight-for-age (WFA) contests. Their reasoning is that the best horses will be entered for these races under WFA conditions, but not if they are handicaps, and certainly it has been vindicated. But there are less desirable corollaries. One is an even greater polarisation of the 'haves' and 'have-nots' of the turf. The best horses are mostly in the stables of the most successful trainers and wealthiest owners, so racing's biggest prizes fall to an ever-contracting plutocracy. Previously a struggling trainer could pay the mortgage on the stables with one win in a rich handicap. This is increasingly rare.[33]

Even before the incursion of WFA conditions into the big handicaps, small trainers were feeling the pinch, because, as O'Hara has pointed out, most of the remaining big handicaps are de facto quality handicaps: races that have a cap set on the top-weighted horse at around sixty kilograms.[34] As the minimum weight has risen to more than fifty kilograms in recognition of modern jockey morphology, the spread of weights in a big handicap has contracted to about eight kilograms, when it was once twenty kilograms or more. Again, this compression of the weights favours the better horses and their connections. Moreover, field sizes have been gradually reduced, purportedly for safety reasons (though causality is not conclusive), and this also hurts the small trainers who provide the majority of the lightly weighted entries that are now balloted out. These circumstances provide the background for the resentment expressed by local connections at the ever-increasing number of overseas horses starting in the biggest prize of all – the Melbourne Cup.[35]

Goodbye to the Inveterate Racegoer

As in all of the established racing jurisdictions, attendance has declined sharply since the 1950s. Saturday crowds in Sydney of around 20,000 people, which prompted alarm in the 1960s, would delight today's officials. The retreat continued until 1986 and became a rout when live racing was screened in hotels and registered clubs, by then also equipped with Totalisator Agency Board (TAB) facilities.[36] A new polarisation emerged. There has been a net decline in racecourse attendances, but the distribution is regular. What has almost vanished is the old-style inveterate racegoer, related perhaps, to Paterson's 'knowledge-box' whose primary motivation was the option of betting with either bookmakers or the tote, and to witness races live. From 1987, he (for the group was primarily male) could do this at the pub or club with equal facility, and most were prepared to accept the loss of the bookmaking option, especially as 'gambling' bookmakers like Bill Waterhouse, prepared to chance a losing book, were in decline. It was these who had previously populated non-feature Saturday and midweek programmes, and their desertion has turned them into ghost-meetings.

In order to remain viable, race clubs began to market their major days as events at which the racing was not the sole attraction (indeed not even the *major* attraction). The target audience became irregular racegoers who perceived their visit to the racecourse as a festive, rather than a racing, occasion. Many are women who are unaware of 'betting options and other aspects of racecourse culture; unfamiliar with individual jockeys, trainers or form, the importance of weight and barrier positions, even of which direction races are run, or at which point on the course they begin.'[37] Ironically there is anecdotal evidence that the often uninhibited behaviour of these irregulars has become a disincentive for the old inveterates (journalist Max Presnell has called them 'dinosaurs') to attend meetings. Those few professional punters who make their living from racecourse betting do so from rooms fitted with computers and communications devices provided by the race clubs.[38] The severance of betting from racecourse attendance has had some unanticipated consequences. In the 1990s, Teletrak proposed to build privately owned straight racecourses in the South Australian outback to provide betting fodder for the Internet. There were to be no grandstands, not betting rings, no bars; in fact, no people, other than connections of horses and company employees. Although a start was made on constructing a track, the scheme failed. Given the advent of computerised 'virtual racing' in Australian betting shops, the question is begged why the backers felt it necessary to construct racecourses at all.[39]

Economic Rationalism and the Closure of Racecourses

Attempts to halt the decline in racecourse attendance include the decentralisation of some Saturday racing between the major carnivals. This has seen the reinstatement of a stand-alone meeting at historic Hawkesbury on Sydney's western hinterland, and promising new Saturday meetings at the Gold and Sunshine coasts in Queensland, and at Scone in the breeding heartlands. Stand-alone meetings aside, however, and with the partial exception of picnic racing noted, bush racing and the tradition of the Saturday country meeting are no longer viable. Well into the 1980s, there were twenty or more 'non-TAB' country meetings each Saturday in Queensland, and almost as many in New South Wales. Sadly, racing regulators and their partners, the off-course totalisator boards, all now privatised, find no *economic* justification for supporting race meetings on which the TABs cannot operate and make money. For this reason the number of country 'community' Saturday race meetings – once important components of the 'liveability' factor of country towns – has been drastically reduced, generating a sense of abandonment akin to those caused by the closure of local bank branches, shops and clubs for similar reasons. In New South Wales there is often just one country race meeting each Saturday. Instead, country meetings are held midweek, or on Sundays, when no metropolitan racing is taking place. In Queensland, in the five years following TAB privatisation in 1999, the number of annual non-TAB meetings fell from 618 to half that figure.[40] Subsequently, the regulator, Racing Queensland, cancelled the popular Brisbane River Valley Friday provincial circuit, in order to programme additional metropolitan meetings. Clubs such as Esk and Kilcoy now have few or no TAB meetings to help to balance their books. These 'Brisbane or the bush' cases are further examples of the ways in which Australia's racing administrators have sacrificed the variety of rural meetings in favour of the homogeneity of city racing.

Racing under the Whip

This chapter has sought to demonstrate the historic centrality of horseracing in Australian culture and how its hegemony has been weakened by recent changes in racing and betting administration. There are yet more challenges to be faced by racing in the future. As in the United Kingdom, North America and other mature racing jurisdictions, the virtual monopoly on betting that horseracing once commanded is being rapidly eroded by sports betting.[41] In 2009–10, while racing betting turnover grew 4.4 percent, sports betting leapt 14 per cent.[42] Some of the (economically) smaller states and territories have allowed freebooter corporate bookmakers to set up ad hoc operations within their boundaries in return for discounted rates of taxation. This affords the bookmakers a hideout from which to raid the racing product of the major racing states. In retaliation, Racing New South Wales introduced a 1.5 per cent turnover tax for the use of the intellectual property represented by its race fields. The corporates, only prepared to be taxed on gross profit, challenged unsuccessfully in the Federal Court. However, they have been granted leave to appeal to the High Court. At stake are more than AUS$120 million already collected and an ongoing income of perhaps $50 million a year.[43] Corporate bookmakers have been given a rails run, but conversely racecourse bookmaking, once perceived as a license to print money but now shackled by operational restrictions not applied off-course, may no longer be viable.

There are biological as well as economic malefactors afoot. In August 2007, an equine virus, believed to have been introduced by shuttle stallions, closed down racing in Sydney and Brisbane for the year and caused governments to ban the movement of all horses across borders and other lines of demarcation. In July 2011, there was a new outbreak of the Hendra Virus, which can kill both people and horses. What is the future of Australian horseracing in these 'interesting times'? Racing is no longer a national sport, and Australia has lost one of its most influential meta-narratives, one that provided a uniting common interest for much of its population throughout the nineteenth and twentieth centuries and is now a nostalgic ideal. But all is not lost. Looking forward with the unshakeable optimism which is the foundation of all racing endeavours, we may find a more diverse set of meaningful symbols around which enthusiasts of all kinds may unite. There is cause for hope in the continued success and relevance of the major carnivals and picnic racing, and the new stand-alone country TAB Saturdays and Sunday country cup meetings taking place before burgeoning crowds. Perhaps a new generation of 'knowledge boxes' will have their first experiences of racing in these diverse environments.

NOTES

1   A.B. Paterson, *Song of the Pen, A.B. (Banjo) Paterson: Complete Works 1901–1941 / Collected and Introduced by Rosamund Campbell and Philippa Harvie* (Sydney: Lansdowne Press, 1983), p. 519.

2   M. Hayes, *The Track: The Story of Good Breeding and Bad Behaviour* (Sydney: ABC Books for the Australian Broadcasting Corporation, 2000).

3   J. Pollard, *Australian Horse Racing* (North Ryde, NSW: Angus & Robertson, 1988), p. 419.

4   M. Twain, 2006. *The Wayward Tourist: Mark Twain's Adventures in Australia* (Carlton, Victoria: Melbourne University Publishing, 2006), p. 60.

5   Hayes, *The Track*, p. 3.

6   A.H. Chisholm, 1965. *The Australian Encyclopaedia* (Sydney: Grolier Society of Australia, 1965), vol. 4, p. 537.

7   In recognition of this, in August 2011, the National Film & Sound Archive Australia added two recordings of Howard calling Melbourne Cups to its 'Sounds of Australia' registry. http://nfsa.gov.au/collection/sound/sounds-australia/. Accessed 4 February 2012.

8   *The Sydney Sportsman*, 5 January 1918, p. 6.

9   J. O'Hara. *A Mug's Game: A History of Gaming and Betting in Australia* (Kensington, NSW: New South Wales University Press, 1988).

10 M. Huggins, *Flat Racing and British Society, 1790–1914: A Social and Economic History* (London: Frank Cass, 2000).

11 A. Lemon. *The History of Australian Thoroughbred Racing* (Strathmore, Victoria: Classic Reproductions, 1987), 51–52; W. Peake, 'The Significance of Unregistered

Proprietary Pony Racing in the Social History of Sydney Horse Racing', *Sporting Traditions*, 20 (2004) 1–18 [quote p. 3].

12 W. Peake, *Sydney's Pony Racecourses: An Alternative Racing History* (Sydney, NSW: Walla Walla Press, 2006).

13 Lemon, *History of Australian Thoroughbred Racing*, p. 107c; Pollard, *Australian Horseracing*, p. 110.

14 Paterson, *Song of the Pen*, p. 519.

15 These analyses foreground those of anthropologist Kate Fox, who, in *The Racing Tribe* (New Brunswick, NJ: Transaction Publishers, 2005), provides a similar taxonomy of racecourse characters in the United Kingdom. 'Anoraks' (pp. 8–9), for example, are Fox's equivalent of 'knowledge boxes'.

16 Paterson, *Song of the Pen*, p. 314; Fox, *The Racing Tribe*, pp. 8–9; NSW Parliament, *Progress Report of the Racing Association Bill Select Committee, Votes and Proceedings of the Legislative Assembly during the Session of 1900* (Sydney: Government Printer, 1901).

17 NSW Parliament, *Report from the Select Committee on the Conduct and Administration of Pony Racing* (Sydney: Government Printer, 1925).

18 J. Andersen *Winners Can Laugh* (Hobart: Libra, 1982), p. 159.

19 R. Ward, *The Australian Legend* (Melbourne: Oxford University Press, 1958).

20 See, for example, *Herald*, 17 July 1953, p. 3.

21 R. Boulter, *Forty Years on, the Sydney Turf Club: A History of the First Forty Years (1943–1983)* (Sydney Turf Club, 1984), p. 224.

22 See *Canberra Times*, 2 May 1952, p. 6, *Sun Herald*, 2 April 1958 and 2 September 1973, p. 3, and Boulter, *The Sydney Turf Club*, pp. 223–24.

23 See *West Australian*, 8 October 1907, p 6.

24 Pollard, *Australian Horseracing*, p. 547.

25 See *Australian*, 28 November 2009, p. 7.

26 Peake, *Sydney's Pony Racecourses*, pp. 180–184; A. Lemon, *The History of Australian Thoroughbred Racing* (South Yarra, Victoria: Hardie Grant Books, 2008), pp. 34–35.

27 Peake, *Sydney's Pony Racecourses*, pp. 83–84.

28 See, for example, *Australian Women's Weekly*, 2 June 1951, pp. 15–17.

29 Personal communication, President of the NSW Picnic Racing Association.

30 For more information about picnic racing, see: www.picnicracing.com.au/AboutPicnicRacing.html. Accessed 4 February 2012.

31 NSW Parliament, *Progress Report of the Racing Association Bill Select Committee*, pp. 1153–57.

32 Peake, *Sydney's Pony Racecourses*, p. 88; W. Hobson, *The Story of the Golden Slipper Stakes* (Gosford South, NSW: Horse-Racing Publishing, 1984).

33 See *Daily Telegraph*, 29 May 2006, p. 38.

34 J. O'Hara, 'Globalisation, historical consciousness and the Melbourne Cup', *Sporting Traditions*, 23 (2007), 33–45 [quote from 39–41].

35 See *The Age*, 2 November 1998, p. 1, and *Herald*, l 4 September 2000, p. 24.

36 Lemon, *The History of Australian Thoroughbred Racing*, p. 220.

37 Peake, 'Unregistered Proprietary Pony Racing in the Social History of Sydney Horse Racing', p. 14.

38 *Herald*, 26 April 2010, p. 16.

39 They also seemed unaware that 1940s legislation had made proprietary rac-
    ing illegal, although an amending bill was passed in 2000; *Daily Telegraph*, 11
    February 1998, p. 78.
40 *Courier Mail*, 14 December 2002, p. 1.
41 See Mark Davies, Chapter 13 in this volume.
42 *Courier Mail*, 4 December 2010, p. 100.
43 *Herald*, 12 March 2011, p. 19.

10

JONATHAN SILVERMAN

Saratoga Style

Sitting somewhere in the friendly bowels beneath the grandstand in plastic seats in front of a television is as good a place as any to start a conversation about the appeal of Saratoga. This particular afternoon I am chatting with an older couple from Rochester and two younger women who live just outside Saratoga. The couple are regular racegoers; the two women are relative neophytes. They have visited the track before, but they need help reading the form, which we do our best to provide. Throughout the afternoon, we search for winners, talk horses and, at my instigation, reflect on the particular qualities of Saratoga. The young women admit that the track provides a social opportunity, the racing more of an afterthought, whereas the couple are there to handicap, for better or worse. They affirm that they believe what many others do (and those from New York *know*): that Saratoga represents the best in American racing. The track draws horses from around the country for its lucrative stakes races, and Kentucky Derby contenders often emerge from the two-year-old races held there the previous summer. The locale in upstate New York is three or so hours from New York City, and its bucolic location provides a welcome change of pace for city dwellers. The grounds themselves are historic and beautiful, a mix of tree-protected seating areas, a grandstand dating from the late nineteenth century and a red and white colour scheme. The town of Saratoga Springs is also a tourist destination, and the track and town support one another in their joyful reinforcement of a nostalgic idea of what horseracing and small towns mean. This atmosphere encourages a wide variety of people to come to the track.

Both the track and the city of Saratoga Springs use nostalgia to draw patrons, preserving the Victorian architecture that gives them their distinctive appearance. As Tower notes:

> The flavor of the place ... hasn't changed all that much, and there remains a sort of common ground for anyone who is drawn to Saratoga these days – nostalgia, perhaps, for a gentler time. The wooden stands with their Victorian

spires are a country fair … I believe that most Saratoga racegoers are in that rickety old stand, mornings and afternoons, because they like the racing and they like the atmosphere of both Saratogas, track and town.[1]

The couple from Rochester confirm that they are attracted to the 'tradition' they see around them, both in Saratoga's architecture and the way people dress. Discussions with patrons and officials alike suggest that the idea of 'tradition' is regularly invoked to account for the track's popularity, but tradition can also exclude if it preserves exclusive and outdated distinctions. Sociologist Paul Kingston has suggested that there are no 'real' classes in the United States, 'at least not strongly so in light of a meaningful realist conception of class'.[2] Kingston is not implying an absence of economic inequality but rather of hierarchical social groupings expressed in different kinds of display.[3] Indeed, we are often left to determine class visually, and imperfectly so, given that the symbols associated with social class are both commercially available and incompletely constructed. Saratoga participates directly in this negotiation. Racetracks and patrons collaborate in a performance of class, both in the architecture of the track and in the human equivalent – fashion – as a type of play that corresponds, albeit imperfectly, with the sport of horseracing on display. Horseracing itself brings together the wealthy – the only people who can afford a serious involvement in racing and breeding – and the rest. This variation is inherently unstable and unresolved, an openness that Saratoga embraces by encouraging a type of class play in its efforts to appeal to a broad variety of patrons.

American Racing

Racetracks in the seventeenth and eighteenth centuries were often simply dirt roads just outside a town centre, although, as Hotaling notes, Saratoga Springs and other towns also ran races in town in a type of match or drag race.[4] Crowds included those who were mounted in carriages or on foot; the rich and the poor; the free and the unfree.[5] The wealthy and the powerful participated in racing as owners: for example, future presidents Thomas Jefferson and George Washington likely raced horses against each other as members of the Alexandria (Virginia) Jockey Club between 1789 and 1791.[6] Vast sums were gambled on colonial racing, but racing patrons emphasised the 'sport' of racing, rather than betting.[7] Horse owners and businessmen began to establish more formal tracks in the nineteenth century, and crowds started to reflect the emergent complexity of distinctions based on wealth, genealogy and race. John Hervey, writing in the 1940s in the Jockey Club–commissioned five-volume epic, *Racing in America*, is particularly concerned with the evolution – and preservation – of class. Writing about the change in manners in the republic, he argues that 'the turf presented a stronger front against the "new spirit" than almost any other form of public diversion as long as Colonial status persisted because of its peculiarly aristocratic organization.' He continues:

> An expression of the spirit of the 'nobility and gentry,' racing and breeding almost exclusively the prerogatives of the upper class, were devoid of commercialism. If a great planter ruined himself in pursuing them, it was quite a la mode and involved no loss of caste; but to make money in other than the sporting way out of his stud or stable was beneath his dignity.[8]

In presenting racing as the last vestige of the 'old spirit', Hervey creates an ideal of colonial aristocratic competition, more imagined than supported by the historical record, and also reflects his anxiety, and that of his peers, that class relationships were changing in the period in which he was writing. The founding of the New York tracks show that racing was not exclusively an aristocratic sport in the United States and that status relied much more on wealth than it did on heredity principles. The immigrant and Jewish Belmont family, for example, was closely involved with founding tracks in New York in the late nineteenth and early twentieth centuries, and Saratoga itself was bankrolled by an Irish immigrant ex-boxer, John Morrissey, who began as a cargo thief and ended up as a congressman. Such concerns made it into the set-up of the tracks themselves. In describing Jerome Park, one of the New York tracks that Belmont helped to create in the nineteenth century, Walter Vosburgh, also writing for *Racing in America*, describes how class and architecture were intermixed: 'The grand stand was double-tiered and divided into three sections, the middle section being reserved for club members.' Vosburgh notes that there were already divisions, made for those in the 'club':

> Manhattan's fairest daughters viewed the racing in a display of costume that caused old-fashioned people to stare at this exhibit of the 'wealth of nations', visiting, as at the opera among the boxes. Then, for the great race of the day, the ladies and their escorts would descend the hill to the members' stand, and all was eminently gentle and well bred.[9]

These tracks were run by recent immigrants who had done well for themselves. Indeed, this fluidity is a crucial part of American horseracing, whose visual affiliations to class are paradoxically loose and definitive.[10]

The first golden age of racing in the United States took place after the Civil War and before the turn of the century, before the Progressive Era. The Progressive Era wiped out those gains, as gambling was prohibited in many states. A number of tracks failed as gambling went further underground.

The implementation of pari-mutuel gambling in the 1930s saved horserac-ing in the United States, as did horses like Seabiscuit, who captured the imagination of Americans.[11] Also in this period, the growth of other sports began to challenge the popularity of horseracing. The Jockey Club was slow to respond to the changing sporting landscape. Three Triple Crown win-ners in the 1970s – the magisterial Secretariat, Affirmed and Seattle Slew – restored some lustre to the sport, but these gains were not protected by the horseracing community.

The current state of horseracing is equally glum. Figures presented at the Jockey Club annual round table conference in 2011 painted a depressing picture of racing, showing a 37 per cent decrease in handle and 30 per cent decrease in attendance over the past decade.[12] A report in preparation by McKinsey and Company suggested that the sport needed to focus on tele-vising the best racing and reforming integrity, retaining core bettors by inno-vating wagering and attracting new fans through 'simplified betting, social games' and 'promoting innovations in on-track experiences and new-look OTBs' (Off-Track Betting parlours).[13] The racino funding model has, at least temporarily, given new life to tracks and state breeding industries, but, as Helmer discusses in his chapter in this volume, this model has the potential to reduce horseracing to a parasitic sideshow to casino gambling.[14] Crist has commented on the sometimes awkward combination of contrasting priori-ties and the fractured image it generates:

> On the one hand, [racing] has the image of the highest social order, replete with aristocrats – both of genetic and professional ascendancy to that designa-tion. On the other hand, because gambling is one dimension of the sport, the turf is seen by some as the habitat of a lower, and corrupt, element.[15]

The development and maintenance of Saratoga offers an insight into how these diverse but related interests may be accommodated. Architecture and dress codes (both official and unwritten) encourage patrons to act out class fantasies. However, the fact that everyone participates in these fantasies sug-gests that a love of the spectacle – and racing – moderates and perhaps hides the inherent difficulties within such dreams.[16]

Saratoga Springs

Saratoga Springs built its reputation on its proximity to history – it was near the site of two crucial Revolutionary War battles – and kept it through tourism that amplifies that relationship. The springs and the location have attracted high-profile visitors since the early nineteenth century. Almost consonant with its history as a tourist locale is gambling, which included casino gaming and horseracing, both before mid-nineteenth century (though the city banned street racing in 1825).[17] Like many tourist areas, Saratoga Springs' fortunes have waxed and waned over the years, with noticeable drops when the springs were overbottled, when Progressive Era reforms limited gambling, and in other times of national difficulty. Today the city is thriving, and unemployment is lower than in the rest of the state.[18]

A trip downtown in the summer of 2011 reveals a well-oiled tourist machine, with shops, restaurants and bars the cogs and gears and historical architecture the casing. With the exception of the high-end Tiznow, named after the only horse to win the Grade One Breeders Cup Classic twice, most of the restaurants are not explicitly horse-related, but all are clearly catering for tourists. Some shops focus on horses, whether this is directly, as in shops that sell horse equipment, or indirectly in the memorabilia shops that tout mugs and dish cloths with equine themes. The city appears more racing-oriented than it did some twenty years ago when I worked there as a reporter. In interviews, residents confirm this impression and also the increase in prices downtown that has taken place during the same period. Inflation is considered a fair trade for the windfall the race meeting brings, which may constitute almost half of the tourism sales annually.

Downtown, Victorian buildings have been renovated and preserved rather than replaced, and new developments are governed by planning principles that recognise the importance of the appearance of the town to attracting tourist dollars. Architecturally, the city and the grandstand echo one another. Both are Queen Anne style, which has a 'loose and wide-ranging repertoire of characteristics' including 'asymmetry, overhanging eaves, wraparound porches, and circular, square or polygonal towers' – the latter a prominent feature of both some city houses and the grandstand.[19] The town has six National Register Historic Districts (including the track) and 900 buildings on the National Register of Historic Places.[20] Some buildings are dedicated to Saratoga's past. The Saratoga Historical Centre is located in Congress Park in Richard Canfield's old casino, a notoriously high-rolling and high-end establishment in the late 1800s. Canfield's casino epitomises the spate of illegal gambling that took place in the nineteenth and twentieth centuries, which is celebrated by the city as part of a colourful (and saleable) past. Like all tourist sites, the city's success is dependent on a certain kind of engaged moderation – one has to recognise its historical nature without drawing so much attention to it that becomes recognisably 'for' tourists and, as a result, inauthentic. Also characteristic of tourist sites is the tension between attracting visitors and protecting locals. In the nineteenth century, illegal casinos banned locals, but now they are active participants in the racing scene.

The track is a part of those efforts, though it has always been operated by an organisation outside the city, the New York Racing Association, albeit with a level of independence (interpreted by some as benign neglect).[21] The track is close to the city, and some people walk the mile or so to get there. Union Avenue is the recognised route: a tree-lined street with Victorian houses on each side. The racetrack seems quite peaceful on the approach from the city – perhaps the trees and grass deaden the noise. People are directed to park on the grass lots close by, though those fill up quickly. There are other ways in – Wright Avenue takes you by the legendary Siro's, a popular après-race hangout, along a route that takes you past more modest homes and apartment complexes. However you reach the track, on arrival it presents you with a world both consonant with and different from the town.

Track

Saratoga racecourse is holding its own, without the racino money that supports many tracks on the East Coast. In 2010, four days of racing were moved from Belmont to Saratoga to swell the festival from thirty-six to forty days, and despite a rainy first day, 'attendance and betting results easily doubled or tripled the activity when the four racing days were held at Belmont'. Daily average all-source handle was a staggering $13 million.[22] This move followed two moves in the 1990s to expand the traditionally August month of racing to five weeks and then, in 1997, to six weeks, increasing the racing days from twenty-four to thirty and then to thirty-six.[23] In 2011, for the first time since 1970, there was no off-track betting in New York, and attendance at Aqueduct and Belmont increased by 50 per cent. Saratoga's attendance was virtually unchanged, but on-track handle increased 5.6 per cent from the previous year, from $114.7 million to $121.1 million, showing the relative resilience of the track. Since the financial crisis in September 2008, racing handle has declined by 8 per cent across the industry, but Saratoga experienced just a 1.7 per cent drop.[24] A few factors may explain this. The track acknowledges its past and celebrates it, is open and accessible to its fans, and has a good relationship with its town, which itself is attractive. The track is beautiful and filled with fans who not only love horseracing but the atmosphere itself. And the atmosphere – and healthy purses – brings excellent racing. It also has several disadvantages – lodging is expensive, the track is a conservative three hours away from the closest major city; it relies on a type of fan that may or may not be familiar with horseracing; it is expensive to eat and drink there. But fans are encouraged to bring coolers, and though a three-hour commute is significant, the popularity of the track draws quite a few daily visitors.

Codified in and demanded by its nationally approved historical status, the track maintains a type of permanent Victorian state. Visitors see this commitment even before they enter the track, in the approaches that link a carefully preserved downtown to the perimeter. The entrances off Union Avenue suggest a carnivalesque atmosphere. We see early on the thematic red and white, and the lettering, which can only be described as 'carnival' font. Just before the entrance itself, people hawk tip sheets and racing forms. Before the entrance structure from Wright Avenue, there are a dozen statues of jockeys holding signs showing the current winners of stakes races in a circular flowerbed. Behind is a stately but friendly entrance, which is white and of classical, Queen Anne appearance. People setting up chairs and coolers line the path – on Travers Day, they set up tents around the picnic tables. Further in, alongside the path, vendors sell horse- and track-related goods, as well as food and drink. The path leads to the grandstand, and to the right is the clubhouse, which is open every morning of the race meeting for breakfast to paying guests and accessible for a small additional fee during racing. To the left is an area called the carousel, another reminder of the track's carnival theme. Of course, the first-time visitor may find this chaotic. Though the grandstand beckons in the background, there are many different paths that lead to other sections of the track – the paddock, the picnic area, a shed with bathrooms and other entrances.

One enters the grandstand by either going up the escalator in the middle of the area below it or by walking through the underground area to the apron. Underneath, the grandstand offers many chances to stop – to eat hot dogs, pizza, popcorn (from a heritage style cart), to drink a variety of hard liquors and beer and to bet. In fact, both the paths to the grandstand and underneath are largely geared towards consumption of one sort or another. Even this least-attractive area (made up mostly of plastic seating, concrete floors and honky-tonk signage that does not always reflect the general aesthetic of the track) still has a sort of spaciousness. The architecture of the racetrack, like many others, fosters an openness that allows people to view the races but also encourages movement and therefore mixing.

Described by its most enthusiastic historians as 'peerless in the integrity of its historical fabric which gives physical expression to over 160 years of continuous evolution', the track imperfectly preserves a number of aesthetic principles.[25] The first is that old – or old looking – is better. This begins with the large trees that grace the landscape inside and outside the track, the sign that declares the racetrack to be a national historic site and the classical entrance. It continues with the sheer volume of wood, some of it old (or old looking) – many of the owners' boxes are constructed of worn wood and the ceilings in the grandstand are wood, as are the paddock fences. A betting shed that lies between the street and grandstand also looks ancient. The second idea is connected to the first – make everything uniform in red and white. The roof is red and white, as is all official track signage. The third characteristic of the track, its carnivalesque atmosphere, is both an unintended consequence of the first two as well as an affect achieved through thematic planning.[26] And there is a type of organised chaos at Saratoga, which can confuse even regular visitors. The grounds between the street and the grandstand are particularly unruly, and only the chauffeur-driven are not subject to the kinds of status confusion and class mixing that carnivals promote. Finally, there is a type of universal, albeit relatively understated, ornamentation. This ranges from basic Victoriana (arches, towers and symmetry) to planting schemes, staff uniforms and popcorn carts. Overall, the grounds present themselves as distinctive and unusual, a gently chaotic, intriguing place to spend an afternoon.

Fashion and Its Contentments

Saratoga's patrons often dress up, especially on weekends and almost always if they are headed to the clubhouse. Ideas about class and dress are complex and unavoidable – one becomes a visual 'text' whatever one wears. Fashion is not simply 'one of the most visible markers of social status and gender' but also 'an indication of how people in different eras have perceived their positions in social structures and negotiated status boundaries.'[27] At Saratoga, where requirements vary, the mixing of historical notions of class further complicates this function of dress. As the Web site indicates:

> The dress code varies at the Saratoga Springs Racetrack depending on where you are planning on sitting. Regular grandstand dress code policy is very casual, and most people wear t-shirts, shorts, tanktops, etc., but there are also some strict dress code policies at the track where you are required to dress more conservatively.[28]

Racetrack staff are uniformed: officials wear ties or skirts and dresses and formal footwear, ticket takers and ushers wear a red vest, white shirt and black trousers or skirts. Patrons are subject to other rules. In box seats, for example, there are 'No jeans, shorts or abbreviated wear permitted. Gentlemen-suits or sports jackets required (ties are not required). Ladies – dresses, skirts or slack outfits'. Racegoers did not describe dressing up, however, as a *compulsion*. People patiently explained to me that they dressed a certain way *because* they *want* to go to the clubhouse; it serves as a costume; they are playing a part. This attitude is not limited to participants: amongst those wearing 'abbreviated wear' in the unrestricted areas of the grandstand there was strong support for dressing up, which was regarded as a kind of indulgence or performance rather than a requirement. In other words, the freedom to dress up was valued by people who had chosen to dress *down* – a sentiment encouraged by the track. And Saratoga tacitly encourages this class play by making it relatively cheap (at five dollars, less than the price of a beer) to enter the clubhouse. However, track policy does not *determine* the atmosphere at Saratoga in any simple sense – instead it is generated by the unique and unprecedented engagements of each meet.

One way Saratoga directly encourages dressing up is through its sponsorship of hat day specifically and hats more generally. The track's Web site expresses this mutual ownership of sartorial standards while capturing the commodification of the past that I have referred to throughout this chapter:

> The summer hats and sundresses of yesteryear are still very much a tradition at this famed Racetrack in Saratoga Springs, NY. Even when not required, many choose to honor these cherished traditions when heading to the track.

By engaging with these kinds of stories, people invest in their own enactment of racing, Saratoga style. And the spaciousness of the track and agreeable attitudes of patrons contribute to what seems like less antisocial behaviour than at tracks with less confident self-images.

Like much else in Saratoga Springs and at Saratoga, this attitude has a historical foundation. Henry James noted the presence of women in Saratoga in the nineteenth century, commenting: 'You are struck, to begin with, at the hotels, by the numerical superiority of the women, then, I think, by their personal superiority. It is incontestably the case that in appearance, in manner, in grace completeness of aspect, American women surpass their husbands and brothers.'[29] James described Saratoga as a social engagement wrapped around horseracing (which he barely mentions). He notes that 'Saratoga is famous, I believe, as the place of all places in American where women adorn themselves most, or as the place, at least, where the greatest amount of dressing may be seen by the greatest number of people.'[30] Saratoga continues to attract relatively large numbers of women.

At all racecourses, women are traditional subjects of a particular kind of 'gaze' encouraged by diverse traditions including Ladies' Day at Ascot and hat day at Saratoga.[31] Note these instructions in the official companion to the 2007 Kentucky Derby, for example:

> Men, wear your Sunday best, make sure you're well barbered and that your shoes are polished to a high gloss. Women, get hold of a dress that you know would look good strolling along the infield at Churchill Downs, and shop here, there, and everywhere for a hat people will look at and do a double take. Almost from the beginning of the Derby women (and men) were turning the Derby walkways into fashion runways, but with the accent on flamboyant, even outlandish hats – crazy chapeaus featuring birds' nests, flowers filled mint juleps, just about anything you could think of. But we can guarantee the overall effect: men used to having their helpmates walking around in jeans and T-shirts will look twice – or more.[32]

This book reproduces a much older idea of male attention as something sought and received by female 'helpmates'. In practice, crowds at racetracks reproduce the proclivities of wider society, and women likely are dressing for themselves as for men, just as men may dress for one another or themselves. Dona McAdams, curator of the 'View from the Backstretch' exhibit at the National Racing Museum, reminds us that 'women like to look at women'.[33] At the racetrack, we are all on display.

Wearing hats is not idiosyncratic at Saratoga. On hat day, women are given numbers, and judges decide which hat is the most 'Saratoga'. At the track, people talked about the tradition of hat wearing as being part of the experience of being at Saratoga, a connection made explicit on the Web site. But the tradition it connects with is ephemeral and diasporic. The famous Ascot racing scene in *My Fair Lady* evokes the pretences of class embedded in the English hat. Eliza Doolittle imitates class pretension (the chorus sings 'everyone who should be here is here' at its outset) through her hat and dress – but ultimately gets excited and reveals her working-class origins by cheering on her horse. In that scene, the women's clothing, though monochrome, is highly ornamental, with a particular focus on the hat, in sharp contrast to the morning suits worn by the men. Saratoga, both on hat day and every day, encourages the type of costume and class dramatisation we see in *My Fair Lady*, in a playful way which reinforces the idea of dress as a type of costume.

Saratoga Style

In one sense, Saratoga represents a certain kind of North American racing. It plays with class, it nods to history, it seeks to draw people for reasons other than gambling. In many ways, it constitutes an ideal – there are high purses, excellent horses, mostly great weather and an enthusiastic public. At the same time, Saratoga looks and sounds like other racetracks. It has a typical dirt track, big grandstands, electronic betting. People talk to themselves while watching television. There can be an aimlessness about the organisation of the grounds. And yet, Saratoga patrons seem to feel a strong loyalty to the track, as ESPN announcer Kenny Mayne discovered when a patron in a Saratoga Spring bar was 'preparing to take a swing' at him for the sin of saying 'nice things about California's storied Del Mar Thoroughbred Club'.[34]

Saratoga does not have a monopoly on fan loyalty: Kentucky fans also have a reputation for partisanship, despite the fact that organised racing in New York long predates Kentucky racing. Keeneland's history begins with a stone wall on the Keene farm that was originally given to the family by Virginia Governor Patrick Henry. But the track itself dates to the beginning of the twentieth century and only opened to the public in the 1930s. Saratoga opened in the 1860s and may be the oldest continually operating sporting venue in the country. Keeneland's particular beauty resides in the formal re-rendering of feudal England with stone and muted greens the dominant decoration. Lettering is formal (if Saratoga has a 'carnival' font, Keeneland has a 'royal' font), and the betting windows look like bank teller windows. The clubhouse is literally a clubhouse; even with a press pass, the guards (!) were reluctant to let me enter to take photos without a sports jacket. The eating area resembles a formal sitting room. Keeneland gets great horses from its breeding hinterland, and the wood and stone, the mix of patrons and the April sunshine rivals Saratoga. At the same time, Saratoga's carnivalesque aura suggests an openness that Keeneland does not have. The flowers symbolise celebration. The picnic tables suggest informality. The whitewashed fences of the dirt paddock evoke the connection to farms. Saratoga is also less concerned with uniformity. The new Shake Shack and barbeque place are the first not to match the red and white of the rest of the site. Signs for Coors beer and other products dot the landscape.

What can we learn from Saratoga, its history and current success? One could argue that Saratoga is an unrealistic model for American racing. It is too popular, its meeting too short, horses are too good, the public too mixed. Other racetracks cannot make the same appeals to history and culture, do not have a downtown like Saratoga Springs, or access to the mix of the wealthy and working classes. However, Saratoga achieves its success by drawing upon whatever local resources exist to make horseracing an enjoyable experience. Given the chance, racegoers will use their imagination

Figure 10.1. Race Track, Saratoga, July 1913. Library of Congress, George Grantham Bain Collection, Prints and Photographs Division, LOT 11146–7.

and 'buy into' a racecourse that produces a confident self-image, and perhaps the content of that image is less important than its openness and the welcome it provides to all comers. Which leads to the question: Hat day at Yonkers anyone (Figure 10.1)?

NOTES

1 W. Tower, *Saratoga: The Place and Its People* (New York: Harry N. Abrams, 1988), p. 141.
2 P. Kingston, 'Are There Classes in the Untied States?' *Research in Social Stratification and Mobility*, 13 (1994), 3–41 [quote taken from p. 4].
3 P. Bourdieu, *Distinction: A Social Critique of the Judgement of Taste* (Cambridge, MA: Harvard University Press, 1984). For descriptions of behaviour on racecourses in the United Kingdom, see R. Cassidy, *Sport of Kings: Kinship, Class and Thoroughbred Breeding in Newmarket* (Cambridge: Cambridge University Press, 2002) and K. Fox, *The Racing Tribe: Watching the Horse Watchers* (London: Metro Publishers, 2002).
4 E. Hotaling, *And They're Off! Horse Racing at Saratoga* (Syracuse, NY: Syracuse University Press, 2005).
5 Hotaling, *And They're Off*, p. xiii. See also J. Hervey, *Racing in America* (New York: Jockey Club, 1940) and W.H.P. Robertson, *The History of Horse Racing in America* (Englewood Cliffs, NJ: Prentice Hall, 1964).

6 J. Hervey, *Racing in America 1665–1865* (New York: The Jockey Club, 1944), p. 117.

7 T.H. Breen, 'Horses & Gentlemen: The Cultural Significance of Gambling among the Gentry of Virginia', *William and Mary Quarterly*, 34 (1977), 239–57.

8 Hervey, *Racing in America*, pp. 129–30.

9 W.S. Vosburgh, *Racing in America: 1866–1921* (New York: The Jockey Club, 1922), pp. 4–5.

10 C. Case, *The Right Blood: America's Aristocrats in Thoroughbred Racing* (New York: Rutgers University Press, 2001).

11 L. Hillenbrand, *Seabiscuit: The True Story of Three Men and a Racehorse* (New York: Random House, 2003).

12 Fifty-Ninth Annual Round Table Conference on Matters Pertaining to Racing. Available at: www.jockeyclub.com/roundtable_11.asp. Accessed 4 February 2012. 'Handle' is the term used for turnover in pari-mutuel betting.

13 McKinsey and Company, *Driving Sustainable growth for Thoroughbred Racing and Breeding*. August 2011. Available at: http://jockeyclub.com/resources%5Cselected_exhibits.pdf. Accessed 4 February 2012.

14 James Helmer, Chapter 7 in this volume.

15 S. Crist, *The Jockey Club's Illustrated History of Thoroughbred Racing in America* (New York: Bullfinch, 1994), p. 6.

16 Fox, *The Racing Tribe*, p. 68.

17 P. Roberts and I. Taylor, *The Spa: Saratoga's Legendary Race Course* (London: Turnberry Consulting, 2011), p. 23.

18 In July 2011, unemployment in the city was 6 per cent. In the rest of the state it was 8 per cent; 'Local Unemployment Statistics Program: Saratoga Springs, NY', *New York State Department of Labor*. Available at: www.labor.ny.gov/stats/laus.asp. Accessed 4 February 2012.

19 Roberts and Taylor, *The Spa*, p. 49.

20 J. Dunning, *Saratoga: The Place and Its People* (New York: Harry N. Abrams, 1988), p. 103.

21 T. Genaro, 'In Keeping with Tradition', *Daily Racing Form Weekend*, 23 July 2011, 8.

22 A. Sichko, 'NYRA pleased with Saratoga attendance, betting levels', *The Business Review*, 27 July, 2010. Average daily all-source handle at Belmont was $9,611,993 in 2010.

23 B. Heller, 'A racing kind of town', *The Thoroughbred Times*, 15 July 2000.

24 J. Bossert, 'Racing officials expect Saratoga attendance, on-track handle to be up without NYC Off-Track Betting', *New York Daily News*, 16 July 2011; M. Cignoli, 'New York Racing Association pleased with 2011 Saratoga Race Course figures, optimistic about the future', *The Saratogian*, 5 September 2011.

25 Roberts and Taylor, *The Spa*, p. 115.

26 M.M. Bakhtin, 'Folk Humor and Carnival Laughter' and 'Carnival Ambivalence', from *Rabelais and His World*, in P. Morris (ed.), *The Bakhtin Reader* (London: Edward Arnold, 1994), pp. 194–226.

27 D. Crane, *Fashion and Its Social Agendas: Class, Gender, and Identity in Clothing* (Chicago: The University of Chicago Press, 2000), p. 1.

28 Extract from Saratoga.com: www.saratoga.com/race-track/dress-code.cfm. Accessed 4 February 2012.

29 H. James, *Portraits of Place* (Cambridge: Riverside Press, 1883), p. 327.

30 James, *Portraits*, p. 329.

31 L. Mulvey, 'Visual Pleasure and Narrative Cinema', *Screen*, 16 (1975), 6–18. The 'gaze' refers to the manner in which male directors represent their female actors as subjects of male desire.

32 P. Bordowsky and T. Philbin, *Two Minutes to Glory: The Official History of the Kentucky Derby* (New York: Collins, 2007), p. 329.

33 In discussion with the author, 27 July 2011.

34 K. Mayne, 'Horseracing at its finest', *ESPN.com*, 10 August 2011. Available at: http://espn.go.com/horse-racing/story/_/id/6831680/kenny-mayne-saratoga-springs-horseracing-finest-espn-magazine. Accessed 4 February 2012.

11

RACHEL PAGONES

The Dubai Connection

According to recent research, 93.9 per cent of today's thoroughbreds descend in tail-male line from the Darley Arabian, one of three 'founding fathers' of the breed, who was imported to Britain from Syria in 1704.[1] The remaining percentages belong to the Byerley Turk, captured, according to racing legend, in battle in 1686, and the Godolphin Arabian, who entered Britain in 1729. British racing historians may think fondly of Aldby in Yorkshire, the expatriate Darley Arabian's home, as the fount from which thoroughbred racing sprang, but to one of Britain's greatest racing enthusiasts, the Middle East will always be the true source of the thoroughbred.[2]

The slogan 'Bringing the racehorse home' is plastered across a billboard at the entrance to Al Quoz stables in Dubai, the winter training grounds of the hundreds-strong string of racehorses who will compete in Britain and other parts of the world for Sheikh Mohammed bin Rashid Al Maktoum, ruler of Dubai. The sheikh, who also holds the titles of prime minister and vice president of the United Arab Emirates (UAE), became Dubai's ruler upon the death of his older brother, Sheikh Maktoum bin Rashid Al Maktoum, in 2006. He, like his horses, descends from a long lineage of male supremacy; the first Maktoum to rule Dubai was Sheikh Maktoum bin Buti, of the Al Bu Falasah sector of the Bani Yas tribe, who along with nearly 1,000 tribesmen seceded from Abu Dhabi in 1833.[3]

Fact and myth blur in accounts of the names given to Sheikh Mohammed's international racing and breeding operations: 'Godolphin' for the racing stable and 'Darley' for the breeding empire. The latter horse's Y chromosome may prevail today, but it is the Godolphin Arabian who holds a special place in the sheikh's heart. A small horse, scarcely larger than a pony, he was found – as legend has it – hauling a cart through Parisian streets, having been shunned after being presented as a gift to the King of France from the Bey of Tunis. Nonetheless, some accounts attribute to him powerful hindquarters and a deep shoulder. Eventually he was brought to England and acquired by Francis, Second Earl of Godolphin.[4] While there is no race record for the bay, he did shape into a remarkable sire. His line peaked in influence around 1760, and remained dominant until about 1785.[5]

Godolphin, Dubai and the Maktoum Family

If it was Sheikh Mohammed's intention to ally his racing stable with the world's greatest historical equine figure, then this showed foresight (along with characteristic bravado). For within just a few years of its inception in 1992, Godolphin became an unstoppable force in British and Irish racing, challenging Coolmore, Irishman John Magnier's more established racing and breeding empire, for dominance. Having won their first British Group One race in 1994 with Balanchine, Godolphin collected twelve Group or Grade One contests the following season, and in 1999 racked up a total of eighteen, a record which still stands. The 1999 victories claimed by Godolphin included eleven Group Ones in Britain and Ireland, as well as the Dubai World Cup and Breeders' Cup Turf trophies, two of international racing's most valuable prizes.

The Dubai World Cup debuted in 1996, just four years after the first race at Nad Al Sheba racecourse was run, paying $2,700 to the winner.[6] The prize money for the inaugural World Cup was $4 million (by 2010, the pot was raised to $10 million). More than a profligate show, the prize was intended to entice Allen Paulson, the American aviation tycoon, to enter his horse Cigar, at the time the world's best dirt runner. The $2.4 million allocated to the winner would be enough to make Cigar the world's highest-earning thoroughbred. Sheikh Mohammed had done business with Paulson before, paying $5 million for a half-interest in the two-year-old colt Arazi shortly before the French-trained horse won the Breeders' Cup Juvenile. He also knew that Paulson, who had established numerous flight records, had an adventurous streak and liked the idea of making history.

As if the sheikh's plans were written in the stars, everything came about as it should. Paulson rose to the challenge, and Cigar duly flew to Dubai and won the inaugural Dubai World Cup in front of the international racing press, despite unexpected and torrential rains that nearly caused the contest's cancellation. He became the world's highest equine earner at the time, with $7,669,015 to his credit, while two other American-based horses, Soul of the Matter and L'Carriere, finished second and third, also picking up lucrative cheques. For Americans, the deal was sealed; Dubai was now a destination to be desired, especially with expenses for horses and connections met by the Dubai Racing Club, and lavish parties and entertainment for participants in the days before the race (including the press, which reported, starry-eyed, on it all). 'Cigar saved the race. Period,' wrote Jay

Hovdey in *The Blood-Horse*, a magazine published by the Thoroughbred Owners' and Breeders' Association in Kentucky. 'Without Cigar, the World Cup would have been nothing more than a multi-million-dollar commercial for a booming Arabian economy. With Cigar, Nad Al Sheba became the center of the sporting universe.'[7]

It may not have been obvious to foreign visitors to the emirate, which until 1952 had no electricity and houses consisting mainly of *barastis* – huts made from palm fronds – but the World Cup was part of a greater plan: to turn Dubai into an international tourist, business and finance hub, on a scale of opulence seen nowhere else in the modern world.[8] The world's first (and self-anointed) seven-star hotel; manmade islands in the Persian Gulf forming the shape of palm trees, with poetry written by the crown prince – Sheikh Mohammed's title before he became Dubai ruler – inscribed in the form of wooden buildings to be visible from the heavens; an indoor ski slope rising insouciantly from the (shopping) Mall of the Emirates; 'cities' and 'worlds' devoted, however ironically, to human endeavours ranging from eco-tourism to health care; a life-sized recreation of the seven wonders of the world, with the perhaps subconscious intent of rendering them less wonderful in comparison to their replication: all of these were planned for the new Dubai.

Dubai and Godolphin rose together. Two models fit the development of both: team effort and brand-building. At one time, from Newmarket, England to Hokkaido, Japan, you could find stablehands wearing royal-blue jackets with the Godolphin slogan: 'All I can say is wow!' In the streets of Britain, small boys were seen in t-shirts exhorting observers to 'Fly Emirates', the reference to Dubai's national airline – a result of a £100 million sponsorship deal struck with Arsenal football stadium in London in 2004. Sheikh Mohammed considers Godolphin as his team, and part of the team's duty is to represent Dubai on the global stage. He also refers to his people as team players for the UAE, the group of former British protectorates that joined in 1971.[9] Speaking to the BBC's Clare Balding in an interview before the Dubai World Cup in 2000, Sheikh Mohammed laid out his raison d'être: 'None of my people have reached how good they are. They have to give me 100 per cent, 110 per cent, and then I want more.... We must strive together, we must go forward, we must invent something, even from nothing. That's what Godolphin is about, that's what Dubai is about, that's what me and my brothers are about.'[10]

It is clear from this proclamation, given on Sheikh Mohammed's home turf as he wore the traditional *dishdasha* (white robe) and *keffiyeh* (headscarf), that Godolphin, Dubai and the Maktoum family are elements of a single project. To understand their interconnectedness, one must first know something of Sheikh Mohammed, the driving force behind them. His public persona, like that of Dubai, is one of shifting, contradictory images, sometimes larger than life. From a rundown skiff powered by a barefoot immigrant on Dubai Creek, you can see his likeness etched several stories high on a gleaming office skyscraper. In the local papers, he is sternly referred to as 'UAE Vice President, Prime Minister and Ruler of Dubai His Highness Sheikh Mohammed bin Rashid Al Maktoum'. In England, his intimates invariably describe him as 'The Boss', while at horse auctions and in press rooms he is informally referred to as 'Sheikh Mo'. He is readily seen at Newmarket races, looking dapper in a suit and tie, watching over a maiden runner, or in jeans and royal-blue t-shirt (the colours of Godolphin) with a baseball cap or sunglasses to shield the glare as he inspects yearlings during the Keeneland September yearling sale in Kentucky. The sales were buzzing the year he was seen strolling hand in hand with a glamorous young woman in jeans who turned out to be Princess Haya of Jordan, holder of an Oxford degree, Olympic show-jumping competitor, and soon-to-be bride of the sheikh. Sheikh Mohammed also has a traditional wife from an arranged marriage in Dubai, mother of his grown children, including the current crown prince of Dubai, Sheikh Hamdan bin Mohammed bin Rashid Al Maktoum.[11]

The Bluegrass and the Desert

The success of Godolphin was spectacular, but Sheikh Mohammed and his brothers, Sheikhs Maktoum bin Rashid Al Maktoum and Hamdan bin Rashid Al Maktoum, had been involved in racing and breeding in Britain for some years before Balanchine's 1994 Oaks victory. Sheikh Mohammed attended his first British race, the 2,000 Guineas at Newmarket, in 1967, and ten years later celebrated his first British winner, Hatta, at Brighton. By the early 1980s, he and his brothers were spending millions of dollars at the Keeneland July yearling sale in Lexington, Kentucky, helping to fuel a bloodstock bubble that saw stud fees rise to nearly $1 million and a record yearling price of $13.1 million.

The Maktoum's reception by the Kentucky breeders was a mixture of welcome and bemusement. Keeneland July Sales in the 1980s featured sumptuous parties and glamorous guests, with jumbo jets from Europe incongruously parked in little Bluegrass Airport. There was a touch of the cosmopolitan to those days, but equally there was a core of insular country thinking amongst horsemen whose families had spent generations in the bluegrass. To them, the Maktoums were collectively 'the Arabs' with an emphatic long 'A', and they represented oil money. The United States has a complicated relationship with oil, which it uses profligately but which renders it dependent on nations that many of its citizens regard with distrust, at best. The oil embargo of 1973 and the consequent sharp rise in energy prices had made Americans uncomfortably aware of this uneasy alliance and touchy about those who they felt were benefiting from their pain. Nonetheless, most Lexington breeders were thrilled at the escalating auction-ring battles between Coolmore, then headed by Robert Sangster and Vincent O'Brien, and Sheikh Mohammed's men. In sum, the arrival of the Arabs was a positive event for Kentucky breeders.

Like Coolmore, the Maktoums shipped their Keeneland yearlings to Europe to train and race. Sheikh Mohammed's stable also included horses bought at British and Irish auctions, as well as those he bred himself. These animals won an increasing number of Europe's most cherished prizes, but the horses were trained by venerable handlers such as Henry Cecil, Andre Fabre, Luca Cumani and Michael Stoute. The outstanding fillies Pebbles, Oh So Sharp and Indian Skimmer, and the top-class colts Carnegie, Old Vic, Opera House, Pennekamp and Singspiel, are remembered in British racing lore more for their athletic accomplishments than for the exotic origins of their owner. In 1985, Sheikh Mohammed was made a member of the Jockey Club, then the ruling body of British racing, and his brother Sheikh Hamdan and half-brother Sheikh Ahmed were added to its roll in 1989 and 1996, respectively. Princess Haya followed in 2007. It was the ultimate mark of acceptance by the establishment.

When Sheikh Mohammed became involved in British racing, he was a recent graduate of Mons Officer Cadet School and Minister of Defence for the UAE. By the mid-1990s, he had taken a much more prominent role in the development of his country, although Sheikh Maktoum, the eldest of the brothers, had been Dubai's official ruler since their father's death in 1990. However, it was Sheikh Mohammed, the third son, who had inherited his father's forward thinking and obsessive attention to detail. He described the filial link himself: 'I do not know if I am a good leader, but I am a leader. And I have a vision. I look to the future, 20, 30 years. I learned that from my father, Sheikh Rashid. He was the true father of Dubai. I follow his example. He would rise early and go alone to watch what was happening on each of his projects. I do the same. I watch. I read faces. I take decisions and I move fast. Full throttle.'[12]

Sheikh Mohammed's decision to winter his horses in Dubai was typically single minded. This iconoclastic move provoked a public rupture with champion trainer Henry Cecil, who had guided many of the sheikh's best horses, after a row involving Cecil's second wife, Natalie. 'Henry Cecil is a very good trainer', Sheikh Mohammed said at Ascot racecourse at the time. 'But I want him to train my horses, not someone else, and particularly not someone who knows very little about Thoroughbred horses.'[13] The British public's sympathy gravitated to Cecil, a beloved and quixotic figure, not least because Godolphin's new trainer was a young man named Saeed bin Suroor, picked by Sheikh Mohammed from Dubai's police force. However, when the colt Lammtarra, who raced for Sheikh Mohammed's nephew Saeed Maktoum Al Maktoum but was trained under the Godolphin umbrella, won the Derby, the King George VI and Queen Elizabeth Diamond Stakes and the Prix de l'Arc de Triomphe after wintering in the desert, the decision was publicly vindicated. Timeform, the hallowed chronicler of British and Irish racing, declared: 'The experiment, to see how horses would react to spending the winter in a warmer climate, has been an unqualified success.'[14]

Yaazer, or Dubai Millennium

The emotional peak came in the year 2000, with a horse called Dubai Millennium. The colt was one of sixty-five foals born at his owner's Dalham Hall Stud, the product of the stallion Seeking the Gold, who stood at Claiborne Farm in Kentucky, and Colorado Dancer, a rangy bay mare who won the Group 2 Prix de Pomone for Sheikh Mohammed. When Dubai Millennium was born on March 20, 1996, there was no sense that it was anything more than a routine foaling. As he grew, he was an ordinary foal to look at. Liam O'Rourke, the stud manager, initially gave the colt a grade of C+ in his development.[15] By the end of his first year, the colt had filled out enough to earn a B, and was sent along with the other foals to Ireland to grow into a yearling, and then to Dubai, where the young horses were broken in over the winter. During this time, he was given the unexceptional name Yaazer.

Dubai Millennium won his first race, on a chilly late October day at Yarmouth racecourse, by five lengths from seventeen others and in such style that the analyst for *The Racing Post*, Britain's daily racing paper, was moved to write: 'He looks like a serious Derby horse.'[16] It was the colt's first and last race for Newmarket-based trainer David Loder, then 'juvenile coach' for Godolphin. In the spring of 1999, he won his first start for Godolphin proper, by nine lengths. The colt had been burning up the gallops at home, and he was next entered in the Predominate Stakes at Goodwood, and won this too. He was obviously talented, but the question was whether he had the stamina to last the Derby trip. Along with the issue of natural stamina, there was one of temperament: Dubai Millennium was large, powerful, and high-spirited, and he could be hard to contain. Godolphin's stable jockey, the irrepressible Italian Frankie Dettori, once described riding him as 'like being on the back of a rhino'.[17]

Everything went wrong on Derby day. Dubai Millennium became excited, or, as his workrider Tony Proctor put it, 'He got very, very horny.'[18] Although the colt had settled down by the time the stalls were loaded, he tried to run off with Dettori in the early stages of the race and faded to finish ninth. It was a tremendous disappointment, but Sheikh Mohammed and his advisors set out a new strategy. The result was victories in two French races, the Prix Eugene Adam and the Prix Jacques le Marois, followed by a run in the Queen Elizabeth II Stakes at Ascot in September. The QEII was delayed by a day of heavy rain, but on a sparkling Sunday afternoon, Dubai Millennium showed his best form yet to win the mile race on heavy ground by six lengths. Afterwards, Sheikh Mohammed entered the press scrum to pronounce calmly that this was the best horse Godolphin had ever had. To the analysts, who had been debating whether Dubai Millennium could be considered a top competitor at a mile, it was a shocking statement, but they knew better than to dismiss a verdict from Sheikh Mohammed. Dubai Millennium would be closely watched when he returned at Nad Al Sheba in March.

The World Cup was held in the cool of the desert night, the finale of a star-spangled and rather decadent evening of Group races and firework displays, with the Dubai locals enjoying family picnics in the grass on one side while champagne glasses, beer bottles and queues for the Portapotties piled up in the 'International Village' on the other. When the horses finally entered the parade ring, Dubai Millennium looked, to Simon Crisford, like a prizefighter ready for battle.[19] As the horses broke from the stalls, Dubai Millennium set off way too fast; he had hooked up with Godolphin's other entry, an American colt called Worldly Manner, and it looked as if the two would burn each other out. But while Dettori could not slow his horse down, he felt he was moving easily. When they entered the notoriously long straight coming out of the final bend, Dubai Millennium seemed to shift into another gear. Touched by Dettori's whip only twice, he sailed across the finish line six lengths in front. The dream had come true. Sheikh Mohammed had told the British racing press that this was his best horse ever. Now his horse was telling the world that Godolphin was the best, that Dubai was the best. The degree to which the two are conflated jumped out in Crisford's words when he spoke of the race later: 'It was the best race that Dubai's ever – that Godolphin's ever won, really.'[20]

Dubai Millennium's next race was the Prince of Wales's Stakes at Royal Ascot. As expected, he won, but it was under American jockey Jerry Bailey, subbing for Frankie Dettori, who had been injured in a small-plane crash in

Newmarket that killed the pilot, Patrick Mackey. It was intended that the colt would seal his reputation as a world champion in the Breeders' Cup at the end of the season in the United States. But here the plan ended, because Dubai Millennium broke a hind leg on the gallops in Newmarket in late summer, and was retired as the winner of nine of his ten races. Ironically, it happened the very day that Godolphin proposed, on the front page of *The Racing Post*, a match race between their horse and Montjeu, the outstanding runner over a mile and a half, who was owned by Michael Tabor, a partner in Coolmore.

The fracture was a serious one, but the Newmarket vets were able to repair it, and by February Dubai Millennium was ready to begin his new career as a stallion at Dalham Hall. His fee was set at £100,000, but the price was largely irrelevant as most breeders took up an unusual offer; they entered into a foal-sharing agreement such that each foal would be jointly owned by the breeder and Darley. The agreement was part of Sheikh Mohammed's newest plan: to set up an unprecedented breeding experiment, by carefully selecting a range of mares from all corners of the globe and with a variety of pedigrees, physical types and talents, although all would have excellent breeding and athletic credentials. The aim was to find out in one year of breeding which type of mare created the best genetic cross with Dubai Millennium.[21]

Attracting breeders was no problem, with all expenses and a trip to Dubai thrown in. Midway through the breeding season, however, the stallion was stricken with grass sickness. The disease is not rare in Britain, but it is unusual amongst thoroughbreds and its cause remains a mystery. It is devastating to a horse's nervous system, particularly the digestive tract, and it is usually fatal. After a week of treatment under a team of vets and pathologists assembled in Newmarket, Dubai Millennium was euthanized. All that was left of him in this world would be his foals, and Sheikh Mohammed set out to procure every one of them. With his focus and finances, the sheikh was able to buy most of the mares that had been bred to Dubai Millennium. While not the initial intent, this allowed a new experiment to begin, in which Darley and Godolphin would manage every aspect of nearly an entire foal crop, from before birth through the horses' racing careers. Thus they would control the highly variable environmental factor of training, estimated by geneticists to comprise two-thirds of racing performance. With the other third, they had done all they could.

The experiment lasted five years, through the horses' four-year-old season, although the majority were retired before their fourth year. The first year got off to a promising start, but despite an exceptional ratio of juvenile winners to foals, there were a disappointing number of repeat winners. All in all, the results of the experiment were inconclusive. Many of the horses did not meet the standards set by either their sire or dam. Two, however, stood out: Echo Of Light, a big, light bay colt in the frame of his sire whom Sheikh Mohammed had chosen as his favourite as a yearling, and who eventually won five Group-level races; and Dubawi, a compact, dark bay who became Dubai Millennium's first winner, and later his best performer. After winning three Group One races, Dubawi was retired to stand at Dalham Hall, where he became one of the leading first-year sires of 2010. Dubai Millennium's legacy would continue.

The Evolution of Darley

Sheikh Mohammed calls the worldwide breeding arm of his operation 'Darley'. The name was certainly prescient, given the dominance of their progeny at British and Irish bloodstock auctions from the 1990s onwards. One of Darley's main purposes is to serve as a source of well-bred runners for Godolphin. Another is to wrestle market share from competitors in the bustling stallion business and in the auction ring, where yearlings by the Darley stallions comprise between 25 and 35 per cent of catalogues at the major sales.[22] A third goal is to own the stallions who earn the highest rank in the annual tables of progeny performance, based on prize money earned, number of winners, and so forth. By 2007, it was clear to both the public and to the Darley and Godolphin executive that the first and third of these goals were not being met.

Godolphin horses won eight Group or Grade One races in 2006, but not one of them was in Britain or Ireland. The following year the team had four British Group One victories, but only six in total, with four going to a single horse, Ramonti, who had been purchased privately from Italy. In 2008, only one of Godolphin's eight Group or Grade One trophies came from Britain, while six were from North America and one from Australia. It was a real letdown from the Dubai Millennium era, when the team had recorded eighteen top-class victories in 1999, eleven in 2000, fifteen in 2001 and sixteen in 2002.[23]

At the same time as Godolphin's performance was declining, Darley's influence in commercial breeding grew. A new generation of breeders viewed Darley as part of the establishment. They could not and did not want to imagine a major auction without the presence of the Maktoums, with their generous spending habits. Racehorse owners around the world also welcomed the approach of Godolphin's bloodstock agents, who regularly made very generous private offers for promising runners. These sales had the potential to stimulate the bloodstock economy, as money gained from them could be reinvested in young horses, breeding stock, or farms. While Sheikh Mohammed had long been known for buying 'made' runners privately, the scope of the purchases increased dramatically with the growth of Godolphin.

He had also increased his consumption of yearlings at auction. Between 2000 and 2006, Darley spent $386 million on almost 700 yearlings in Europe and North America. The net gain was five individual Group or Grade One winners who won five such races, and only a single stallion. Coolmore, Darley's chief rival, had a better record; the Irish company bought 343 yearlings during the same period for $261 million, which produced fifteen individual Group or Grade One winners who won thirty-five such races, and yielded eight stallions for Coolmore.[24] Moreover, Coolmore sires, most of them homegrown, overwhelmed the British and Irish stallion tables. The dynamic between Darley and Coolmore had become increasingly unfriendly, and one result was that the Maktoums began, in 2005, a boycott of yearlings sired by Coolmore stallions. Coolmore largely reciprocated, although neither side ever confirmed the boycott publicly. After 2006, a year in which Coolmore's agent Demi O'Byrne outbid Sheikh Mohammed's adviser John Ferguson for a two-year-old colt who cost $16 million at an auction by the Fasig-Tipton company in Florida, the two stopped bidding against one another entirely. The price, for a horse called The Green Monkey who ran only three times and did not win, marked the height of the most recent bloodstock bubble. Stallion valuations continued to soar for another two years, however.

In 2007, with no serious Godolphin contenders for the Classic races in Britain, Ireland or the United States, Darley began buying the stud rights to the top three-year-old colts campaigned by other owners. It bought the rights to the Derby winner Authorized and to the first and second finishers in the Kentucky Derby, Street Sense and Hard Spun. By mid-August, Darley had acquired the stud rights of nine outstanding horses, including three from the United States, three from Britain and Ireland and one each from Australia, Germany and Japan. Darley also purchased significant shares in three established stallions. It was especially remarkable that the three stallion prospects from Britain and Ireland were sired by Coolmore horses, creating a way into the desirable bloodlines that Sheikh Mohammed had been avoiding at auction.

Sheikh Mohammed had also been aggressively pursuing an owner's licence from the Japan Racing Association since the early part of the decade. Concurrently, Dubai, through its various investment arms, particularly Dubai International Capital (DIC), Sheikh Mohammed's global investment fund, had launched a spate of acquisitions of foreign business icons, including

Madame Tussauds, Peninsular and Oriental Steam Navigation Co. (P&O) and Travelodge. One of DIC's major acquisitions in 2007 was a stake in Sony, the Japanese consumer electronics maker; the deal was announced the day after Admire Moon, a top Japanese runner Sheikh Mohammed had bought earlier in the year, won the country's most famous race, the Japan Cup.[25] The racing licence, upon which the Japanese government places stringent requirements, would have allowed the expansion of Darley Japan, a nascent breeding endeavour. The Japanese had been amongst the most enthusiastic visitors to the Dubai World Cup, and one of the desirable outcomes of enhancing the Dubai brand in Japan would be increased tourism and trade. Obtaining the document proved a byzantine process, however, and Darley Japan ended up relinquishing a license it was granted in 2007 after only four months.[26]

The global reach of the equine acquisitions mirrored a vast expansion of Darley. While Sheikh Mohammed had for years owned breeding properties in Japan and Australia as well as in the United States, France, Britain and Ireland, the size and scope of his international bloodstock holdings leaped forward in 2008. In spring of that year Darley purchased the Woodlands Stud holdings of Bob Ingham and brothers in Australia, including several properties and around 500 horses, along with the services of Woodlands' trainer and 230 employees. The price, $415 million, made it the most valuable bloodstock deal in history. It was also revealing of the way Sheikh Mohammed does business; according to Ingham, he had no plans to sell until approached 'out of the blue' by Darley with an offer too good to refuse.[27] Around the same time as the Woodlands deal, a previously unknown company called Synergy Investments Ltd bought the oldest thoroughbred auction company in the United States, Fasig-Tipton. Synergy Investments, based in Dubai, was headed by Abdulla Al Habbai, described in a Fasig-Tipton's press releases as a 'close associate of Sheikh Mohammed'. In September 2008, Darley acquired the Stonerside Stable of Texans Robert and Janis McNair, including a farm, training centre, and approximately 250 horses. The McNairs, owners of a football team, had developed one of the most successful breeding and racing operations in the United States.

Reality Check

The end of 2008 marked the bursting of the most recent bloodstock bubble. Week two of the fortnight-long Keeneland September yearling sale, the main U.S. yearling auction for international buyers since the July sale was closed down in 2003, coincided with the collapse of Lehman Brothers. It was the start of a precipitous global slide which the bloodstock markets did not escape. Within the next two years, the bloodstock market lost between 30 and 50 per cent in value, stud fees were slashed, broodmares disposed of, slow horses abandoned and farms lost.[28] Dubai, dependent on dreams and credit, was also affected. Fortunately, it had the backing of Abu Dhabi, capital of the UAE and source of most of its oil, and in 2009 Dubai received a $20 billion loan from Abu Dhabi. Nonetheless, the Dubai government was forced to cancel close to 500 development projects, about half those that had been planned, according to the *Financial Times*.[29]

With the breeding industry in crisis and Dubai's troubles appearing regularly in the press, racing feared that Sheikh Mohammed and his brothers would reduce their spending. At this time, the importance of the Maktoums to the full cycle of breeding, buying and racing became starkly apparent. To the relief of the industry, Sheikh Mohammed continued to inject vast amounts of money into public auctions, particularly the Tattersalls October yearling sales in Newmarket. His contribution to this auction was such that in 2008, when he received a special order of merit at the Cartier Awards (the annual celebration of achievement in British racing), he was lauded for his role in supporting British bloodstock sales.[30] In the United States, his role was more complicated; having invested in Fasig-Tipton, he increased his spending significantly in subsequent years at that company's primary yearling sale at Saratoga, in New York. The effect on Keeneland, the rival auction house, was not clear as the Maktoums had reduced their budget there rather dramatically beginning in 2007, the year of the multiple stallion acquisitions.

At home, Meydan Racecourse, a grandiose replacement for Nad Al Sheba, escaped the slowdown on developments and was opened in 2010. The same year, Godolphin appointed a second trainer, Mahmood Al Zarooni, and received planning permission to expand its Newmarket stables – reassuring signs for a bloodstock industry beginning to stabilise after the recession. Sheikh Mohammed has made an indelible mark on racing and breeding worldwide, through his bold initiatives and grand gestures, his international scope and his linking of Dubai to every aspect of the game. A considerable number of owners and breeders have described his influence in their lives – through the generous terms of Godolphin's purchase of their horses – as life-changing. Yet the very dynamism that defines the sheikh continues to confound an industry that is inherently conservative but has allowed itself to become dependent on his unpredictable actions. People who might have known nothing of Dubai are now watching its fortunes closely as they wonder how he will respond to the upheavals in the world economy and the politics of the Middle East. That in itself is another triumph for Sheikh Mohammed.

NOTES

1 M. Binns and T. Morris, *Thoroughbred Breeding: Pedigree Theories and the Science of Genetics* (London: J.A. Allen, 2010).

2 For a discussion of the origin stories of the three founding fathers, see D. Landry, *Noble Brutes* (Baltimore: Johns Hopkins University Press, 2008).

3 C. Davidson, *Dubai: The Vulnerability of Success* (London: Hurst & Company, 2008), p. 13.

4 For a discussion of the motivations for attributing particular origins to the founding fathers of the thoroughbred, see R. Nash, '"Honest English Breed": The Thoroughbred as Cultural Metaphor' in K. Raber and T. Tucker (eds.), *The Culture of the Horse: Status, Discipline, and Identity in the Early Modern World* (Oxford: Palgrave, 2004), pp. 245–72 and Richard Nash, Chapter 1 in this volume.

5 Morris and Binns, *Thoroughbred Breeding*.

6 G. Wilson, 'Sheikh, Rattle and Roll', *The Blood-Horse*, 16 March 1996.

7 J. Hovdey, 'Horse of the World – Cigar Conquers Dubai', *The Blood-Horse*, 6 April 1996.

8 Sheikh Mohammed's official Web site (www.sheikhmohammed.com) includes an account of Dubai history. The description of Dubai prior to 1952 is from the 'Old Dubai' section.

9 The UAE was founded in 1971 with six member states, including Abu Dhabi, Ajman, Dubai, Fujairah, Sharjah and Umm al-Quwain. The seventh, Ra's al-Khaimah, joined in 1972. The capital is Abu Dhabi, the largest and richest emirate because of the size of its oil reserves, discovered in 1958. Abu Dhabi possesses four-fifths of the UAE's oil.

10 From unedited BBC video archives, 2000, quoted by R. Pagones in *Dubai Millennium: A Vision Realised, A Dream Lost* (Compton: Highdown, 2007), p. 23.

11 Sheikh Mohammed's arranged marriage to Sheikha Hind bint Maktoum Al Maktoum is referred to in Davidson, *Dubai*, p. 145.

12 Quoted by Pagones, *Dubai Millennium*, p. 17.

13 R. Henwood, 'A Kingdom for their Horses', *The Blood-Horse*, 16 March 1996, quoted by Pagones, *Dubai Millennium*, p. 41.

14 *Racehorses of 1995* (Halifax: Timeform, 1996).

15 Personal interviews, Newmarket, May 2006.

16 Quoted by Pagones in *Dubai Millennium*, p. 49.

17 Personal interviews, Newmarket, September 2006.

18 Personal interviews, Newmarket, August 2006.

19 Personal interviews, Newmarket, May 2006.

20 *Ibid.*

21 The breeding experiment is described in full in Pagones, *Dubai Millennium*, pp. 127–38.

22 R. Pagones, 'Surge in Demand a Global Feature of Sales Season', *Racing Post Bloodstock Review*, 8 December 2006.

23 Details of Godolphin's Group One wins by season can be found at: www.godolphin.com/WinnersGroup1ByYear.aspx. Accessed 4 February 2012.

24 R. Pagones, 'Clash of the Titans', *The Blood-Horse MarketWatch*, 5 October 2007.

25 R. Pagones, 'Change of Game Plan', *Racing Post Bloodstock Review*, 17 December 2007.

26 For more on the saga of Sheikh Mohammed's quest for a Japan Racing Association licence, see the archives of *The Racing Post* (www.racingpost.co.uk), *The Blood-Horse* (www.bloodhorse.com) and *Thoroughbred Times* (www.thoroughbredtimes.com).

27 Ingham quoted in R. Chapman, 'Darley Buys Woodlands Stud', *The Blood-Horse*, 25 March 2008. See also R. Thomas, 'How the Dubai Sheikh bought Woodlands stud for $500million', *The Telegraph* (Australia), 25 March 2008.

28 For analysis of the North American, British and Irish bloodstock markets during the recession, see *Thoroughbred Daily News* columnist Bill Oppenheim at: www.thetdn.com.

29 S. Kerr and R. Wigglesworth, 'Half of Dubai's Property Projects Scrapped', *The Financial Times*, 27 September 2010.

30 The organisers of the Cartier Awards create videos in honour of the recipients of special merit awards. The video honouring Sheikh Mohammed made reference to his support of the British bloodstock sales, the first time to the author's knowledge that a buyer's contribution at auction was so recognised.

12

MARK GODFREY

Racing in Asia

Harry Sweeney: Pioneer

Few people who peruse the racing pages in Europe will bother to look for the winners from the 3.45 in Tokyo. Maybe they should. Until the financial crisis hit in 2008, the Japan Cup, a mile-and-a-half invitational turf race run every November at Tokyo racecourse, was the richest race in the world. In 2012, prize money will be ¥521 million (about $6.5 million), making it the third-most valuable race, behind the Dubai World Cup and the Melbourne Cup. As well as a mega race, Japan produces some of the largest betting markets in the world.

One man who has long appreciated the wealth of Japan's racing scene is Dr Harry Sweeney, a Japanese-speaking veterinarian from County Louth in Ireland who runs Paca Paca, one of Japan's most successful breeding farms. In 2011, Sweeney was hopeful that one of the farm's products, Deep Brilliante, would win the 2012 Japan Derby: 'well, that hope is certainly making the Winter shorter for us!' he joked. Deep Brilliante lived up to expectations, winning the Derby by a nose from Fenomeno and crowning Sweeney's achievements in Japan thus far. Sweeney is remarkable for the path-finding role he has played in Japanese racing. He was the first outsider to buy agricultural land for the purposes of setting up a thoroughbred breeding farm and the first foreigner to be granted an owner's license by the Japanese Racing Association (JRA). I open this chapter with his story because it is suggestive of the combination of opportunities and challenges that characterise the most promising and frustrating jurisdiction of all: China.

Paca Paca – the name is a Japanese expression used to describe the sound of horses galloping – is set in 550 acres on Hokkaido, the northern island where many of Japan's bloodstock farms are located.[1] In hill land known as Niikappu, Sweeney's farm is home to up to 180 horses at peak season and is also where composer and horse lover Andrew Lloyd Webber and several

Arab sheikhs stable horses which race in Japan. Cooled in the summer by winds off the Japan Sea and the Pacific, Hokkaido is by far Japan's largest prefecture. A short hop east of Russia, the island is linked to the main island of Honshu by the famous Seikan Tunnel, the world's longest rail tunnel. The island has been Sweeney's home for nearly two decades since he left a job on the Curragh for an adventure in one of the world's lesser-known racing scenes. The enormity of what he found convinced Sweeney to extend his stay and to learn Japanese.

The central place of horseracing in Japanese society has been maintained by the illegality of virtually all other forms of gambling, and the monopoly enjoyed by the semi-state authority and sole official operator the Japanese Racing Association (JRA). Japan conducts approximately 20,000 horse races each year on 26 tracks. The ten premier tracks are overseen by the JRA, which was formed in 1954 and is both the monopoly pari-mutuel operator and also responsible for regulation.[2] Prize purses for JRA-graded stakes races start at about $800,000. Lower-grade races are run on another sixteen tracks under the auspices of the National Association of Racing (NAR), which was formed in 1962.[3] Purses at NAR tracks reflect local conditions and can vary between metropolitan and country tracks by as much as a factor of twenty. In both cases, turnover is boosted by the most enthusiastic bettors of any racing jurisdiction in the world. According to figures compiled by the International Federation of Horseracing Authorities (IFHA), Japan's turnover is twice that of second-place Australia and 6 per cent of this turnover is returned to racing. Once thought of as the strongest market for horseracing betting in the world, Japan has experienced a decline in turnover of approximately 5 per cent each year for the past ten years. The decline has caused concern among racing administrators, who have been forced to seek sponsorship of the most prestigious races, including the Japan Cup, for the first time. Despite the waning popularity of the sport, in 2010, punters bet more than $33 billion on racing in Japan.[4]

As well as Deep Brilliante, Sweeney's career in Japan is associated with star horses like the 1993 winner of the mile championship Shinko Lovely and Japanese Horse of the Year Taiki Shuttle, who won the Prix Jacques le Marois in 1998. His success is based on his willingness to adapt and a sharp eye for opportunities. He also believes his Irish veterinary background is 'an enormous asset'. Sweeney grew up on a farm near Dundalk and took his veterinary degree at University College Dublin before completing a doctorate at the University of Edinburgh. While a young veterinarian at the Curragh practice of since-deceased Kieran Bredin, he got an unsolicited phone call asking if he would be interested in managing the breeding program at Taiki Farm, a newly established breeding centre in Japan whose owner Yoshiki

Akazawa had ambitions to win races in Japan, train in Ireland and breed in North America. That was 1990, and Sweeney ended up staying five years at Taiki with his wife Anne and three young sons. By 1995, Taiki Farm ranked seventh in the owners' table at JRA tracks with winnings of 730 million yuan ($6.6 million).[5] Having enjoyed great success at Taiki, Sweeney moved on to handle pre-training at Machikane Farm, also on Hokkaido. After three and a half years at Machikane, he spent some time trading horses. 'In the 1980s, during the boom, Japanese paid big money for mares and when the bubble burst there was a market to purchase these and repatriate them to the US and Europe', he explained.

In 2000, after a decade spent at various farms, Sweeney decided to go it alone. In order to set up a farm, he had to overcome nearly a century of tradition at the JRA, which had never before handed an owner's license to a foreigner. Becoming the first foreign member of the JRA owners' club was an honour Sweeney earned through persistence and commitment to the country – and help from the Irish embassy and officials, he recalls gratefully. Buying land was also a huge challenge, as Sweeney explains, 'Because of the scarcity of arable land in Japan, I was only the first foreigner licensed to purchase agricultural ground.' Today he speaks Japanese, is a permanent resident and visited by Japanese industrialists and Middle Eastern Sheiks who stroll through the pristine, white-walled stables and gardens of cherry blossoms to watch Paca Paca racing stock work on the farm's run-out track. As a member of the Japan Race Horse Association (JRHA), he is able to enter young horses in the sales, where he has enjoyed great success. According to the racing press, he sells young horses for an average of $396,000 a piece.[6]

Japan's racing purse is twice as big as that on offer in Hong Kong, and racing operates on a vast scale, as Sweeney explains: 'Japan follows only US and Australia in terms of scale and training.' And yet, it is Hong Kong that is better known within the international racing scene. Sweeney puts this higher profile at least partly down to cultural reasons, Japan being 'secure and insular in itself ... it is impenetrable in lots of ways.' Hong Kong, by contrast, has long made its name as a trading port, British colony and gateway to China. Sweeney thinks that while bloodstock and other industries are easier to enter in bilingual Hong Kong, 'it's far more competitive than Japan which is hard to enter but full of opportunities.'

According to Sweeney, Irish horsemanship commands a great deal of respect amongst Japan's racing establishment. This mutual regard is expressed in several joint initiatives including the annual Ireland Trophy Stakes, sponsored by the Irish Thoroughbred Breeders Association and hosted by the Irish Embassy in association with the JRA. In 2011, Japanese racing fans turned out in numbers to cheer Irish jockey Johnny Murtagh, who rode in Japan for a period in 1999, win the World Super Jockey Series in December at the Hanshin racetrack.[7] Sweeney thinks Irish equestrian talents should look to Japan for work opportunities. He points approvingly to a placement programme which allows students from the University of Limerick and University College Dublin to spend between six and eight months in Japan. 'They'll get all the training they'd get at home but also the scale of the racing industry in Japan.' Japan has also been interested in Irish horses. Sweeney points out that the sales topper of the 2009 yearling sales was a $1.5 million colt sired by Rock of Gibraltar, an Irish legend trained by Aidan O'Brien.[8] Vodka (JPN), the highest earning female racehorse of all time, now resides at the Aga Khan-owned Gilltown Stud: 'She won the Japan Derby twice and is now based in Ireland since her Japanese owner wants her to breed from Irish champion Sea the Stars,' says Sweeney.[9]

While Sweeney's license signalled change, international personnel continue to face particular challenges in Japan. Foreign trainers are effectively excluded by a Japanese-language exam, while jockeys can ride for only three months a year in local races. The breeding scene remains dominated by local players including the Shadai bloodstock farms held by three Yoshida brothers, Katsumi, Terry and Haruya. Sweeney was ahead of others trying to breed horses in Japan, amongst them Dubai's ruler Sheikh Mohammed bin Rashid al-Maktoum. In order to enter the game, foreign owners like Al-Maktoum have bought local horses, including Japan Cup winner Admire Moon, who won the Dubai Duty Free Stakes, the Takarazuka Kinen and the Japan Cup in 2007.[10] In 2011, Sheikh Mohammed was one of only five people resident outside Japan to be registered as owners by the JRA.[11]

Just as foreign owners seek a slice of Japan's prize money, so Sweeney sees Japanese buyers in recent years becoming 'very active' in European bloodstock sales. The Yoshida brothers have kept an eye on Ireland, last year buying champion mare Sarafina from the Aga Khan's Irish breeding centre.[12] This year, Sarafina was joined by Cozi Rosie, a multiple Grade Two winner bought for $525,000 at Keeneland.[13] These purchases, paid for with some of Shadai's ¥3,249,360,000 ($39 million) winnings from Japanese racing in 2011, will bolster the Yoshidas' total dominance of Japanese racing.[14]

While the Yoshidas have become important global players, there are, however, worries that Japanese punters, like counterparts in other racing territories like the United Kingdom and Ireland, are losing interest in betting. Globally, betting turnover was down 1.4 per cent in 2010, according to IFHA data, and although Japan remained at the top of the global rankings in betting revenues, the slide there was a more pronounced 6 per cent. In response, the JRA loosened restriction on foreign horses competing in local races, hoping that big names would pull punters back to the tracks.[15] The government also submitted a bill which would allow regional race organisers to increase the returns on popular bets.[16] As well as taking steps intended to stabilise demand at home, Japanese racing (like the broader Japanese economy) also sees its future increasingly driven by the giant next door – China.[17] China is already factored into the plans of breeders like Sweeney who has exhibited at Chinese equestrian trade shows. He sees Chinese investment as a theme for the future for Japan, with possible investment in racing farms – given that foreign investment in agricultural land is allowed. Likewise, he wants to see racegoers from nearby China, connected by several flights a day into Tokyo, visiting for races: 'Wealthy citizens of cities like Beijing and Shanghai can enjoy the glamour and luxury of Tokyo and be back in their own beds the same night.' And he believes that wealthy Chinese will embrace the sport: 'Racing is the ultimate status symbol, get you up close with royalty like Queen Elizabeth or the Aga Khan or Sheikh Mohammed.' 'Racing will be a win-win for China and for racing when it happens,' says Sweeney.[18]

Wuhan: Pony Rides and Raffles

Despite the ban on betting on the mainland, demand for racehorses has risen as China has produced a new class of super-rich.[19] Having spent fourteen years selling horses to owners from Macau and Hong Kong, in 2005, Kiwi bloodstock agent Brian Ridley formed Race Horse International to import thoroughbreds from Australia and New Zealand on behalf of Chinese buyers. Based in Shenzhen, a mainland city near Hong Kong, Ridley ships these horses to Hong Kong and Macau to race. 'I started the business when I began bumping into Beijing natives at Hong Kong's Sha Tin track several years ago', he explained in 2009 'and I quickly saw the potential to sell horses to mainland Chinese who would house their horses at the Jockey Club at Sha Tin.'[20] Ridley oversees care of the horses and informs owners of their progress. He describes his customers as syndicates consisting of drinking or business acquaintances who are eager to have a horse run in their names but unable to do so on the mainland. The solution? To buy a horse to race in Hong Kong or Macau. Prices paid for what Ridley terms ready-to-race 'entry-level' three-year-old New Zealand imports vary between 500,000 yuan ($79,377) and 1.5 million yuan ($238,133). 'Horses with a track record of wins sell for multiples of that figure,' he adds. The quality of the imported horses is paramount: 'We don't want to sell them cheap horses, we want them to win something.' Ridley has sold horses for between 1 million yuan ($158,755) and 4.2 million yuan ($666,773).

By 2009, Ridley was confident that he would eventually export horses to mainland tracks, encouraged by the development of Wuhan, a central Chinese city, with a track built by a Hong Kong real estate developer Jacky Wu and the Oriental Lucky Horse Group Co. The Wuhan Jockey Club was nothing if not ostentatious: a 200-metre-long seven-storey glass-encased grandstand housed spectators at the 1.6-kilometre sand track. Racegoers wanting a close-up could view the action on a gigantic 480-square-metre screen. 'The logic of a racecourse in Wuhan is that it's far away from the seat of government, which banned gambling in 1949,' Ridley explained. Regulators will eventually relent, he predicted, 'because people want it and also because Beijing government officials have looked admiringly at how much the Hong Kong Jockey Club gives to Cantonese society in taxes and philanthropic activity.' Ridley estimated tracks like Wuhan would eventually require up to a thousand horses to sustain a meaningful racing calendar. And he was convinced that local breeds would not excite potential buyers who are familiar with racing outside China – 'the best Mongolian and Yili [local breed] horses will be two hundred yards behind a thoroughbred on the track.'[21] This suggests demand for imported horses. Ridley said strict management, big prize money and good foreign bloodstock have made big-money racing synonymous with Hong Kong, a model that Chinese tracks should seek to emulate. He also believed it was vital that locals – and not the Jockey Club – owned the horses: 'private owners will put pressure on the Jockey Club to keep high standards and raise the prize money.' In 2009, Ridley believed that on-track betting was imminent at Wuhan and that 'when people start talking about it', there would be a huge explosion of demand. The government would see windfalls in tax and jobs and the future of the betting industry would be secured. However, as of August 2011, visitors to the track could watch horses racing, but were limited to winning shopping vouchers in raffles: not quite the high-rolling action that widely travelled and wealthy Chinese expect.[22]

The current crop of horses and level of prize money would also be a disappointment to Ridley and to all of those who believe that high-quality racing will guarantee integrity and audience interest. In 2012, the club took delivery of 90 Mongolian ponies, bringing the Club's horse population – all Chinese breed horses rather than thoroughbreds – up to 380. A club official said that the club will eventually house 600 horses. A race in March 2012 featured twelve Mongolian ponies, pootling along a state-of-the-art racetrack like a herd of escaped Shetlands. Track officials suggested that races featuring privately owned thoroughbreds were also a regular feature, but no clear calendar of such races has been fixed for 2012. Currently, there are between four and six twelve-horse races scheduled every Saturday. Raffles for spectators take place between races. Prize money for trainers and jockeys – all Chinese – was 300 yuan ($47). Two races during the eight-day festival held in November will again test the boundaries of current policy by offering a modest cash prize to anyone guessing the winning horse. The club also supplements its income by offering riding lessons on its horses in an on-site equestrian centre.[23]

Tongzhou: Mixed Messages and Local Trouble

The growth of the racing industry in China has been hampered by the historical ban on horseracing, the contemporary ban on betting, the absence of an indigenous thoroughbred population and the costs of creating infrastructure in the face of such uncertainty. A recent report by the Kentucky China Trade Centre suggests that resistance to the legalisation of betting comes primarily from central government, fearful that betting will accentuate the widespread problem of corruption.[24] Investments are thus vulnerable to the whims of notoriously fickle politicians who seem content to prolong the uncertainty surrounding betting despite the loss of millions to offshore and domestic illegal operators. It will take some time for China to get its racing scene in place, Alastair Donald, chief executive of the International Racing Bureau, a UK-based agency for racing authorities worldwide, explained: 'This is not like a casino where you just need a roulette. It's like an Olympic village.... You need an equine population and you have to look after it.' Some of the perils of this unique structure are evident in the rise and fall of Tongzhou racecourse.

Tongzhou was still a dusty backwater village when I first visited in the spring of 2004, but the scale of Hong Kong-backed Beijing Jockey Club investment was impressive. The buildings looked like any Chinese warehouse – white rectangular blocks hooded by blue steel-sheeted roofs – but there was a military regularity and this was a hive of activity. Workmen and women pushed brushes, pulled wheel barrows of hay and dung, polished leather tack and carried buckets of water. Irish club manager Kevin Connolly was proud, and confident in the future, watching his jockeys, perched on horses galloping around the track. It was a Monday in February, just after the Spring Festival, and the jockeys were prepping their mounts for the start of the racing season in March. The racetrack seemed to be fulfilling its promises to the local economy, bringing jobs and visitors. The villagers were welcome on the track, and sold egg pancakes and bowls of soup to hungry punters who attended the weekly races. Locals also accounted for most of the 1,000-worker payroll that fed and tended the horses and weeded the 2-kilometre dirt track.

Visiting the Beijing Jockey Club in 2004 was remarkably similar to a day out at a Western racetrack. The track bussed punters in from downtown Beijing to its summer season of racing in a rural pocket, one of the few remaining. The Club also had plans for a grandstand modelled on Hong Kong Jockey Club's Happy Valley track. But several years later the grandstand remained an architect's model in a glass case coated in dust in a corner of the boardroom of the Beijing Jockey Club. The project had run aground after disputes with authorities over unsanctioned betting activity. Punters were turned away in 2005 after local authorities told the Jockey Club its model of allowing punters to 'guess the winning horse' was gambling in all but name. A visit in the spring of 2012 revealed weeds and withering long grass choking the gates of the once-impressive Jockey Club. The sign remained, in yellow Chinese characters on a blue horseshoe-shaped arch which spelled the club's name. But the long-term future of the Jockey Club and its horses seems bound up with both local disputes and the legalisation of on-track betting.

The Beijing Jockey Club facility was developed twelve years ago by YP Cheng, a Hong Kong manufacturing tycoon who foresaw another fortune in bringing horseracing to mainland China. Connolly and a staff of Australian vets were hired, along with more than 100 local jockeys. Expensive horses were shipped in from all over the world. The track opened in 2001 and by 2003, according to Connolly, was operating a form of pari-mutuel betting which generated a modest daily turnover of 500,000 yuan ($62,000), apparently sanctioned by the local government.[25] The sudden closure of the track by the local public security bureau in 2005 was unexpected. Hundreds of horses were reported to have been euthanized and seven hundred personnel were dismissed. The $100 million invested by Cheng appeared to have been wasted.[26]

According to Connolly, the future of the track is now threatened by a local dispute about the rental value of land. Tongzhou is no longer the backwater it was when the leases for 150 hectares of land on which to build a racetrack were signed in 1997. Soaring prices have prompted the villagers to demand its return. In August 2009, villagers chained bicycles to the gates and laid siege in shifts of picketers who blocked supplies from entering the club for more than a month. Thirty horses died of starvation. Connolly claims he was locked out, forced to spend several weeks at home while his horses starved. The picket was lifted in October when authorities removed the villagers, promising them the issue would be resolved after the National Day festivities. Dozens of horses are slowly returning to health but will always bear the marks of starvation, hip bones protruding through dun-coloured skin. The only horses which appear to have escaped the ordeal are the club's two dozen stallions, champions purchased in order to create a dynasty of competitive racers for the Tongzhou track. Behind the white perimeter walls, now graffitied with villagers' protests, Connolly continues to oversee 1,750 thoroughbred horses in the hope that they will race or breed. Breeding is possible – Connolly sells an average of 150 horses a year to Chinese buyers. But racing appears unlikely. The success of this venture depended on Beijing legalising gambling, and this has not transpired. As Connolly says, 'putting on a race is an expensive business, and the club will only race if there's a return.'

The Royal Nanjing Jockey Club

A ban on gambling means that the traditional model of trackside betting is currently impossible in China.[27] But a Hong Kong-based coterie of wealthy investors has an alternative, non-gambling model that it hopes will enable racing to flourish. RS Management (RSM) has spent a reported $280 million on two tracks and a clubhouse at the Royal Nanjing Jockey Club (RNJC), which was scheduled to open in 2012 when the project was announced in 2009. The clubhouse has been completed, but racing appears unlikely in 2012 because of difficulties in securing local financing for the project, explained Amir Steven Johan, Corporate Strategy Adviser and Interim CEO at RSM. The Chinese government's tightening of credit in order to cool a bubbly housing market meant that securing cash has been harder than in the past year, said Johan. 'We are slowing down the race track development and in the meantime our members can enjoy the clubhouse until we're ready for racing.' But the original plans remain in place, he added. When the track opens, members will be able to watch twice-weekly (mid-week and weekends) race meetings from luxurious clubhouse seats scattered off a bar-restaurant on a 72-million-square-feet ecological resort planted with poplar trees and organic gardens in the outskirts of Nanjing, once capital of China.

Five racetracks were constructed in China during the 1990s, only to fail when the 'Strict Forbidden Order on Horseracing Gambling' was issued by five ministries (interpreted as a strong show of unanimity) in 2000. More recently, Tongzhou and Wuhan have also been unsuccessful. The RNJC hopes to avoid their fate by operating according to a system that can survive *without* support from betting revenues, traditionally conceived. In this way they maintain a first-entry presence in what could be an immense market if the law on betting should change at some point in the future. In the meantime, the RNJC will provide an exclusive facility for the growing numbers of newly wealthy Chinese.

According to the original design for the track, local executives will be able to entertain in corporate boxes facing the track, while individual members will watch the races from trackside leather chairs or an adjacent members-only bar and restaurant. A public grandstand will accommodate up to 5,000 punters whose race ticket also includes a buffet meal and a drink served up in the public area. In addition, a one-off prize will be shared between those who pick the winning horse. 'Local authorities don't mind, as long as we're not taking money from people to gamble,' Johan suggested. In place of official betting, horses owned by members will race for prize money at the track, in which RSM has a 60 per cent stake. Cash prizes at Nanjing will be sponsored by corporations with the right to name particular races: there will be a prize pot of $50,000 per race, with bumper $1 million prizes for special occasions such as Chinese New Year. RSM will earn stabling fees for looking after the horses of club members: Johan predicted that there will eventually be 4,000 horses on site as each horse will be restricted to a maximum of two races a month on grounds of health and well-being.

Despite the absence of a structure that facilitates betting in order to return some of the proceeds to racing, prize money is forthcoming: according to Johan, fifty of one hundred corporate memberships of the RNJC, each priced at $15.2 million, have already been sold: 'Its association with wealth makes racing a winner in China.' Johan predicts that 90 per cent of Nanjing members will be wealthy local businessmen. But there will also be outsiders: in addition to the RNJC, RSM is responsible for the Richman's Club, a worldwide chain of exclusive members clubs which sells memberships for up to $30 million, which buys access to yachts and horseracing clubs around the world.

No expense has been spared in Nanjing. RSM brought in experts from Australia and Qatar to oversee the laying of two tracks (one turf course, one sand all-weather surface) which will take two years to settle in. Although, initially, bloodstock will be kept 'affordable', 'these won't be Mongolian horses or any old rubbish, these are Arab and Thoroughbred horses', said Johan. The RNJC, which is licensed to import horses, will look for younger horses priced between 100,000 yuan ($15,875) and 200,000 yuan ($31,751). It is anticipated that betting members will wish to own at least five to six horses each. The club will have separate races for Arabs (thought to handle daytime heat) and thoroughbreds (which will race in the cooler evening and weekend meets). The Melbourne Equestrian Hospital will be responsible for the running of the Nanjing club's on-site equine clinic.

Johan is not betting on gambling being legalised anytime soon, and instead RSM plans to expand its membership-driven model to other cities by targeting the racing rights at China's other jockey clubs, including Beijing and

Guangzhou. While other territories in the region are turning to gambling to ease economic woes – Taiwan is building horseracing tracks and Singapore has opened casinos – China is the glaring absence on a list of members of the Asian Racing Federation, which includes relative minnows like Mauritius. The Nanjing model of China's rich paying membership fees to race for corporate-sponsored prize pots may work in Beijing, but Johan has also hedged his bets: Nanjing will also be ready in the event that gambling is legalised: 'Government will want to know there's a system in place to collect tax, a system that can be audited. We have that system.'

And finally … Welcome to Horse City!

One of the most intriguing recent developments in China's racing scene was the announcement in 2010 by the Dubai-based Meydan development company that it would build an equestrian city in Tianjin.[28] The joint enterprise of Meydan City Corporation (Dubai, United Arab Emirates), TAK Design Consultants (Malaysia) and Chinese partners Zhouji Jiye and Tianjin Farm Group would 'hold international and domestic professional horse races, promote and impart equine culture and knowledge to youths, provide tourism services for the public, and protect the wellbeing and interests of equines.' Horse City was also to offer apartments and offices, all in a comparative backwater belt of Tianjin which is an industrial city better known for its petrochemicals plants and factories. The proposal contained a mixture of optimism and reserve.

There were several reasons to suggest that the project might be successful. It enjoys a favourable location, close to Beijing, one of China's wealthiest cities and home to the greatest concentration of equestrian clubs, according to the Chinese Equestrian Association. Land is also relatively cheap in Tianjin, which is linked to the capital by a thirty-minute high-speed rail connection. One of the local partners, the Tianjin Farm Group, is a state-invested firm, suggesting good connections to local policy makers. Tianjin also has a track record as a testing ground for off-beat sports. China's first baseball stadium after the Communist Revolution in 1949 was built here – by the U.S.-based Dodgers team. The city has also been used by the government as a trial zone for financial innovations such as venture finance. On the other hand, the fortunes of Wuhan and Tongzhou suggest that betting is at best temporarily tolerated in its most innocuous forms, and that this tolerance may be withdrawn at any time and without warning. Without properly financed racing there seems less chance of success for a five- to seven-star international hotel with a capacity of 3,600 guests. It is difficult to imagine the international super-rich coming to China in order to watch pony racing and enter raffles. Even at the Dubai World Cup, the flagship event in a country where betting is also illegal, racegoers can enter the free Pick 7 competition for a cash prize.

The official announcement in 2010 noted that 'commencement of the construction of a horse racing field will depend on the decision of the State on commercial horse racing.' In particular, Meydan and its local partners promised to 'pay attention to and make proposals on the policy of the State in respect of commercial horse racing, seek the support of the State and local governments'. It seems that this dialogue may not have yielded the results intended, in the short term at least. According to the original plan, an equestrian college, stud and feedstuff plant were to be completed by the end of 2011. By the end of 2012 a horse-trading centre, hotel, clubhouse, shopping and entertainment centre were to have been completed. However, there was no evidence of these developments in Tianjin in the spring of 2012 – a failure to launch confirmed by calls to Meydan and design consultants on the project, TAK. The promise of 10,000 jobs, 'hundreds of millions of taxes and profits to the State within five years' and franchises across China will have piqued the interest of local officials. However, in 2012, officials in both Ninghe and Tianjin municipality declined to comment on the status of a project which is constrained by the same uncertainty that holds Wuhan and Tongzhou in a state of suspended animation. It remains to be seen whether the Royal Nanjing Jockey Club will buck the trend, but while its membership model may be one of the few legal ways to make a profit from racing in China currently, it will not replace traditional, illegal, low-stake betting as practiced by millions of Chinese, every day.

NOTES

1 In 2010, 82% of the 1,053 stud farms with broodmares stabled were to be found in the Hidaka area of Hokkaido, and 88% of the 256 thoroughbred stallions in Japan stood in Hokkaido. Additionally, 7,112 foals were produced in Japan in 2010. Production peaked at 10,188 in 1992 and has been in decline notably since 2003 – an effect attributed to shift from quantity to quality and also a decline in racing by local governments. Figures are taken from www.japanracing.jp. Accessed 13 March 2012.

2 Information about Japanese racing and the Japanese Racing Authority (JRA) can be found at: www.japanracing.jp/en/index.html. Accessed 13 March 2012.

3 Information about the National Association of Racing (NAR) can be found at: www.keiba.go.jp/guide/english/index.html. Accessed 13 March 2012.

4 Facts and figures about wagering can be found on the Web site of the International Federation of Horseracing Authorities at: www.horseracingintfed.com/wageringDisplay.asp?section=4. Accessed 13 March 2012.

5 Statistics taken from 'Taiki Farm' entry at: www.breederscup.com/bio.aspx?id=1992. Accessed 16 March 2012.

6 R. Pagones & J. Hickman, '"How to be a successful Irish breeder in Japan" by H. Sweeney', *The Racing Post*, 11 July 2003.

7 'John Murtagh wins 2011 world super jockey series title', *Horse Racing in Japan: News*, 4 December 2011. Available at: www.japanracing.jp/_news2011/111204-02.html. Accessed 13 March 2012.

8 R. Pagones, 'Rock Of Gibraltar colt stars on day one as new buyers contribute to "amazing figures"', *The Racing Post*, 14 July 2009.

9 The latest news about Vodka and her Sea the Stars colt can be found at the Gilltown Stud Web site: www.agakhanstuds.com/news/news_display.asp?NewsId=618. Accessed 16 March 2010.

10 In a novel race format, runners in the Takarazuka Kinen are selected partly by popular vote.

11 'Sheikh Mohammed attends racing at Tokyo racecourse on Derby Day', *Horse Racing in Japan: News*, 30 May 2011. Available at: www.japanracing.jp/_news2011/110530-02.html. Accessed 13 March 2012.

12 Blood-Horse Staff, 'Yoshida purchases top mare Sarafina', *Blood-Horse Magazine*, 20 January 2011.

13 J. Nevills, 'Cozi Rosie to Shadai Farm for $525,000', *Thoroughbred Times*, 10 January 2012.

14 For a recent interview with Teruya Yoshida, see *The Thoroughbred Daily News*, 'Q and A: Teruya Yoshida: July 12 2010', available at: www.thoroughbreddailynews.com/members/pdf/qna/qna100712.pdf. Accessed 16 March 2012.

15 'All JRA flat graded races have been opened to foreign-trained horses since 2010' in Japan Association for International Racing and Stud Book, *Horse Racing in Japan 2011* (Tokyo: Japan Racing Association, 2011), 14. A complete list of JRA Graded Races and other races open to foreign-trained horses is available at: www.japanracing.jp/en/information/jra-graded-races/index.html. Accessed 13 March 2012.

16 Y. Shimbun, 'Horse racing to get needed spur', *Daily Yomiuri Online*, 26 February 2012. Available at: www.yomiuri.co.jp/dy/national/T120225003116.htm. Accessed 16 March 2012.

17 Five Chinese officials, including Han Guocai, vice chairman of the China Horse Industry Association, visited stud farms in Hokkaido in December 2011. K. Funaki, 'Hokkaido racehorse breeders bet on China', *The Japan Times*, 27 January 2012.

18 A version of this material appeared in *The Market*, February–March 2012. It has been updated and expanded for the purposes of this chapter.

19 McKinsey have predicted that by 2015, China will account for 20% of all luxury sales worldwide. Y. Atsmon and V. Dixit, 'Understanding China's wealthy', *McKinsey Quarterly*, July 2009.

20 Sha Tin is the larger of the two racecourses in Hong Kong. It was built on reclaimed land in 1978. Happy Valley, the oldest, was built in 1845 by the British, for the British. Both are managed by the Hong Kong Jockey Club. For information about racing in Hong Kong, see www.hkjc.com/home/english/index.asp. Accessed 19 March 2012.

21 According to the Kentucky China Trade Centre, China has two breeds: the small domestic breed known as the Mongolian horse, which is used for farm work; and the larger Sanhe or Yili, improved breeds produced from imported stock. Kentucky China Trade Centre, *Chinese Equine Industry Overview* (2009), pp. 6–7. Available at: www.kentuckychinatrade.com/index.php?option=com_docman&task=doc_view&gid=12&Itemid=72. Accessed 13 March 2012.

22 D. Van, 'When will the horses run?' *China Daily*, 8 July 2011.

23 In 2012, an hour-long lesson cost 360 yuan, or $57.

24 Kentucky China Trade Centre, *Chinese Equine Industry Overview*, p. 3.

25 M. Jamieson, 'A China horseracing punt goes to put', *The Shanghaiist*, 23 November 2005.

26 N. Godfrey, 'Huge cull of racehorses at Beijing track', *The Guardian*, 22 November 2005. L. Sheng, 'Taking a gamble', *Global Times*, 1 July 2011.

27 Although gambling is illegal, it is also popular. For a helpful recent insight, see D. Eimer, 'China's secret gambling problem', *The Telegraph*, 9 January, 2010. Available at: www.telegraph.co.uk/news/worldnews/asia/china/6942975/Chinas-secret-gambling-problem.html. Accessed 13 March 2012.

28 The full announcement is available on the Dubai Racing Club Web site at: www.dubairacingclub.com/media-centre/news/meydan-joint-venture-develop-tianjin-horse-city-china. Accessed 18 March 2012.

13

MARK DAVIES

Global Markets, Changing Technology: The Future of the Betting Industry

Betting entered the twenty-first century largely unaltered over a period of forty years, but the next decade brought dramatic change. Whether evolution or revolution, for better or worse, was hotly debated, but one thing was beyond dispute: new technologies had changed the world of betting forever. How does racing, predicated as it has been for years on betting income, capture its slice of the funding pie now that anyone can place a bet on a race from a handheld device anywhere in the world? How can revenue be captured when markets and audiences are global and connected through flows of information that operate at lightning speed? How will these new forms of gambling affect the future of horseracing in the United Kingdom and elsewhere?

Few in horseracing, worldwide, initially paid the Internet much attention. Bookmakers first began to offer horseracing online in 1998, four years after gambling became available, but at the time, the Internet was no more than an additional channel of delivery – like the telephone, decades earlier – simply opening a new shop window onto a larger world. The basic betting product remained as it had been since the 1960s – a choice between traditional fixed-odds betting, where a bookmaker made a price; or the pari-mutuel system of the Tote.[1] This chapter focuses on the revolutionary potential of new technology, the threats and opportunities that it presented to horseracing and some of the results of the sport's incremental response to the rapidly changing world. I begin by reflecting upon the momentous changes brought about by betting exchanges.

Betting Exchanges

In June 2000, six companies came to market in quick succession with the same basic premise: that disintermediation – matching bets directly between customers, rather than having the betting operator carry a bet's risk – could deliver significantly better pricing to the market.[2] The model needed the

Internet, with its super-fast technology and its means of allowing thousands of people to interact simultaneously. It enabled punters to bargain over price in a way that had been impossible before.[3] Dubbed 'exchange betting', it was at the forefront of a host of developments in sports betting.[4]

In theory, exchange betting was not new, but brought the industry full circle: in the eighteenth century, bets on horseracing had been 'exchanged' between people gathered around a post on course, and only from 1800 onwards were individuals licensed to stand as a common counterparty.[5] Modern exchange betting brought significant new challenges which were compounded by the globalisation of betting and its attendant increase in players on an international scale, much greater competition, and significantly lower margins. They impacted sports betting in general, but the Sport of Kings was shaken it to its core.[6]

The mechanics of exchange betting hardly suggest they would produce a seismic shift in the landscape. Exchanges are promoted as platforms which allow customers to 'bet directly with each other'.[7] In reality they are bookmaking operations with sophisticated risk-management technology: the service provider accepts a bet only if it can pass on its full risk to a customer (or set of customers) with an equal and opposite view.[8] Traditional bookmakers managed risk through a 'field book' – a mechanism which gave them a picture of their liabilities across a selected range of their shops. The composition of shops was carefully chosen to ensure a representative sample of liabilities, and selected shops relayed each bet placed with them to the bookmaker's head office, where the field book was assembled. The operator could manage his overall position as it saw fit, often by sending money to the racecourse to back any horse(s) on which it had been 'filled in'.[9] More recently, the system was replaced in most traditional bookmaker shops by automated Electronic Point of Sale (EPOS) software.[10]

Exchanges, in contrast, used proprietary technology to accept and match bets only if their risk balanced perfectly, or accept in principle and advertise the availability of those bets on a Web site if they did not. The effect was that customers were seen to choose their own price, and to bet with each other; but in fact, the exchange could stand as counterparty to all bets (and could even decide to take risk) without the 'front end' of the Web site looking any different, and no price which is 'off-market' could be matched.[11] Although it is argued that because exchanges act only as agents in a manner not true of traditional bookmakers, or that in charging a commission on winnings (rather than building the cost to the customer into their overall book), the model differs fundamentally, in fact the similarity of the structural process by which bets are placed and settled is easy to demonstrate. The professional punter, Alan Potts, wrote five years before the creation of the first betting exchange: 'The bookies act as agents for the market and take a percentage of the losers' money before redistributing it among the winners. ... The crux is that winning punters do not take their profits from the bookies, but from the losing punters' – a description that applies equally to the traditional bookmaking operators as it does to the exchanges.[12]

There were other innovations in the industry: price comparison sites such as Oddschecker had blown apart what had been described as bookmaking's 'cosy cartel', allowing a host of new bookmaking brands such as Paddy Power and Bet365 to threaten the supremacy of the traditional 'Big Three'.[13] But the pioneer of the exchange, Betfair, was at the forefront of every part of the developing industry.[14] It was at once the most competitive offering in a world increasingly driven by competition; the easiest way to take a position either side of an outcome (leading many, despite it being *possible* on other platforms, to state that exchanges allowed 'every person to act as a bookie' and causing arguments to rage over whether it was 'right' to 'make money out of horses losing races'); and the catalyst to further innovation, such as the ability – almost unknown in the twentieth century – to bet 'in-running', from the 'off' right up until the first horse crossed the line.[15]

Regulating Innovation

More crucial than innovation, however, was competitiveness, which was built into the exchanges' structure in a way that is still rarely understood. Exchanges immediately passed bets between counterparties, so they had no need to add the traditional model's risk margin of perhaps 1.5 to 2 per cent per runner. That left only the operator's commercial margin (charged, usually, as a commission on winnings). This was often confused with an overall fall in commercial margin which was being driven, independently, by market competition – a separate phenomenon in which Betfair undoubtedly had some impact, but arguably no more than other online players.[16] The effect, of course, was the same whatever the cause, and the commercial challenge soon combined with moral, political and regulatory objections.

Traditionally, bookmakers had been regulated, rather than their customers, but the arrival of exchanges, offering options of 'back' and 'lay', suggested that the distinction between the two had been dulled, at best. Claiming that the failure to license those who could oppose horses led to integrity problems for the sport, Racing and the established betting industry called for exchange customers to be regulated as if they were bookmakers.[17] The three-year scrutiny of the UK Gambling Act 2005 took place in the midst of heated debate worldwide: the febrile atmosphere bordered on hysteria.[18]

In Britain, much of the argument centred around allegations of race fixing culminating in two high-profile cases in March 2004. The first involved then-champion jockey Kieren Fallon 'dropping his hands' and losing a nineteen-length lead aboard Ballinger Ridge at Lingfield Park. The second alleged that Sean Fox 'stepped off' Ice Saint after the ninth fence of the Beginners' Chase at Fontwell six days later, and was carried in a front-page photo-story in *The Sun* under the headline 'Jump Jockey!'[19] In this and other articles, an apparent increase in instances of race fixing was linked to the potential for unlicensed and unregulated 'layers' to bet against a horse.

Arguing that they could track every detail of every bet, Betfair established a Memorandum of Understanding with the Jockey Club in June 2003.[20] This led to information-sharing agreements between other operators across Europe and further afield, marking a fundamental change in an industry in which client confidentiality had been sacrosanct.[21] This was not the end of the debate, however. In 2004, Ladbrokes' Chief Executive Chris Bell suggested to the BBC that 'a race a day [was being] fixed', at least in part because of the failure to regulate all layers.[22]

The Parliamentary Joint Scrutiny Committee which looked at the Gambling Act believed that 'the image of the exchanges has been tarnished, however unfairly, as a direct consequence of the fact that they were the preferred betting medium in a number of recently publicized cases involving suspicious betting patterns', but also stated that 'we have no wish to put in place unduly onerous obligations on the operators of betting exchanges.' In its response, the government 'confirmed that persons using betting exchanges in the course of business would require an operating licence', and required all customers of exchanges to be registered with the operator, as those in operation by that time were already doing.[23] In their turn, exchanges argued that the word 'layer' had falsely become synonymous with bookmaking: in context, it simply meant betting on an outcome 'not to happen' – the mathematical equivalent of betting on the remaining outcomes to occur. Backing and laying, they claimed, were two sides of the same coin.[24]

This outcome failed to settle the dispute. Although concerns about integrity had been dismissed by many within the racing establishment by the time the Gambling Act passed in April 2005, the financial impact of the exchanges continued to exercise many Racing minds.[25] The problem became acute as the decade turned, with levy yields on British racing falling dramatically from their 2007–08 peak.[26] Two principal causes were mooted: an acceleration in the movement of bookmaking offshore, and the existence of would-be Levy payers acting 'as bookmakers' on exchanges without a commensurate payment in dues.[27] The argument that racing was losing market share to other products was largely rejected on the grounds that the overall quantum of horseracing betting was continuing to increase, but it was clear from bookmakers' annual reports that singles bets on football (previously not offered owing to fears of potential match fixing), the introduction of Fixed-Odds Betting Terminals (FOBTs) (seen by some as turning High Street bookmaker shops into mini-casinos) and the increasing popularity of 'virtual racing' were eating significantly into racing's dominance of punters' activity.[28] Between 1999 and 2004, the proportion of bookmaking revenues generated by racing fell from approximately 60 per cent to approximately 40 per cent; by 2011, it had fallen below 30 per cent.[29]

Changes in legislation brought no clarity, because arguments about claimed 'bookmaking' were firmly entrenched on both sides. Neither the passing of the Gambling Act nor the publication later that year of a Treasury report into the issue convinced Racing to declare the case closed, with so much at stake.[30] A Levy Board consultation in July 2010 invited further submissions: the rejection of that motion for change in turn – through a casting vote from Chairman Paul Lee in June 2011 – led the Chairman of the British Horseracing Association Paul Roy to comment that the Levy Board had a 'lack of balls' when it came to dealing with bookmakers and betting exchanges.[31] At the time of writing, it seems unlikely that the last of the debate has been heard. Little has changed since it was first alleged that exchange layers 'drove a cart and horses through legislation', except the overall level of business done by Betfair; but the prevalence of professional punters – a class never previously taxed or licensed, while long having its existence documented both in law and anecdote – is on the rise.[32]

The Future of Funding for Racing

Bets, like other kinds of promises, are immaterial. This has made it especially difficult for governments to contain betting within their national borders and is a particular challenge to traditional state-based betting monopolies. In France, Hong Kong and Japan, customer demand for broader product or keener pricing has resulted in the growth of black markets estimated to be worth at least as much as the legitimate offering.[33] In Britain, with greater competition, the black market is less of a threat, but the impact on horseracing of losing customers to other betting products has been just as pronounced. Around the world, the horseracing industry has fought a rearguard action to arrest a decline rooted principally in the loss of almost two-centuries-long hegemony.[34] What new challenges face racing at this juncture, and how are they being met?

Mature racing jurisdictions have sought to 'dig in' against the ravages of competition, with varied success. Statistics published in 2004 demonstrated that among the major horseracing nations, the return to owners was greater in Hong Kong, Japan and France than in Australia, Britain and Ireland – the latter three open to competition to a greater or lesser extent.[35] The question is what effect so-called 'punter power' will have over the longer term with the Internet making it increasingly difficult for governments to put barriers around their preferred domestic product. It is too early to say whether the maintenance of higher-margin betting product in those countries that return the most money to racehorse owners constitutes a successful defence of the status quo or an extension of a final few hours in the sun.

The decline of margin may be an inevitable corollary of competition to which horseracing will have to adapt. Some argue that falling commercial margin should not be seen as an issue: a drop should not, in itself, be a problem if turnover rises by a commensurate amount.[36] But the difficulty for horseracing is that it cannot, casino-like, spin the wheel an unlimited number of times: the quality of fixtures remains important, the horse is a living creature, and the sport is expensive to produce.[37] Commercial reality may therefore dictate that in a world with multiple products the trend away from horserace betting will continue.

The impact of competition from other sports can hardly be overstated. Outside Britain, both empirical and anecdotal evidence suggests that horseracing's betting supremacy is under threat.[38] Hong Kong legalised football betting in 2003, and within a few years it had a third of the overall market share by turnover.[39] Governments in Europe have, since 2005, moved closer towards regulatory systems that allow betting on a variety of new products. Some, such as France, have protected the horseracing industry by restricting the number of betting operators that can offer bets on its product, but they have not, in turn, limited the number of sports upon which those other licensed operators unable to make prices on horseracing can offer bets instead.[40] Several horseracing authorities worldwide are trying to move towards a system whereby betting operators need to pay for the 'right to bet', following a model successfully adopted in various states in Australia, but here, too, debate rages: there is argument over what constitutes intellectual property, what Racing has to 'sell' other that pictures (discussed later in the chapter) and what is the most suitable way to charge for the 'right', if one is created and accepted.[41]

Some argue that the solution lies in pari-mutuel betting, where a percentage is taken from the pool of bets to cover the operator's costs (and, if allowed, profit), and whatever is left is given back to winning punters (weighted by the amount of money in the pool that was placed on each of the horses placed). A fixed percentage of the pool is taken out, whatever the pool's size; thus, a tax on the take-out produces returns which rise commensurately with the pool's growth, and horseracing receives a consistent return. In reality, the return's predictability is not dependent on the bets being in a pool, but on the tax being levied on turnover rather than profit. That system in turn relies on the existence of a single operator, which is why it remains in place where totalisator betting is offered in a monopoly format. It breaks down as the world becomes more competitive and a betting provider (either of a pool or of fixed-odds) cuts its price.[42]

Racing authorities worldwide have argued forcefully that this is the betting operators' problem and not theirs.[43] But it becomes a racing problem if the solution for the betting operator is to offer its customers a different product. The central point is this: demanding payment on the basis of turnover is an invitation to operators to keep prices high, because raising margin reduces turnover. This in turn makes the horseracing product relatively uncompetitive compared with alternative betting products which charge either on the basis of gross profit (thus allowing price competition) or not at all.

The solution, for some in horseracing, has been to seek turnover-based payments across the board, forcing bookmaking to maintain uniform (but artificially high) margin, and to remove the incentive for punters to bet on other sports or products. But as this chapter has shown, responses such as these seek to hold back the Internet tide, and ignore the black market operators. They also run counter to the consumer-orientated strategies of most governments, and are unlikely to find political support in the long term except in the most hierarchical (and closed) racing jurisdictions.

How might Racing meet these challenges? Some are urgently seeking funding models not predicated on betting, and one solution – inspired by the success of the English Premier League after its launch in 1990 – has been to focus on monetising the rights to television pictures, which, it is clear, has been important to bookmakers since their introduction in the 1980s.[44] It is widely accepted that racing pictures get punters 'through the doors' of betting shops; but the unhappy irony for Racing is that their success has accelerated the diversification inside shops to products which compete for the punter's pound.

The relevance of pictures online was established more slowly: betting had been available online for the better part of a decade before Web sites first streamed pictures – partly for the obvious reason that Internet customers often bet at home while watching television. This was another difficulty for racing: until bookmakers embraced live streaming, the 'use' of pictures was already paid for by personal subscription by the bookmaker's customer – a frustration compounded by the knowledge that in-race pictures were crucial in facilitating the major growth area of betting product in the last decade – in-running betting.[45] A key difference between how punters can bet today and what was possible a decade ago lies in the ability to place or lay off bets right up until the moment that the winning horse crosses the line.

From 1986 until 2006, all UK racecourses sold their pictures to one company, Satellite Information Services (SIS), which in turn was the sole supplier to betting shops, via its television channel, FACTS.[46] SIS was (and remains) partly owned by the United Kingdom's largest bookmakers.[47] As such, until 2006, the bookmaking industry effectively enjoyed a monopoly on the purchase and supply of horseracing pictures. Eventually a consensus formed amongst a number of British racecourses that lack of competition in the process of negotiating product rights meant that they were being undersold, so half the UK racecourses advanced a plan that they hoped would monetise their media rights more effectively: they created a rival to SIS in the market, establishing a joint venture between Racing UK – a shareholding comprising thirty of the sixty British racecourses – and technology company Alphameric Plc, which they called Turf TV.

The intention was to foster competition in the market: racecourses would be paid more for their rights if the rival broadcasters had to bid against each other for contracts. But the respective ownerships of the competing broadcasters – with SIS perceived to be 'bookmaker-owned' and Turf TV 'racing-owned' – led to dispute, and the UK government had to intervene as a referee when the bookmakers questioned the validity of Turf TV's contracts.[48] Despite early difficulties, however, competition has resulted in media rights' payments to the British racing industry increasing dramatically: by 2011, its growth was sufficient for prize money to rise, despite a significant drop in the levy.[49]

The World

As we enter the second decade of the twenty-first century, attention turns to the international market, where the export of media rights alongside pool betting may present British horseracing with a significant opportunity. In many horseracing jurisdictions, a sole pool-betting operator remains the dominant (sometimes only) legal outlet for consumers to bet on races; and in partnership with the UK Tote operator, racecourses are attempting to facilitate global 'co-mingling' of pools. Though the concept is still relatively new, media rights may prove to be the key to such deals. The ambition of British Racing is to allow international pool operators access, as a package, to both the UK pool and the live stream from UK courses – thereby allowing international punters both to watch races and to bet on them. The sale by government, in June 2011, of the Horseracing Totalisator Board (the 'Tote') to the Manchester-based bookmaker Betfred now means that two independent commercial organisations will need to sell the combined betting-and-pictures product jointly, but doing so successfully would present British racing with a significant commercial windfall.[50] The combination of technology and media rights opens up a new and potentially lucrative revenue stream.

The value of pictures, whether sold domestically or internationally, is, however, considered by most in racing to be an additional revenue stream rather than an alternative to a betting-related one (although the bookmaking industry, in turn, believes that pictures are all that Racing actually has to 'sell'), and a replacement for the levy, by 2011 widely viewed as an anachronism, remains at the forefront of both Racing and government agendas in Britain.[51] The Department for Culture, Media and Sport launched a consultation in May of that year, suggesting a series of alternatives, including a 'right to bet' which closely followed the system adopted for sport under French legislation.[52]

Is Britain leading the world into a modern betting future, or being slow in following other countries in establishing proper protections for horseracing? The bookmaking industry believes that adopting the French model enshrines a non-existent 'right' and fails to take into account the likely reaction of consumers confronted with costs which would not be levied by unlicensed but easily accessible operators globally. Racing believes that the rest of the world is succeeding in protecting long-established industries in the face of commercial behaviour bordering on piracy as part of a 'race to the bottom'. Which side will win the argument remains to be seen, but the battle lines have long since been drawn.

What can be learned from these reflections? Twenty-five years after Jocelyn de Moubray wrote about the impact of the cheap movement of racehorses by air upon the international pattern, the paddock at Royal Ascot reflects the contemporary internationalism that has produced the modern thoroughbred racehorse.[53] This revolution is less fully realised in the funding of racing. Administrators and operators have yet to grapple with the essentially fluid and global market for betting that the Internet has created, while ongoing culture clashes between Racing and the old and new betting industries retard progress in finding innovative and equitable solutions to funding problems. Media rights and commingling may bring new markets, but if racing is to enter a new and profitable cosmopolitan era, energy currently spent resisting perceived threats will have to be redirected towards building alliances with colleagues and customers, wherever they may be.

NOTES

1. The main Act which regulated betting in the United Kingdom before the Gambling Act 2005, including defining a 'bookmaker', was the Betting, Gaming and Lotteries Act 1963. However, betting shops were legalised in 1961.

2. The six companies were Betfair, Flutter, Intrade, Betswap, Betmart and Play2Match. By December 2001, only Betfair remained – the result of a merger between the original Betfair and the investment funding behind their rival Flutter. The remainder went bust.

3. Bets with any bookmaker can, in theory, be haggled over. Students of Contract Law learn in *Carlill v. Carbolic Smoke Company* (1893) about the 'invitation to treat', which applies equally to a bookmaker's price on a board: the price is an invitation to make an offer to the bookmaker, which may be declined (or declined in part).

4. The name was coined within weeks of Betfair's launch, although it is not clear where it first appeared. Despite their parent company being called 'The Sporting Exchange', Betfair initially called their product-offering 'Open Market Betting'.

5. C. Sydney, *The Art of Legging* (London: Maxline International, 1976). There were illegal 'street bookies' until shops were legalised in 1961.

6. 'Exchanges tear at the very core of racing's heartbeat', *The Australian*, 15 October 2004.

7. 'Betting exchanges [...] enable punters to bet directly with each other, rather than with bookmakers.' *Research Paper 04/79*, House of Commons library, 28 October 2004, p. 33.

8. M. Davies, L. Pitt, D. Shapiro and R. Watson, 'BetFair.com: five technology forces revolutionize worldwide wagering', *European Management Journal*, 23 (2005), 533–41.

9. 'At small race meetings, when the market is weak, a hedging bet of as little as several hundred pounds may be sufficient to significantly affect the odds', William Hill Share Offer, Price Range Prospectus, May 2002, p. 30. Available at: www.global-documents.morningstar.com/documentlibrary/document/8722daf31b9a2871.msdoc/original. Accessed 6 February 2012.

10. Alphameric claims that 5,000 shops in Britain now use this system; see: www.alphameric.com/epos-solutions. Accessed 6 February 2012.

11. 'Betdaq has created a separate company, Exchange Trading Strategies, to trade markets whose aim will not be in making money, but in kickstarting trading while avoiding any financial conflict', Betdaq owner Dermot Desmond quoted in *The Racing Post*, 7 January 2005. Any exchange can stand as counterparty to bets without any optical change. Indeed, Betfair's international business is linked to its UK-facing business through Betfair Malta matching bets on one side and delivering them the other.

12. A. Potts, *Against the Crowd* (London: Aesculus Press, 1995), p. 15.

13. A. Salmond MSP, 'Power Play Deserves to Succeed', *The Scotsman*, 27 July 2002. 'The Big Three' are Ladbrokes, William Hill and Coral.

14. Betfair's order-driven exchange concept, modelled on the New York Stock Exchange, was created by the company's co-founder, Andrew Black. *The Racing Post* described it as synonymous with its product: 'Betfair is to betting exchanges,

[what] Sellotape, Hoover and Biro once were to sticky tape, vacuum cleaners and ballpoint pens' (21 October 2003).

15 A. Aitken, 'Exchanges: a foe to be used, not feared', *South China Morning Post*, 22 January 2003. Comments by the Classic-winning trainer John Gosden and BHB Chairman Peter Savill, quoted in *The Herald Sun* (Melbourne), 19 October 2004.

16 Betfair, *The Funding Question*, 24 November 2003.

17 Who runs horseracing is often debated, but collectively its various factional elites are conventionally described as 'Racing'. Capitalisation refers to the sport's hierarchy, as opposed to the sport itself. By the end of the decade, the British Horseracing Association (BHA) was leading this position publicly; but its then chief executive, Greg Nichols, confirmed to the author that, behind the scenes, it took a strong line from the start, lobbying ministers from 2004.

18 Australian Racing Board CEO Andrew Harding said that allowing exchanges would be 'like taking a suicide pill' (*The Australian*, 23 September 2004), while Tasmanian Shadow Racing Minister Sue Napier said it would 'sound the death-knell (sic) for the racing industry' (Press release, 5 April 2005). See also 'Racing for Ribbons: Exchanges to reduce prize money by 75%', *Daily Telegraph* (Sydney), 27 July 2004; 'Racing primed for war', *Herald Sun*, 25 July 2004; 'UK race-fix scandal fuels betting exchange bonfire', *Sydney Morning Herald*, 3 September 2004; and "Internet deal will 'devastate' racing", *Illawarra Mercury*, 23 July 2004.

19 'Sean Fox comes neatly off his mount', *The Sun*, 9 March 2004.

20 The MOU came into effect on 16 June. At the time, the Jockey Club was responsible for regulation.

21 Ladbrokes signed an agreement with the Jockey Club in the United Kingdom in January 2004. William Hill declined to give names relating to betting on Man Mood, a horse which underperformed at Warwick on 5 November 1996, citing the Data Protection Act. See D. McCrystal, *The Observer*, 13 October 2002 and an episode of the BBC investigative program *Panorama* broadcast in 2002. Available at: www.news.bbc.co.uk/1/shared/spl/hi/programmes/panorama/horse_racing/html/number3.stm. Accessed 6 February 2012.

22 *The Money Programme*, BBC2, 2 June 2004.

23 'We think betting exchanges are a good thing. They must not be forced abroad by unnecessary regulations', John Greenway, MP, announcing the publication of the report by the Joint Committee on the Draft Gambling Bill in 2004. Available at: www.parliament.uk/business/committees/committees-archive/jcdgb/jcdgb-press-notice-10/. Accessed 6 February 2012.

24 *Betfair briefing notes*, 13 February 2004 and 27 October 2009.

25 'I think the betting exchange is quite good because it will show up who is actually not playing the game right', jockey Frankie Dettori quoted in *The News of the World*, 5 November 2004; 'The real watershed for racing was betting exchanges because they didn't cause corruption, they brought it out into the open and exposed what was already there', Paul Scotney, Director of Security at the BHA, quoted in *The Guardian*, 29 August 2007.

26 'Levy falls by 8%', *Horserace Betting Levy Board Press Release*, 15 July 2007. The 46th Levy Scheme returned approximately £153 million; the 47th scheme, £146 million.

27 The Joint Scrutiny Committee was the first to consider the concept of 'non-recreational layers' in their 2004 report. See paragraphs 537–541 of the Joint Committee on the Gambling Bill, available at: www.publications.parliament.uk/pa/jt200304/jtselect/jtgamb/63/63.pdf. Accessed 6 February 2012. These two causes are the most commonly identified, but not exhaustive. Racing has also cited 'loopholes' in the current system, including 'threshold rules originally set up to exempt only small independent high street bookmakers', and even, most controversially, the fact that 'no Levy is received from bets being placed in Britain on overseas racing'. 'British racing unites to secure fair return from betting'. Available at: www.racingunited.co.uk. Accessed 6 February 2012.

28 'Racing's market share […] is in serious decline', *Sydney Morning Herald*, 3 November 2010. According to the *Telegraph*, the number of planning applications for licensed bookmaker premises in the United Kingdom rose from 39 in 2001 to 340 in 2004, an increase commonly attributed to the introduction of FOBTs. R. Evans, 'Betting shop gaming machines cause concern', *The Daily Telegraph*, 4 March 2005. For more reaction to FOBTs, see Lord James of Blackheath, *Hansard*, Vol. 695, No. 132, 11 October 2007, p. 395 and C. McKenzie, 'BHA Boss Roy wants Breeders Cup in 2012', *The Daily Mail*, 22 October 2007.

29 *Ladbrokes Annual Reports*, 1999, 2004 and 2011.

30 *The Taxation of Betting Exchanges and Their Customers* (London: HM Treasury Review, 2004).

31 The consultation finally ended as a result of two votes: the first, passed five against three, asked whether to accept two independent Queen's Counsels' opinions and not to go to court for a ruling on the matter; the second, with Lee breaking a four votes to four outcome, decided whether to pursue exchange customers for Levy. The Board comprises three independent members (including the Chairman), three appointed by the racing industry, one from the Bookmakers' Committee, and the Chairman of the Tote. For a full report, see G. Wood, 'Racing is burying its head in the sand with Paul Roy's bunker mentality', *The Guardian*, 27 June 2011.

32 John Brown, Chairman of William Hill, on Channel 4's *Morning Line*, 27 July 2002. The phrase was used repeatedly in the coming months, notably by ABB Chief Executive Tom Kelly to the author (see www.markxdavies.com/2010/03/10/abb-agm/). For case law relating to professional gamblers, see *Graham v. Green* (1925). Patrick Veitch claims to have made 10 million pounds betting with traditional bookmakers in *Enemy Number One: The Secrets of the UK's Most Feared Professional Punter* (London: Racing Post, 2009).

33 A government-commissioned report into the opening of the French Gambling Market by Bernard Durieux estimated in March 2008 that 5,000 gambling Web sites were available to the French. EU Internal Markets Commissioner Michel Barnier put the number at 15,000 by May 2010, and a Barclays Capital research note published on 8 June 2010 quoted the Web site www.investir.fr as saying that 20,000 now targeted France. The French regulator, ARJEL, had issued fewer than forty licences by 2011.

34 See J. Ashton, *The History of Gambling in England* (London, 1898), pp. 173–84.

35 *The Racing Post*, 6 October 2004. Argentina came first, with Hong Kong sixth, Japan nineteenth, France twenty-first, Australia twenty-seventh and Britain thirty-seventh out of forty-seven nations. The statistics were supplied by each country and presented to the International Federation of Horseracing Authorities' annual conference in Paris. Similarly, French racing's annual report of 2005 lists 'average prize money per horse' in Hong Kong at €53,829, against €24,726 in Japan, €12,570 in France, €7,899 in Great Britain and €6,685 in Australia. The most recent (2009) data can be found at: www.horseracingintfed. com/resources/Annual_Report_2009.pdf. Accessed 6 February 2012.

36 D. Paton, D. Siegel and L. Vaughan Williams, 'Gambling Taxation: A Comment', *Australian Economic Review*, 34 (2001), 437–40.

37 L. Mottershead, 'Quantity not quality is the key to success for racing', *The Racing Post*, 1 September 2011.

38 See footnote 29.

39 *Hong Kong Jockey Club Corporate Results, 2009–10*. Available at: www.cor-porate.hkjc.com/corporate/operation/english/09-10-results.aspx. Accessed 6 February 2012. Racing's turnover was HKD 71,647 million; football accounted for HKD 38,908 million.

40 Horserace betting in France is legal only through the totalisator *Pari Mutuel Urbain* (PMU) under the April 2010 law. Punters can, however, bet with a variety of licensed operators on any other sport.

41 In any case, only in Hong Kong does Racing get the proceeds. In other jurisdictions with a 'Right to Bet', the fee goes to the relevant sport.

42 For example, if a betting operator is taxed at 3 pence in the pound, and his take-out is 30 pence in the pound, you can say he is being charged 3% of turnover or 10% of profit. But if, through price competition, he drops his take-out to 18 pence and his tax remains at 3 pence, then, while still paying 3% of his turnover, he will pay 18% of profit.

43 This point was made repeatedly at the 2010 Asian Racing Conference in Sydney, most notably by the Australian delegates. A round-up of news from the conference can be accessed at: www.ifhaonline.org/newsDisplay.asp?story=676. Accessed 6 February 2012. Racing New South Wales CEO Peter V'Landys has been particularly vocal on the subject of betting exchanges and corporate (i.e. non-state) bookmakers, declaring that 'if we don't put a stop to it now, we are bloody idiots' (quoted in *The Sydney Morning Herald*, 23 July 2004).

44 M. Armytage, 'Nic Coward calls for a substantial levy increase', *The Telegraph*, 9 January 2008.

45 First offered by Betfair in early 2002.

46 Satellite Information Services (Holdings) Ltd (SISH) is based in Corsham Street, London. For more information, see www.sis.tv/sis-facts. Accessed 6 February 2012.

47 J. Moore, 'The battle for TV rights in racing', *The Independent*, 25 July 2007. See also *Owner*, 43 (July–August 2004).

48 Department of Culture Media and Sport Statement, *47th Horserace Betting Levy Determination*, 2008. Competition Case Note, *Bookmakers' Afternoon Greyhound Services vs. Amalgamated Racing Services*, Monckton Chambers, 2008.

49 Horseman's Group Chairman, Alan Morecambe, told *The Racing Post* that prize money would rise from £139 million to £152 million in a year. 'Even with a levy that's reducing we have other income streams, like media rights, that are increasing very fast. [...] This cake [...] looks like it might get bigger next year.' (J. Lees, 'Tariff levels could rise next year as Horseman's Group eyes media rights income', 29 July 2011).

50 A joint venture between the two British broadcasters, Racing UK and At the Races, called GBI, was formed to sell the picture rights internationally on 1 March 2010. For more information, see www.gbiracing.com. Accessed 6 February 2012.

51 And long before in some quarters. See 'The Abolition of the Levy', *Owner*, 41 (February–March 2004).

52 CMS 173473/DC, dated 5 May 2011.

53 J. De Moubray, *The Thoroughbred Business* (London: Hamish Hamilton, 1986).

14

CHRIS MCCONVILLE

Horseracing: Local Traditions and Global Connections

Invented in 1855 by Admiral Rous, the dictatorial handicapper for the English Jockey Club, the weight-for-age scale (WFA) has shaped global racing and breeding for more than 150 years. A remarkably resilient measure, WFA cemented an all-pervasive 'Englishness' across the sport and Rous's scale still ensures consistent global standards in thoroughbred racing. Rous arrived in Sydney Harbour in 1827, a British naval captain commanding the frigate *Rainbow*. He had soon formed a thoroughbred-importing firm in Launceston. Rous stood his own English stallion, Emigrant, so as to improve the colonial-breds, and after a posting to India, returned to Sydney with the thoroughbred mare, Iris. He then acquired 5,000 hectares of good horse pasture near today's Canberra.[1] Despite such colonial opportunities, Rous turned his back on New South Wales, sailing for England in 1829 where he survived a court martial, before turning to a career as steward and handicapper with the Jockey Club.[2]

On the one hand, Rous embodies the English character of racing, disseminated from Ascot and Newmarket to far-off corners of the globe. On the other, in his brief Antipodean sojourn, Rous's breeding efforts hybridised the thoroughbred and played a part in the divergent trajectory of racing and breeding in Australasia and Asia.[3] For unlike other sporting spectaculars, thoroughbred racing has benefited from a long tradition of globalising figures, Rous amongst them. Some aspects of this globalism are no doubt intensifying. Fees paid for services by shuttle stallions or the riches lavished on winners of events like the Japan Cup point to a global commerce in racing, breeding and increasingly in gambling. By the same token, alongside such signs of global interchange, we can still find places in which horses and horsepeople inhabit an intensely familiar landscape, where horizons are narrowing rather than broadening. Looking over a lush Ballydoyle in Ireland, Vincent O'Brien, one of the guiding hands in the global Coolmore bloodstock business once confided, 'I could never leave here.'[4] Racing people have acquired the language of globalism and yet their dreams can remain unshakeably localised.

Other sports have found themselves thrust from parochial settings into global contests very recently and very rapidly. Horseracing, in contrast, can look back to a long history of globalism, so that an interconnected world appears neither threatening nor enticing. Rous's experiments with weight scales and colonial breeding fitted with a trade in horses and a racing network that quickly hybridised English origins. English racing was initially mimicked around the globe. Its subsequent absorption into local folkways resulted eventually in racing owners and professionals setting out from distant parts for England itself, intent on competing in the home of horseracing. Others were content to build up regional networks for horse sales and racing. Understanding the complexities of the global and the local in racing requires us to look back to these reworkings of English precedent, to attempts at creating a global racing system and to the regional and local networks of today's thoroughbred world.

Adaptation and Innovation

Historians are firmly committed to depicting horseracing as a cultural practice whose origins flowed from the core of imperial England to colonial and other peripheral places.[5] Equally significant were the steps taken in India and elsewhere to modernise racing without relying on either English precedent or American commercialism. Initially, English racing structures were adopted in the United States and France, as historians insist. With more than eighty stallions from Britain imported to the United States between 1830 and 1839, together with the transition from an elite pursuit to a moneymaking trade, through bodies such as the Kentucky Import Company, racing in the United States, as Huggins reminds us, had taken on a transnational identity before 1840.[6] By century's end, English jockeys were riding in the United States and U.S. trainers, horses and owners became familiar figures in English racing centres like Newmarket.

In France, Japan and Latin America, regions outside the Anglophone sphere, racing was organised with 'an acknowledgement that England is the place where racing standards were set'.[7] English race promoters, Lemon noted, had themselves moved beyond the boundaries of empire, setting up racetracks in France early in nineteenth century, with a track at St Malo ready for racing in 1840. Perhaps less controversially than in the newly democratic United States, the Restoration enabled English and aristocratic ways to be adapted to post-revolutionary France. By mid-century, Robert Black claimed that thoroughbred trainers in France were English 'to a man' – with more than a score working at Chantilly alone.[8] Indeed, only an untimely demotic mob had forestalled thorough anglicisation of French horse sports before 1830:

> But for the Great Revolution which interfered with so many possibilities and probabilities, horse-racing on English principles might have become naturalised in France before the commencement of the nineteenth century, instead of having to wait for the revolution of July 1830, the patronage of the popular Duke d'Orléans, son of Louis Philippe, and the foundations of the French Jockey Club in 1833.[9]

Once English ways were established in France, England's own classic races became targets for French owners, so that European horses eventually took on races including the Derby – an integration welcomed in elite circles but rejected amongst more proletarian racegoers.[10]

Argentina's elite also took to the model of the Jockey Club in pursuit of a patrician French identity, a process described as an acquisition of 'English culture and achievement through French mediation'.[11] Needell saw 'the decision to found a jockey club – the epitome, of course, of such emblematic aristocratic English phenomena as horseracing and the gentleman's club – was taken by four members of the Argentine elite at a Parisian restaurant after attending the Derby at Chantilly'.[12] The Jockey Club building in Calle Florida, Buenos Aires and the 1908 Beaux-Arts grandstand at the Palermo track (for a time Argentina's only turf track) stand as signs of both French acculturation and English standards in sports and gentlemanly exclusiveness.[13] Local hierarchies were thus cemented by 'national elites whose self-legitimisation entailed successful replication of the style and achievements of foreign elites'.[14]

In gambling, French racecourses brought about their own innovation – the now globalised totalisator was a form of gambling originating in France as the pari-mutuel and mechanised in New Zealand by George Julius, son of an anti-gambling Anglican bishop.[15] The English preference for the bookmaker and fixed odds remained a more localised, almost eccentric racetrack spectacle, and even in India observers pointed to gambling by way of lotteries and sweeps rather than totes and bookies' odds.[16] When race clubs in India eventually did turn to a mechanised tote, they sought out the Julius design and bought their equipment from Adelaide, South Australia, rather than from Europe.[17]

Indian racing had commenced as the exclusive possession of the elite of the British Army's officer corps and the English-allied masters of local principalities. But here, too, a degree of hybridity characterised race meetings. When Edgar Britt began riding in India, he was surprised to find that race programmes at Poona were divided into two classes, with Arabians running more than six furlongs – where they were three seconds slower than the thoroughbreds and more difficult to keep on racing pace.[18] Any cosy reproduction of an imperial structure was further subverted through introduced Cape ponies from South Africa and then 'Walers', tough stock horses from New South Wales and Queensland.[19] Australian-bred thoroughbreds followed, so that in 1934 this long historical association struck its high note with Ethics, ridden by the Australian jockey E.J. Morris and trained by the Australian horseman Alec Higgins, winning the Viceroy's Cup and the King Emperor's Cup in Calcutta.[20] The imperial and racing establishment had reservations – with some good cause – about these colonial interlopers. Edgar Britt recalled his battles with Colonel John Pape, Mysore Steward:

> A tall and dignified-looking Englishman, who had a reputation for not being over-impressed with Australians in general and Australian jockeys in particular. His antipathy to Australian riders possibly was caused by an incident in Secunderabad, when a jockey's ring, organised by an Australian, fixed a race. If Colonel Pope disliked Australian jockeys, the feeling was mutual so far as we were concerned.[21]

Racing Adventurers

'"A rolling stone gathers no moss." Well granted that it does not, what good is moss to a stone anyway?' wondered the globe-trotting 'turfite' Samuel Griffiths in 1933.[22] As a self-styled rolling stone of the turf, Griffiths was reflecting, somewhat cryptically, on half a century of racing employment. Samuel Griffiths was speaking for that small band of racing adventurers who had made the most of an uneven nineteenth-century development in their sport. These horse buyers, jockeys, trainers, course managers and gamblers took their chances, sometimes working the racing outposts of the southern hemisphere, making quick raids on dispersals in North America and Europe, or else seeking new opportunity in Asia, India in particular.

In his recounting of India's racing scene, Hayes thought that the social framework could be best identified in the horsy enthusiasms of young fit Englishmen, most of them junior army officers, although by the time Griffiths arrived on the subcontinent, Indian owners had made their way to the top of the game. Hayes too sensed that thoroughbred racing, whilst retaining critical elements of its English origins, would soon diverge from the sport as carried on at Epsom. During Griffiths's sojourn in Edwardian and interwar India, Mathradas Goculdas, a textile magnate, became the leading Indian owner. Goculdas extended his racing stable to England and now has an Indian classic race named in his honour.[23] Griffiths himself was called to the Aga Khan's Indian palace to advise on the formation of one of the twentieth century's most successful, ultimately French-based, racing and breeding enterprises. By 1930, the Aga Khan's horses were regularly winning or placing in English classics.

It is to India that we might further turn to distinguish racing's syncretic growth, in which peripheral locations rather than a European core took the lead. Hayes may well have been correct to recall the role of junior army officers at early race meetings. But up to the Second World War, Indian racing cast a wide net in chasing administrators, jockeys and trainers, as much as in importing horses.[24] The Royal Calcutta Turf Club actively sought out Australian administrators, men like Harvey Roulston, 'experienced, astute and forthright', whose peculiarly Australian qualities were defined by an 'efficient professionalism'.[25] The club gave up on English starting gates and turned to the Australian 'Gray' gate. One of the principle patrons of the track – and later leading owner in England – the Maharada of Baroda, hired Edgar Britt, the Sydney Cup-winning jockey, who followed the Maharada to England where he rode the winners of two Oaks, two St Legers, two One Thousand Guineas and one Two Thousand Guineas, before the Maharada sacked him. Britt returned to Australia and a career in racing journalism.[26]

By the end of the 1930s then, a close body of trainers, jockeys and officials had moved from Australia to India, bringing good horses with them. The presence of Australian jockeys was put down to the difficulty of getting a riding licence in England where they had to have a stable lined up before applying.[27] Alongside jockeys and trainers, a significant Australian figure at Indian tracks included D.J Leckie, a retired hotelier who had close connections with the Royal Calcutta Turf Club and A.E. Glassock, who cornered much of the bloodstock trade.[28] The quality of horse was constantly improving, and J. Kenny, an Australian handicapper at the West Indian Turf Club, vouched for the success of Australian horses and jockeys.[29] Indian racing officials went so far as to lay out an Australian-style cinder or sand track for monsoon-season racing and employed the architect of one of Sydney's modernised racetracks, Theo Marks, to provide grandstand designs.

As Lemon pointed out with regards to colonial thoroughbred racing, 'a sportsman in Brisbane in Queensland might have been equally interested in what was happening on the racetrack in Calcutta or Hong Kong as he was in what happened in Gympie or Rockhampton'.[30] In South Africa, New Zealand and Australia, just as in India, the first racetracks were more or less controlled by British regimental officers on colonial duties. In New South Wales, Lemon noted that Captain Ritchie's horse won the first race of Sydney's first meeting. 'As well as Ritchie', remarked Lemon 'there was a brace of Majors and Captains who raced horses at this first meeting.'[31] In South Africa also, militarised racing persisted to at least the end of the Boer War. Nomadic owners like Samuel Griffiths, however, had little respect for the quality of South African racing as, 'with few exceptions, the seventy or eighty racehorses and ponies I took to South Africa were moderate or low priced animals yet most of them won races'.[32] Such moderate horses, when interbred with Cape ponies, were still capable of winning in India, Mauritius and elsewhere – a hybridity that differentiated racing from Europe and North America. The same could be said of Argentine racing where thoroughbred imports in turn stimulated stud book records for locally bred and Andalusian-influenced 'criollos'. In some of these places, just as at the Poona race meetings noted by Britt, a separate standard in horses competed on the same tracks but with an entirely more plebeian ownership than thoroughbreds. Former colonies also supported pony circuits for smaller horses.[33]

The export of the English model was then overlain by local and regional syncretism in racing with peripheral locations able to bring their own innovations to the sport. The more secure these vernacular diversions became, the more confident were wealthy horse owners from around the globe, several of whom eventually did seek to win English races. In part they drew on the hubris of the newly rich from lands newly settled. In part their remigration seemed an inevitable extension of localised racing success. Horses weighted out of handicap victories in South Africa or New Zealand, for example, could be brought to England to prove themselves. Indian maharajas, South African Randlords like Solly Joel, Australian graziers and U.S. merchants like Pierre Lorillard all sought out the most prestigious English races and racetracks. For this self-styled peripheral elite, victory in an English classic race, even an appearance at Ascot itself, set the seal on their rise to wealth and prominence. Before the end of the nineteenth century, U.S. merchants, led by the tobacco magnate Lorillard, were sending horses back to England, culminating in Iroquois's wins in the 1881 Derby and St Leger.[34] Yet for all their self-importance, such men remained a marginal, eccentric, possibly even grotesque sidelight to the characteristic adaptations made within and between distant colonies, rather than in the racing centre of England.

To an extent, the transnational connections made by these bullish parvenus before the Second World War reflect the core-periphery hierarchy common to analyses of cultural imperialism in the later twentieth century.[35] But, just as these newly enriched owners brought horses to England, unquestionably aristocratic English horsepeople were eyeing French classic races. Some colonial jockeys and trainers also felt more comfortable racing at continental courses rather than in England. In the interwar years, they and English trainers and owners often looked to England alone. After the war they could turn to the Prix de l'Arc de Triomphe – first run on 3 October 1920 – as a likely victory. In its very first running it was won by an English owner, Count Evremond de Saint-Alary, whose training stables were located in France. The winning horse, Comrade, with bloodlines entirely British, was ridden by the Australian Frank Bullock. The race had some additional English winners before the Second World War, although since then winning owners have come increasingly from the Middle East whilst winning trainers might just as easily be English or Irish. Since 1980, more or less half of the trainers and almost half of the owners have been based in France itself – a success that may be related to the state pari-mutuel's monopoly, affirmed recently in European courts despite challenges from corporate bookmakers, and from which gambling commissions are returned to the racing and breeding industry.

At the same time, French owners were crossing the Channel to chase success in England. Despite their efforts and those of owners from across the globe, the English Derby has remained a race usually won by horses trained in either England or Ireland.[36] Perhaps the English St Leger demonstrates a broadening globalism more clearly than the Derby. For more than a century, horses were British and owners titled.[37] Then in 1865, the French horse Gladiateur (ironically nicknamed the Avenger of Waterloo) won, and was the first French horse to win the English Triple Crown.[38] South African-enriched but East End-born Jack Joel's horse Black Jester won in 1914, his brother Solly's Pommern in 1915. Apart from wins by the Aga Khan's horses in 1924, 1935 and 1940, the race was regularly captured by titled Englishmen, until in 1947, Edgar Britt won on Sayajirao for the Maharaja of Baroda.[39] Untitled English owners then began to win the race. Since 1995, Godolphin, and Middle Eastern owners generally, have dominated the St Leger, reflecting the current hierarchy in world racing.

Global Competition Comes of Age

'A horse race has sprung up that is modern as a jet and just about as hectic.'[40] So Roger Kahn welcomed the race that he dubbed the 'Olympics for thoroughbreds' and forerunner to the Breeders' Cup. The Washington DC International was set to become the world championship for horses, claimed Kahn. Occasional adventurous forays by owners and jockeys into Europe and Britain, the more systematic connections between colonial breeders and trainers in the early twentieth century and the Latin American adaptation of English and American style seemed entirely sporadic when compared to the International which emerged between 1959 and 1982 as the first serious attempt at a regular international race between the world's best horses. Since 1982, the Washington DC International has evolved into the Breeders' Cup run to close the North American racing season and used as the source of ratings for global Horse of the Year voting. The Washington DC International was genuinely international – even, for one running, attracting two contestants, instead of a single one invited, from the Soviet Union. As the International and Breeders' Cup it has been won by horses from all the principal racing regions.[41]

By 1991, the Breeders' Cup had become a full programme of races. A record total of twenty-one horses from Canada and Europe were amongst the ninety-one entered. For the first time, horses either bred or trained in other countries were entered in all seven races on the Breeders' raceday card.[42] Also in the 1990s, a closed Japanese racing industry gradually opened to international competition.[43] At the beginning of the 1990s, the Japan Cup seemed a genuinely international contest, with winners from Europe, North America, Australia, New Zealand and, in 1995, Lando from Germany. But over time the race has become localised, at least in the winner's circle, with Japanese-bred, owned and trained horses winning in most years since 1999. Other racing regions followed suit, with race managers trying to secure an international if not a fully globalised gloss for what might otherwise have remained purely localised racing carnivals. The Dubai World Cup was first run in 1996 with fields of invited international champions. It has been won once by a Brazilian horse trained in France, but in the race's fifteen-year existence, five winners have come from the United Arab Emirates. Despite its cosmopolitan beginnings, The Breeders' Cup can look more like those 'World Series' contested exclusively by American teams than like Kahn's equine Olympics. For most of its history, this event has been won by American or Irish horses.[44]

Elsewhere, the four international races run annually at Sha Tin in Hong Kong – the Hong Kong Cup, Mile, Vase and Sprint – are promoted as the richest turf races over their distance. The Cup is now one leg of the World Series Racing Championship and displays a global roll call, with winning owners, trainers and jockeys from disparate parts of the world.[45] Billed as the world's handicap staying championship, the Melbourne Cup had for several years produced winners from a widening geographic area. In 2006, the Japanese horse Delta Blues won. In 2010, an Australian-owned but French-bred, ridden and trained horse, Americain, won.[46] The 2011 Melbourne Cup marked what may be a turning point. Australian owners and trainers turned away from traditional sources in New Zealand and scoured Europe for likely contenders. European trainers, tempted in part by a rising Australian dollar, and gradually coming to terms with the race's handicap conditions and Australia's quarantine regulations, were comfortable sending good horses to Melbourne. By Cup Day, in a field of more than twenty, fifteen were either Northern hemisphere horses trained in Australia or European-trained horses, many of them part-owned by Australian syndicates. All places were filled by European horses, and immediately after the race, bookmakers installed third placegetter, Lucas Cranach, discovered in Germany by Melbourne trainers, the Freedman brothers, as a favourite for the 2012 Cup.[47] The 2010 winner and 2011 topweight, Americain, ran again in Melbourne, was transferred to a local stable (along with his dedicated French stablehand) and prepared for a final campaign in Australia's 2012 autumn, before going to a local stud. The 2011 Cup winner, French-trained Dunaden, went on to win the Hong Kong International Vase, over 2,400 metres, with the English horse he managed to edge into second place at Flemington, Red Cadeaux, finishing third.[48]

The existence of 'mega' races, a world championship race series spread across four continents and international racehorse rankings create a global layer of racing management. The rankings are devised by the International Federation of Horseracing Authorities, formed in 1993 and preceded by other attempts at transnational co-operation dating from the Paris Meeting in October 1961 of the International Joint Secretarial Liaison Committee.[49] Results of Group One contests are brought together by the International Federation in a ranked table. In mid-2011, the leading horse was the British-bred Frankel with the Australian horse, Black Caviar, second. Of the top ten ranked horses, four were bred in Ireland, two in Australia, one in New Zealand and three in Britain. One, Black Caviar, is trained in Australia, another in Ireland, Rocket Man is based in Singapore and another of the ten is trained in France. Six of the horses are trained in Britain. This snapshot captures a group of quite narrowly located champions within an apparently rapidly globalising industry and suggests that the racing world is not yet borderless or fully internationalised.[50] For various historical reasons, national and regional bodies continue to make important and influential decisions about the nature of racing in their own jurisdictions.

Shuttles and Natives

International races like the Hong Kong events or the Japan Cup are tied inevitably to the fee structure of breeding in which prize money can have a direct impact on a stallion's nomination fees. Some of the more lucrative global breeding opportunities have emerged in recent years in the trade in shuttle stallions, occasionally allied to success in one or other of the richest global challenge races. By 2003, more than sixty shuttle stallions had arrived in Australian breeding barns in migrations spread over more than a decade.

However, stud managers in the Hunter Valley noted that up to 2000, shuttle stallions commanded lower fees than did locals. Eliza Park Stud's Dennis Roberts pointed out: 'Just because they work in Europe doesn't mean they are going to work here.'[51] Less than 10 per cent of Australia's annual foal crop (the world's largest outside the Unites States) is by shuttle stallions.

Other southern hemisphere breeding regions still depend on northern hemisphere bloodstock, even if they are no longer enamoured of the shuttle horse. South Africa's leading sires by the twenty-first century had moved some distance from the inferior stock brought by Griffiths and had drawn on stallions from around the globe – amongst the top earners in 2007 were Jallad, Western Winter and Ford Wood, all from the United States, as well as three Canadian stallions and a German horse.[52] Southern hemisphere racing and breeding seems to have long suffered from a characteristic pattern: cycles of despair at local quality, followed by importation of sires and then reliance once again on improved local progeny. It goes without saying in all of this that the dams were not internationalised in the manner of sires. Perhaps the most astute and selective use of northern hemisphere stallions has occurred in New Zealand. Kiwi trainers made historically canny purchases of champion English and Irish horses, with occasional imports from North America, to underpin a proud tradition in breeding. The all-time leading sire remains Foxbridge, whose progeny dominated racing in New Zealand in the 1940s. Imported by Seton Otway of the Trelawney Stud, Cambridge, Foxbridge's journey from Europe was tracked like that of visiting royalty. Journalists dutifully registered his safe landfall from the Rangitata in Wellington and monitored both his road trip by float to Auckland and the health of the broodmares awaiting him in Cambridge.[53] On earnings in New Zealand, the current leading sire is the British Volksraad, although when overseas races are included, locally bred Zabeel dominates. New markets for New Zealand breeders have opened up in Asia. However, the number of horses exported from New Zealand has actually fallen – from more than 2,000 in 1964 to fewer than 1,500 in 2009–10.[54]

Towards the end of the twentieth century, racing, like other aspects of entertainment and agribusiness, began to open up to global possibilities. Transnational breeding and racing conglomerates, including Godolphin-Darley and Coolmore, for example, shaped bloodstock and race entries in all of the key centres. Coolmore, now the world's largest thoroughbred breeding enterprise, had set out to take advantage of low yearling prices in the United States following the 1987 stock market crash. But then, changing fashions and costs could be determined by circumstances more volatile than increased globalisation. The late-twentieth-century decline in Kentucky's sales, for example, has been attributed to exchange rates and taxation – microeconomic differences that undermine any simplistic notion of a global market for bloodstock.[55] At the same time, the number of sales throughout the United States became concentrated in Kentucky, marking an intensified localism in breeding. In 1991, 17 per cent of U.S. foals were born in Kentucky. By 2009, this figure had risen to 28 per cent.[56]

Internationalism and Regionalism

'It is important to recognise that the greatest future for racing lies in the international arena with close cooperation between all participating parties.'[57] Such confident assertions typify accounts of racing today. Certainly results are now presented instantly to fans around the world. Air transport of horses, pioneered in India during the Second World War, has brought racetracks closer together and allowed the shuttling of stallions between northern and southern hemispheres.[58] At its highest level, horseracing relies on global corporate sponsorship. There are increasing signs of globalised pools for punting on major races, as Mark Davies describes in this volume (Chapter 13).

Part of the story of horseracing must reflect this recent integration. At the same time we need to resist the idea that racing is a wholly international genre and that horses, trainers and jockeys move without friction between geographically distant but culturally identical places of work. Of the thousands of races run every year, few draw horses from across one nation, let alone internationally. Races such as the Dubai World Cup or the Hong Kong Internationals are won, regularly, by local trainers and owners, even if their winning horses are bred through transnational bloodlines. In this and in many other ways, horseracing remains highly localised. A handful of stallions might be transported around the globe, but most stand in tightly circumscribed localities with their own distinctive cultures and traditions: Kentucky, Newmarket, the Hunter Valley or Cambridge, New Zealand.[59] Broodmares rarely travel far from home paddocks. Racing has its peculiar club structure in each place, its distinctive track designs and training and riding techniques. National governments, through racing authorities, gambling commissions and quarantine regulations, all limit global movement.

What is often packaged as 'internationalism' could equally be described as a strengthening of the historical regionalism described in this chapter. Australasian, Hong Kong and Singapore races are increasingly connected. Australian and New Zealand horses supply the bulk of the racing stock to Malaysia, Singapore, Hong Kong and increasingly to Macau, China and Korea. Racing and breeding in England, Ireland and France appears increasingly integrated, whilst trainers in North America turn more often to Argentina and Chile for dirt-track runners. Barriers such as quarantine, tax treatment of equine investment and exchange rates militate against any broader integration.[60] One critic of the simplistic argument that modern sport is inevitably transnational noted that 'the self-contained, local system continues to exist, by carving out a niche where there is sufficient nourishment and no external competition'.[61] Racing may not meet these strict criteria, but limits on global competition are many. Most obviously, the dangerous and expensive business of flying sensitive, valuable horses from one continent to another must be carefully weighed up against local prize money and competition. Trainers of even the best horses often conclude that the risk is just not worth it.

Sporting historians Andrews and Ritzer, whilst deferring to the influence of the global, also point out that in sport there is an 'interpenetration of the global and the local, resulting in unique outcomes in different geographic areas'.[62] Racing, with its long history of what Huggins called 'proto-globalisation', seems particularly well placed to have such different geographically circumscribed outcomes. Horseracing has shown little sense of starting anew. Traditions count, and lineage, expressed most clearly in the national stud books, remains an unalterable foundation around the globe. And yet there are some horses which obtain iconic status in local racing cultures precisely through defying the logic of globalism. Takeover Target took wins and placings in England, Japan and Singapore at the same time as embodying a particularly local racing stereotype: to fans in Australia, both horse and owner were 'battlers'.[63] The star sprinter was owned and trained by a sole operator and taxi-cab driver Joe Janiak. Janiak bought the broken-down horse for a little more than AUS$1,000. Even the name of the sprinter suggested a defiance of corporatised owners. More fashionably bred Australian horses such as Miss Andretti or Choisir have probably raced as well if not better than Takeover Target at Ascot. But it is the struggling ('battling') trainer and the blue-collar horse who remain dear to racegoers' hearts.[64] Such cultural identities are not those of an aristocratic ownership of WFA champions or of the ambitions of breeding empires. They are not even the stuff of dreams of the new rich of the provinces returned to the Old Country.

In 1855, Rous initiated a worldwide standard in racing. His horse Emigrant was in the vanguard of English thoroughbreds brought to the southern hemisphere, to be succeeded by many others, including Foxbridge, who travelled by boat and Danehill, who flew. The progeny of Danehill were in turn sent to Hong Kong to form the basis of a breeding industry. Horseracing is a sport spread around the globe but intensely followed in few locations. It accommodates global businesses as well as backcountry clubs, and struggling owners and trainers with a few horses and ambitions confined to provincial cups run against other local horses. Its strongest networks are regional and its breeding industry clusters in cherished fields and farms. Most racing people have, at some point, leaned on a paddock rail looking at a favourite horse, dreaming of global domination. They are encouraged in this dream not least by the historically deep and geographically extensive connections evoked by their horse's pedigree. However, their dream is pursued within distinctive local conditions. These govern horse ownership and racing success in a manner far more concrete than the events taking place half a world away, in the paddocks of Newmarket, the racecourses of Dubai or the committee rooms of Paris.

NOTES

1 L.T. Daley, 'Rous, Henry John (1795–1877)', *Australian Dictionary of Biography* (Canberra: Australian National University), available at: www.adb.anu.edu.au/biography/rous-henry-john-2611/text3597. Accessed 22 February 2012.

2 W. Vamplew, *The Turf: A Social and Economic History of Horseracing* (London and New York: Allan Lane, 1976); T.H. Bird, *Admiral Rous and the English Turf* (London: Putnam, 1939).

3 Daley, *Australian Dictionary of Biography*.

4 P. Robinson and N. Robinson, *Horsetrader: Robert Sangster and the Rise and Fall of the Sport of Kings* (London: Harper Collins, 1993), p. 57.

5 Vamplew, *The Turf*.

6 M. Huggins, 'The Proto-globalisation of Horseracing 1730–1900: Anglo-American Interconnections', *Sport in History*, 29/3 (September 2009), 367–68.

7 A. Lemon, 'Horse Racing: An English or an International Sport? Le Jockey Club, El Jockey Club, Jokey Kulubu', in C. McConville (ed.), *A Global Racecourse: Work, Culture and Horse Sports* (Sydney: Australian Society for Sports History, 2008), p. 7.

8 R. Black, *Horse-Racing in France; a History* (London: Sampson Low, Marston Serle and Rivington, 1886), p. 53.

9 *Ibid.*, p. 5.

10 *Ibid.*, p. 230.

11 R.D. Needell, 'Rio de Janeiro and Buenos Aires: Public Space and Public Consciousness in fin-de-siecle Latin America', *Comparative Studies in Society and History*, 37 (1995), 519–40. *Ibid.*, p. 521.

12 *Ibid.*

13 J. and L. Newton, *Historia del Jockey Club de Buenos Aires* (Buenos Aires: Ediciones, 1966) and W.H. Koebel, *Modern Argentina* (London: Francis Griffiths, 1907), p. 55, quoted in Needell, 'Rio de Janiero and Buenos Aires'.

14 Needell, 'Rio de Janeiro and Buenos Aires', p. 540.

15 *Sydney Morning Herald*, 4 April 1929.

16 H. Hayes, *Indian Racing Reminiscences* (London: W. Thacker, 1883), pp. 40–43.

17 W.G.C. Frith, *Royal Calcutta Turf Club: Some Notes on Its Foundation, History and Development* (Calcutta: Royal Calcutta Turf Club, 1976), p. 82.

18 E. Britt, *Post Haste* (Stratford-on-Avon: Shakespeare Head Press, 1967), p. 51.

19 F. Carruthers, *The Horse in Australia* (North Sydney: Random House, 2008), pp. 247–48.

20 *Sydney Morning Herald*, 28 December 1934, 17 December 1934.

21 Britt, *Post Haste*, p. 54.

22 S. Griffiths, *A Rolling Stone on the Turf* (Sydney: Angus and Robertson, 1933), p. i.

23 *Ibid.*, pp. i–iii.

24 Britt, *Post Haste*, p. 51.

25 Frith, *Royal Calcutta Turf Club*, p. 109.

26 Britt, *Post Haste*.

27 *Sydney Morning Herald*, 10 March 1937.

28 *Ibid.*

29 *Ibid.*, 6 April 1938.

30 Lemon, 'Horse Racing', p. 3.

31 A. Lemon, *The History of Australian Thoroughbred Racing*, vol. I (Melbourne: Classic Reproductions, 1987), p. 55.

32 Griffiths, *A Rolling Stone*, pp. 96–97.

33 W. Peake, *Sydney's Pony Racecourses: An Alternative Racing History* (Sydney: Walla Walla Press, 2006).

34 Huggins, 'Proto-globalisation', p. 385.

35 B. Houlihan, 'Homogenization, Americanization and Creolization of Sport: Varieties of Globalization', *Sociology of Sport Journal*, 11 (1994), 356–75.

36 R. Mortimer, *The History of the Derby Stakes* (London: Cassell, 1962); Epsom Downs Racecourse Derby History, available at: www.epsomdowns.co.uk/racing/derby-history. Accessed 22 February 2012.

37 For St Leger statistics, see The National Horseracing Museum's archive, available at: www.horseracinghistory.co.uk/hrho/action/viewRaces?id=5. Accessed 22 February 2012.

38 View Gladiateur's profile at the National Horse Racing Museum's Horseracing History Web site, available at: www.horseracinghistory.co.uk/hrho/action/viewDocument?id=870. Accessed 22 February 2012.

39 Britt, *Post Haste*, p. 91.

40 R. Kahn, 'Olympics for thoroughbreds', *Saturday Evening Post*, 11 July 1959, p. 232.

41 For Breeders Cup statistics, go to http://stats.breederscup.com/. Accessed 22 February 2012.

42 *New York Times*, 1 November 1991, p. 12.

43 'Odds Against', *Economist*, 29 June 1991, 320, 7713.

44 Breeders Cup statistics, http://stats.breederscup.com/.

45 Past winners of the Hong Kong Cup are listed at: www.hongkong-cup.com/past-winners. Accessed 22 February 2012.

46 Statistics for the Melbourne Cup are available at: www.races.com.au/melbourne-cup/. Accessed 22 February 2012.

47 *Sportsman*, 30 October 2011.

48 Melbourne *Age*, 12, 13 December 2011; *Racing and Sports*, 30 October 2011, Melbourne *Herald Sun*, 2 November 2011.

49 Information about the International Federation of Horseracing Authorities can be found at: www.horseracingintfed.com/. Accessed 22 February 2012.

50 World thoroughbred rankings are available at: www.horseracingintfed.com/racingDisplay.asp?section=22. Accessed 22 February 2012.

51 Melbourne *Age*, 13 February 2004.

52 *South African Racing Fact Book* (2008–09), p. 37.

53 New Zealand *Evening Post*, 13 April 1935.

54 Statistics can be found at New Zealand Racing, the official site for NZ thoroughbred racing, available at: www.nzracing.co.nz/. Accessed 22 February 2012.

55 P. Karungu, M. Reed and D. Tvedt, 'Macroeconomic Factors and the Thoroughbred Industry', *Journal of Agricultural and Applied Economics* (July 1993), 165–73.

56 The Jockey Club, *Kentucky Fact Book: A Statistical Guide to the Thoroughbred Industry in Kentucky*, 2011, p. 5.

57 F. Holland and C. Andressen, 'Australia's Thoroughbred Racing Industry: The Australia-Asia Connection', *Australian Society for Sports History Bulletin* 32 (August 2000), 7.

58 J. Blancou and I. Parsonson, 'Historical Perspectives on Long Distance Transport of Animals', *Veterinaria Italiana*, 44 (2008), 28.

59 R. Cassidy, *Horse People: Thoroughbred Culture in Lexington and Newmarket* (Baltimore: Johns Hopkins University Press, 2007).

60 Houlihan, 'Homogenization, Americanisation and Creolization of Sport', 372.

61 T.H. Eriksen, 'Steps to an Ecology of Transnational Sports', *Global Networks*, 7 (2007), 165.

62 D.L. Andrews and G. Ritzer, 'The Global in the Sporting Local', *Global Networks*, 7/2, (2007), 135–53.

63 C. McConville, 'Cyklon and the Caulfield Cup', in C. McConville (ed.), *A Global Racecourse: Work, Culture and Horse Sports* (Australian Society for Sports History, ASSH Studies), 23, (2008), 15–23.

64 C. McConville, 'Jockeying for the Lead: War, Sport and Vernacular Identities in Australia, 1915–2006', *Sporting Traditions*, 23 (May 2007), 52–53; L. Carlyon, *Chasing a Dream, the Les Carlyon Collection* (Melbourne: Raceplay, 1988), p. 25; L. Crisp, *Takeover Target – the Best $1375 Joe Janiak Ever Spent* (North Sydney: Ebury, 2009).

A GUIDE TO FURTHER READING

Barich, B. *Laughing in the Hills*. St Paul, MN: Hungry Minds Press, 1980.

Barnard, J. *Talking Horses*. London: Fourth Estate, 1987.

Beyer, A. *Beyer on Speed: New Strategies for Racetrack Betting*. New York: Mariner, 2007.

Binns, M. and T. Morris, *Thoroughbred Breeding: Pedigree Theories and the Science of Genetics*. London: J.A. Allen, 2010.

Breen, T. 'Horses & Gentlemen: The Cultural Significance of Gambling Among the Gentry of Virginia', *William and Mary Quarterly*, 34 (1977), 239–57.

Caine, G. *The Home Run Horse*. Chicago: The Daily Racing Form, 2004.

Case, C. *Down the Backstretch: Racing and the American Dream*. Philadelphia: Temple University Press, 1991.

Chinn, C. *Better Betting with a Decent Feller*. Hemel Hempstead: Aurum, 1991.

Clapson, M. *A Bit of a Flutter*. Manchester: Manchester University Press, 1992.

Conley, K. *Stud: Adventures in Breeding*. New York: Bloomsbury, 2008.

De Moubray, J. *The Thoroughbred Business*. London: Hamish Hamilton, 1986.

Edwards, P., K. Enenkel and E. Graham (eds.) *The Horse as Cultural Icon. The Real and Symbolic Horse in the Early Modern World*. Leiden-Boston: Brill, 2011.

Fox, K. *The Racing Tribe*. London: Metro, 1999.

Francis, D. *Banker*. London: Pan, 1982.

Hagedorn Auerbach, A. *Wild Ride: The Rise and Tragic Fall of Calumet Farm Inc, America's Premier Racing Dynasty*. New York: Holt Paperbacks, 1995.

Harrison, F. *Early American Turf Stock, 1730–1830*, Vol. II. Richmond, VA: The Dominion Press, 1935.

Hervey, J., W. Vosburgh and R. Kelly. *Racing in America* (6 volumes: 1665–1979). New York: The Jockey Club, 1922–1980.

Hill, C. *Horse Power: The Politics of the Turf*. Manchester: Manchester University Press, 1988.

Hill, E. and P. Cunningham, 'History and Integrity of Thoroughbred Dam Lines Revealed in Equine mt Variation', *Animal Genetics*, 33 (2002), 287–94.

Hillenbrand, L. *Seabiscuit: The True Story of Three Men and a Racehorse*. New York: Random House, 2003.

Hotaling, E. *The Great Black Jockeys: The Lives and Times of the Men Who Dominated America's First National Sport*. New York: Prima, 1999.

They're Off! Horse Racing at Saratoga. Syracuse, NY: Syracuse University Press, 2005.

Huggins, M. *Flat Racing and British Society 1790–1914*. London: Frank Cass, 2000.

Horseracing and the British, 1919–1939. Manchester: Manchester University Press, 2003.

Lambton, G. *Men and Horses I Have Known*. London: Thornton Butterworth, 1924.

Landry, D. *Noble Brutes: How Eastern Horses Transformed English Culture*. Baltimore: Johns Hopkins University Press, 2008.

Leach, J. *Sods I Have Cut on the Turf*. London: Victor Gollanzc, 1961.

Leicester, C. *Bloodstock Breeding*, 2nd ed., revised by H. Wright. 1957; London: J.A. Allen, 1983.

Lemon, A. *The History of Australian Thoroughbred Racing*. South Yarra, Victoria: Hardie Grant Books, 2008.

Maynard, J. *Aboriginal Stars of the Turf*. Canberra: Aboriginal Studies Press, 2007.

McClelland, T. *Horseplayers: Life at the Track*. Chicago: Chicago Review Press, 2007.

McConville, C. (ed.) *A Global Racecourse: Work, Culture and Horse Sports*. Melbourne: ASSH, 2008.

McIlvaney, H. *McIlvaney on Horseracing*. London: Mainstream, 1995.

Mooney, B., G. Ennor and G. Kelly, *Complete Encyclopaedia of Horseracing*. London: Carlton Books, 2006.

Mortimer, R. *The Jockey Club*. London: Cassell, 1958.

Munting, R. *Hedges and Hurdles*. London: J.A. Allen, 1987.

Nack, W. *Secretariat: The Making of a Champion*. New York: Da Capo Press, 2002.

O'Hara, J. *A Mug's Game: A History of Gaming and Betting in Australia*. Kensington, N.S.W.: New South Wales University Press, 1988.

Olsen, S., S. Grant, A. Choyke and L. Bartosiewicz (eds.) *Horses and Humans: The Evolution of the Human-Equine Relationship*. Oxford: BAR, International Series 1560, 2006.

Pagones, R. *Dubai Millennium: A Vision Realised, A Dream Lost*. Compton: Highdown, 2007.

Peake, W. *Sydney's Pony Racecourses: An Alternative Racing History*. Sydney, N.S.W.: Walla Walla Press, 2006.

Potts, A. *Against the Crowd*. London: Aesculus Press, 1995.

Prior, C. *The History of the Racing Calendar and Stud Book*. London: The Sporting Life, 1926.

Raber, K. and T. Tucker (eds.) *The Culture of the Horse: Status, Discipline, and Identity in the Early Modern World*. Basingstoke: Palgrave, 2004.

Reiss, S. *The Sport of Kings and the Kings of Crime: Horse Racing, Politics and Organised Crime in New York 1865–1913*. Syracuse, NY: Syracuse University Press, 2011.

Robinson, P. and N. Robinson, *Horsetrader: Robert Sangster and the Rise and Fall of the Sport of Kings*. London: Harper Collins, 1993.

Rosecrance, J. 'The Invisible Horsemen: The Social World of the Backstretch', *Qualitative Sociology*, 8 (1985), 248–65.

The Degenerates of Lake Tahoe: A Study of Persistence in the Social World of Racehorse Gambling. New York: Peter Lang Publishing, 1987.

Runyan, D. *The Racing World of Damon Runyan*. New York: Constable, 1999.

Simon, M. *Racing through the Century: The Story of Thoroughbred Racing in America*. Irvine, CA: Bow Tie Press, 2002.

Smiley, J. *Horse Heaven*. New York: Ballantine Books, 2001.

A Year at the Races: Reflections on Horses, Humans, Love, Money and Luck. New York: Anchor, 2005.

Sydney, C. *The Art of Legging*. London: Maxline International, 1976.

Thibault, G. 2001. *Un siècle de galop, 1900–2000*. Paris: Filipacchi, 2001.

Thornton, T. *Not by a Long Shot: A Season at a Hard Luck Horse Track*. New York: Public Affairs Books, 2007.

Vamplew, W. *The Turf*. London: Allen Lane, 1976.

Vamplew, W. and J. Kay, *Encyclopaedia of British Horseracing*. Abingdon: Routledge, 2005.

Warner, M. and R. Blake, *Stubbs & the Horse*. New Haven, CT and London: Yale University Press, 2004.

Watson, S.J. *Between the Flags: A History of Irish Steeplechasing*. Dublin: Allen Figgis, 1969.

Welcome, J. *Irish Horse-Racing: An Illustrated History*. London: Macmillan, 1982.

Wilkinson, D. *Early Horse Racing in Yorkshire and the Origins of the Thoroughbred*. York: Old Peg Publications, 2003.

Wright, H. *Bull: The Biography*. London: Portway Press, 1995.

INDEX